GRESS, July

LARAT

'RESENTATIVES O

TATES OF AM

AL CONGRESS ASSE

Events, it becomes necessary for one People "to dissolve the Polit
nong the Powers of the Earth, the separate and equal Station "
cent Respect to the Opinions of Mankind requires "that they shou

self-evident, "that all Men are created equal," "that they are
; these are Life, Liberty, and the Pursuit of Happiness--That to
n the Consent of the Governed," that whenever any Form of Go
olish it, and to institute a new Government, laying its Foundat
ikely to effect their Safety and Happiness." Prudence, indeed,
it Causes; and accordingly all Experience hath shewn, that Man
ng the Forms to which they are accustomed. But when a long T
uce them under absolute Despotism, it is their Right, it is their
Such has been the patient Sufferance of these Colonies;" and such
The History of the present King of Great-Britain is a History of
Tyranny over these States. To prove this, let Facts be submitted
ome and necessary for the public Good.
nediate and pressing Importance, unless suspended in their Opera
nd to them.
dation of large Districts of People, unless those People would rel
dable to Tyrants only.
nusual, uncomfortable, and distant from the Depository of their

for opposing with manly Firmness his Invasions on the Rights of
ns, to cause others to be elected; whereby the Legislative Powe
remaining in the mean time exposed to all the Dangers of Invasion
States; for that Purpose obstructing the Laws for Naturalization
onditions of new Appropriations of Lands

DECLARING INDEPENDENCE

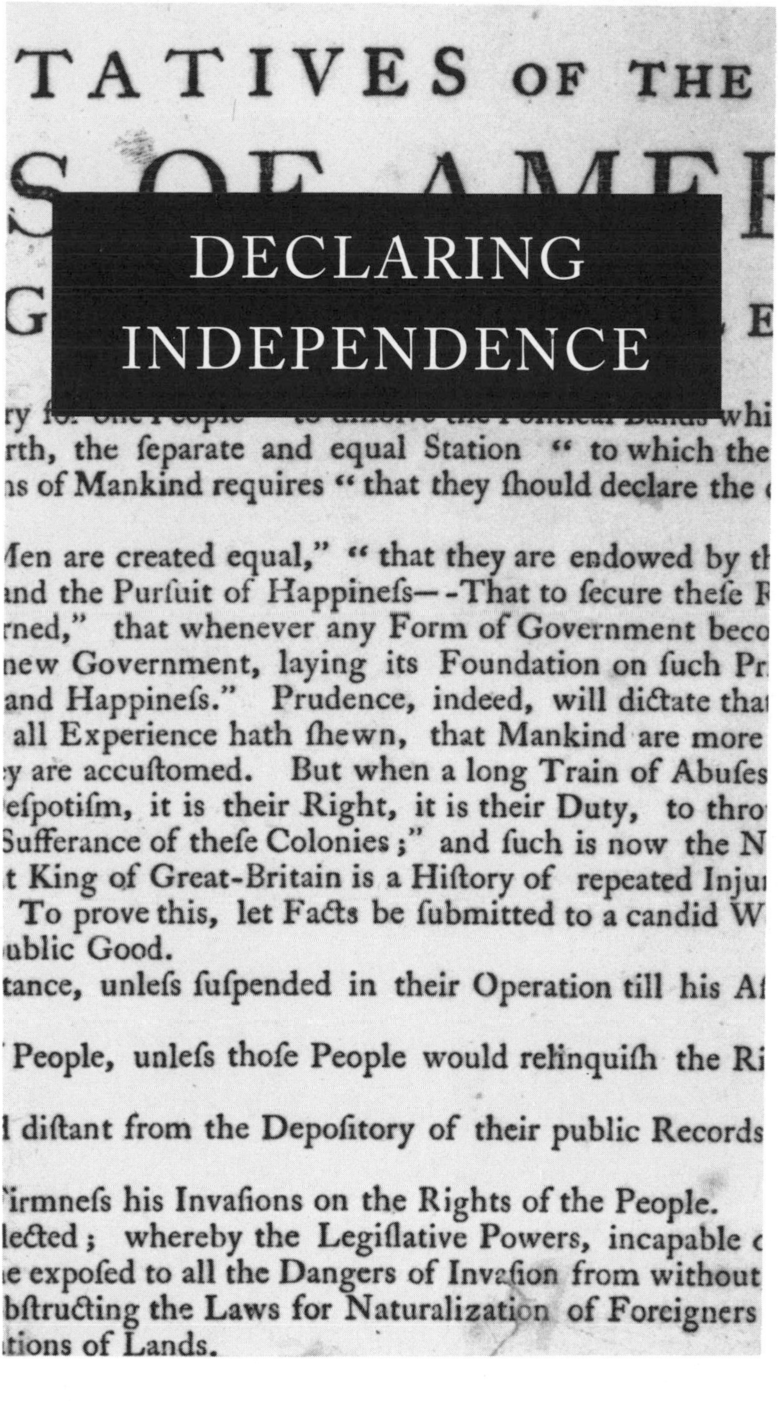
TATIVES OF THE

S OF AMER

G E

ry for one People to dissolve the Political Bands whi
rth, the ſeparate and equal Station " to which the
ns of Mankind requires " that they ſhould declare the

Men are created equal," " that they are endowed by th
and the Purſuit of Happineſs—-That to ſecure theſe R
rned," that whenever any Form of Government beco
new Government, laying its Foundation on ſuch Pr
and Happineſs." Prudence, indeed, will dictate that
all Experience hath ſhewn, that Mankind are more
y are accuſtomed. But when a long Train of Abuſes
eſpotiſm, it is their Right, it is their Duty, to thro
Sufferance of theſe Colonies;" and ſuch is now the N
t King of Great-Britain is a Hiſtory of repeated Inju
To prove this, let Facts be ſubmitted to a candid W
ublic Good.
tance, unleſs ſuſpended in their Operation till his A

People, unleſs thoſe People would relinquiſh the Ri

diſtant from the Depoſitory of their public Records

irmneſs his Invaſions on the Rights of the People.
lected; whereby the Legiſlative Powers, incapable c
e expoſed to all the Dangers of Invaſion from without
bſtructing the Laws for Naturalization of Foreigners
tions of Lands.

Jefferson, Natural Language, & the Culture of Performance

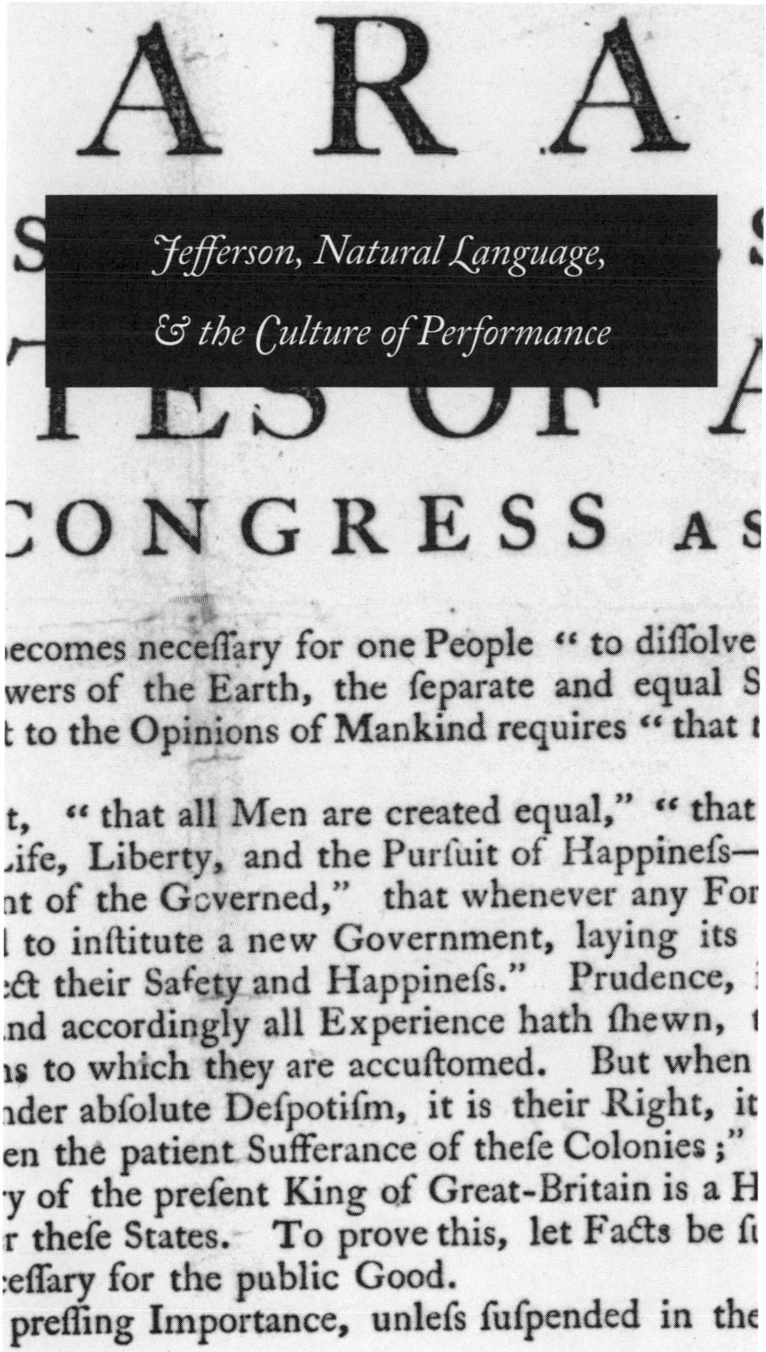
ARA
S S
TES OF A
CONGRESS AS
ecomes neceſſary for one People " to diſſolve
wers of the Earth, the ſeparate and equal S
t to the Opinions of Mankind requires " that t
t, " that all Men are created equal," " that
Life, Liberty, and the Purſuit of Happineſs—
nt of the Governed," that whenever any For
l to inſtitute a new Government, laying its
ect their Safety and Happineſs." Prudence,
nd accordingly all Experience hath ſhewn,
ns to which they are accuſtomed. But when
nder abſolute Deſpotiſm, it is their Right, it
en the patient Sufferance of theſe Colonies ;"
y of the preſent King of Great-Britain is a H
r theſe States. To prove this, let Facts be ſu
eſſary for the public Good.
preſſing Importance, unleſs ſuſpended in the

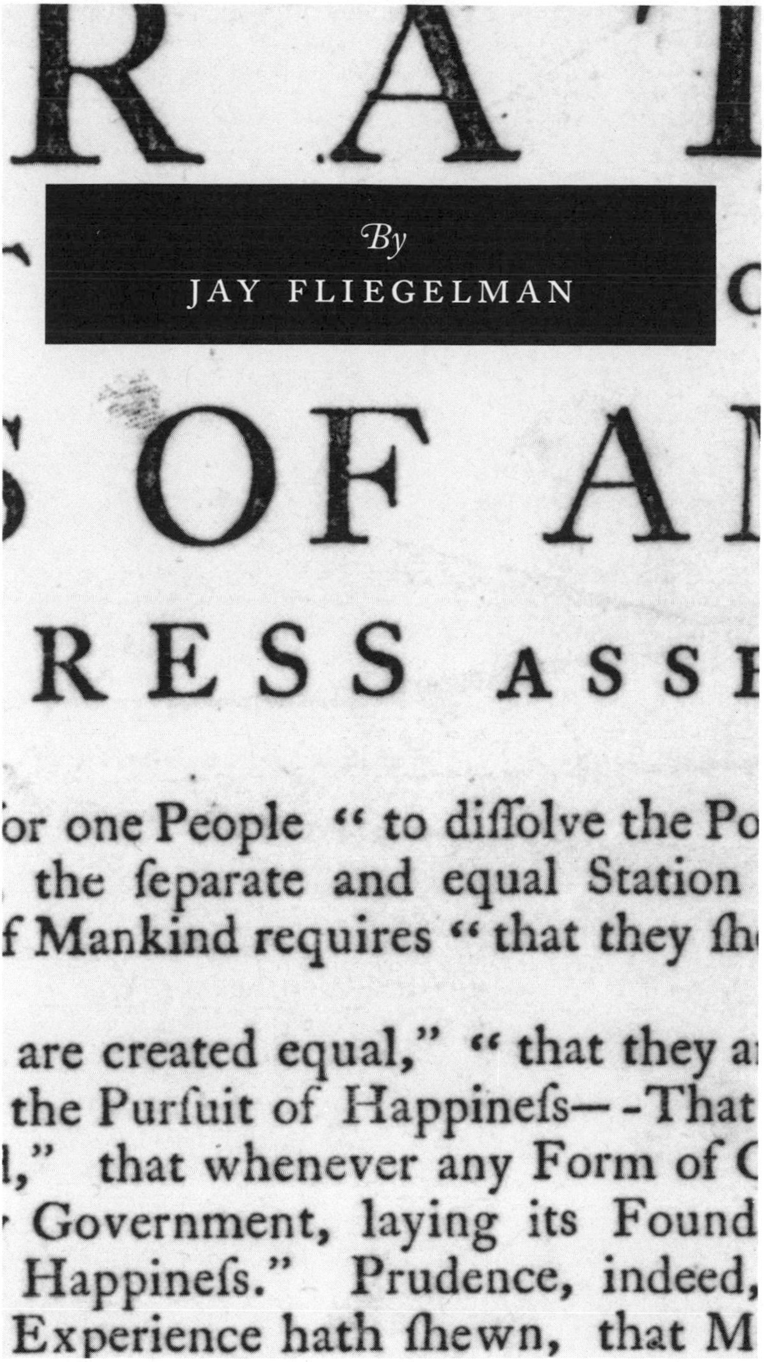
R A T
S OF A
RESS ASS
or one People " to diſſolve the Po
the ſeparate and equal Station
f Mankind requires " that they ſh
are created equal," " that they a
the Purſuit of Happineſs—-That
," that whenever any Form of
Government, laying its Found
Happineſs." Prudence, indeed,
Experience hath ſhewn, that M

By
JAY FLIEGELMAN

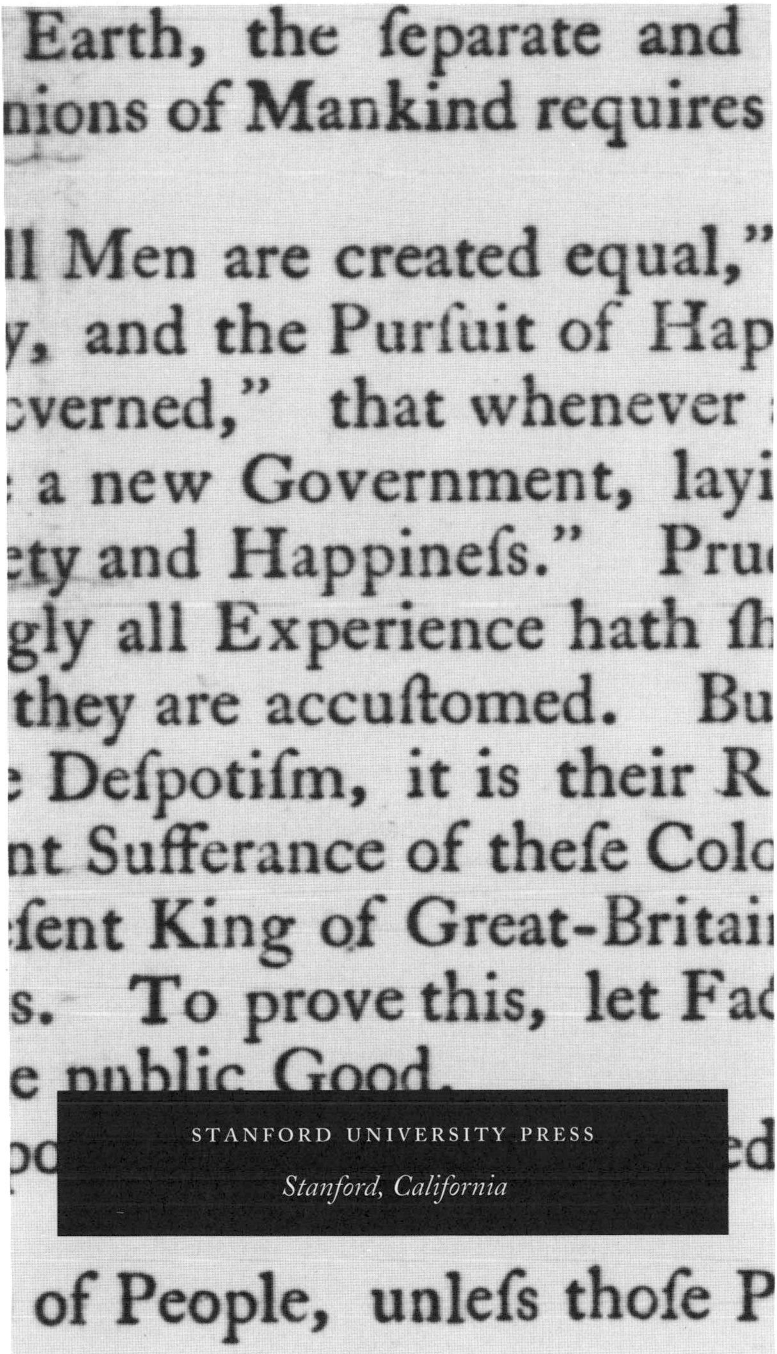
Earth, the ſeparate and
nions of Mankind requires
ll Men are created equal,"
y, and the Purſuit of Hap
verned," that whenever
a new Government, layi
ety and Happineſs." Pru
gly all Experience hath ſh
they are accuſtomed. Bu
Deſpotiſm, it is their R
nt Sufferance of theſe Colo
ſent King of Great-Britai
s. To prove this, let Fa
e public Good.
of People, unleſs thoſe P

STANFORD UNIVERSITY PRESS

Stanford, California

Photographs in title sequence:
Details from the unique proof copy
of John Dunlap's broadside printing
of the *Declaration of Independence.*
Courtesy of The Historical Society
of Pennsylvania.

Stanford University Press
Stanford, California

Printed in the United States of America

CIP data are at the end of the book

Original printing 1993
Last figure below indicates year of this printing:
05 04 03 02 01 00 99 98 97 96

Stanford University Press publications are
distributed exclusively by Stanford University Press
within the United States, Canada, Mexico, and
Central America; they are distributed exclusively by
Cambridge University Press throughout the rest of
the world.

For Renée

ACKNOWLEDGMENTS

This book began a number of years ago as an essay I wrote during a fellowship year at the Stanford Humanities Center. Subsequently I worked on it in conjunction with several incarnations of my graduate seminar on the American Enlightenment. Most recently I received extremely useful feedback from the participants in the Stanford Faculty Seminar on Enlightenment and Revolution. My colleagues John Bender, Bliss Carnochan, and Jack Rakove read early drafts of the whole and gave me the benefit of their considerable learning. George Dekker meticulously read through two versions of the manuscript. For his generous encouragement and savvy practical advice I am, as always, deeply grateful. Albert Gelpi, Thomas Moser, David Riggs, Seth Lerer, Steven Watts, Jim Carson, Laura Rigal, Jenny Franchot, and Donald Weber offered useful suggestions, and Mitchell Breitwieser, as reader for the press, read the manuscript with extraordinary care and engagement. In addition, Helen Tartar of Stanford University Press has been an exemplary and tireless editor. Nancy Lerer and Lynn Stewart nicely expedited the publication process, Bud Bynack raised copyediting to the level of rhetorical art, and Cope Cumpston designed a handsome book. Finally I want to thank my sister Jane for her dear and lifelong friendship. My greatest debt, however, is to my wife Renée Santifaller, whose love, keen intelligence, and exuberant example inspire and sustain me.

CONTENTS

Figures

Declaring Independence

DECLARING INDEPENDENCE

Introduction

In 1948 Daniel Boorstin published *The Lost World of Thomas Jefferson*, a book that sought to locate Jefferson's political ideas and social theory within the largely unexplored context of eighteenth-century physiology, natural history, and philosophical materialism. In the last 45 years a number of other "lost worlds" of Thomas Jefferson have been reconstructed. Notable among such studies has been Garry Wills's *Inventing America*, which makes a powerful argument for the centrality of Francis Hutcheson's communitarian thought, rather than the individualist philosophy of John Locke, to the Declaration of Independence. In *Declaring Independence* I seek to recover yet another lost world, one that makes possible a new way of understanding the Declaration, specifically, and Jefferson and late eighteenth-century American culture more generally. That lost world is the world of eighteenth-century theories and practices of rhetoric, the classically derived art of persuasive communication that prescribed the codes and character of public speaking in England and America.

In the mid eighteenth century that world was revolutionized by an intensified quest to discover (or theorize into existence) a natural spoken language that would be a corollary to natural law, a language that would permit universal recognition and understanding. According to the rhetoricians of what came to be called "the elocutionary revolution," that new language was composed not of words themselves, but of the tones, gestures, and expressive countenance with which a speaker delivered those words. Consequently, an orator's primary obligation was no longer to communicate thoughts and feelings. Rather it was to display persuasively and spontaneously the experiencing of those thoughts and feelings.[1] The elocutionary revolution made the credibility of arguments contingent on the emotional credibility of the speaker. Preoccupied with the spectacle of sincerity and an intensified scrutiny of the body as an instrument of expression, the quest for a natural language led paradoxically to a greater theatricalization of public speaking, to a new social dramaturgy, and to a performative understanding of selfhood. By altering the dynamics of persuasion and, by extension, the dynamics of political authority, the new eloquence played a key role in the American revolution John Adams famously described in 1815 as having taken place within the "minds and hearts of the people" before any shots were fired.[2] In addition, it reflected and contributed to a heightened self-consciousness about the relationship of public and private selves, and thus about what it meant to "be oneself" and to speak in one's own voice without abandoning the conventional forms of a social or civic language.

I treat Jefferson less as the autonomous subject of this study than as a witness to, and conflicted participant in, a new affective understanding of the operations of language, one that reconceives all expression as a form of self-expression, as an opportunity as well as an imperative to externalize the self, to become self-evident. He is an especially sensitive register of the social costs and benefits of such a view of language. Insofar as the form of that externalization is prescribed and determined by a set of rules and expectations, the natural self that is ostensibly revealed is, in fact, concealed by or collapsed into a theatricalized social construction. What especially intrigues me are precisely those rhetorical and performative situations, behaviors, and strategies that reveal the paradoxical mutuality of self-assertion and self-concealment, the systole and diastole of polarization and elision whereby roles and identities are set in opposition and then blurred. In the period of American history most sensitive to the competing claims and attractions of subjection and independence, such a complex pattern characterized a wide range of cultural phenomena, a pattern summed up in the problematics of declaring independence and in the oratorical revolution that accompanied the effort to do so.

Defining independence as a rhetorical problem as much as a political one, much of this book is concerned with recovering the conditions of speaking and writing operative in 1776: what was assumed, but not spoken, in the domain of action and speech. Such a recovery involves engaging, from a number of different perspectives, the complex dialogue between the natural and the artful that dominates so many disparate eighteenth-century discourses. That recovery also opens up a host of other related issues. Primary among these is the changing nature of authorship—from a view that sees the editorial and authorial functions as versions of one another to one that stresses the primacy of originality and imagination. Questions of authorship, I argue, raise larger questions about the character of personal and historical agency (what it means to be an "actor" in history); they also shed light on the often gendered dialogue between active agency and passive instrumentality so central to much of the period's prose. From such questions of agency I move to a discussion of eighteenth-century debates over the nature and extent of personal responsibility and accountability. In these sections, which deal with a number of texts but always spiral back to an accretive contextualized reading of the Declaration, I view the history of rhetoric as it relates to the larger history of the social and psychological meanings and consequences of self-expression. I conclude with a discussion of how the oratorical revolution and the culture of performance were used to define the distinctiveness of Americans, a distinctiveness that excluded African-Americans from that definition.

Insofar as I offer "explanations" of certain of Jefferson's attitudes and actions, those explanations tend to be cultural and social rather than biographical. Rather than posit a "personality" as an explanatory category, I examine Jefferson and his Declaration in the context of the emergence of personality as a concept. In this "lost world," Jefferson's fascination with Homer, Ossian, Patrick Henry, and the violin is of greater significance than his indebtedness to Locke or Hutcheson. And the fact that the Declaration was written to be read aloud becomes a crucial clue to elements of its meaning. Indeed, throughout the book I am concerned with rethinking and expanding the kinds of "facts" that are traditionally judged to be relevant to understanding a major historical document. In the case of the Declaration, those facts include, for example, the structure of a fugue, the particular design of a chair, the way Jefferson wrote the letter *s*, accusations that Milton's *Paradise Lost* was plagiarized, and the eighteenth-century assumption that blacks are unable to blush. But as my title suggests, my concern is not just with the Declaration as artifact, but with "declaring" as performance and with "independence" as something that is rhetorically performed. Assuming an interactive culture in which political ideas are present in nonpolitical texts and vice versa, this study proceeds by associative progression rather than by the isolation of different discourses for separate treatment. In a similar spirit, the book is written as a single continuous essay, divided into titled sections but not broken into chapters.

Jefferson's Pauses

Mostly silent in debate and preferring to express himself in writing, Jefferson was throughout his career an anxious orator. When he began to speak in public his voice, as eulogist William

Wirt put it, "sank into his throat" and became "guttural and inarticulate."[1] John Adams recollected, "During the whole time I sat with him in Congress, I never heard him utter three sentences together."[2] Indeed, hoping that his *Summary View of the Rights of British America* would be read by the infinitely more talented orator, Patrick Henry, Jefferson became "conveniently ill" with dysentery on his way to the Virginia Convention in the summer of 1774.[3] Even in his youthful prepolitical career as a lawyer (which consisted mostly of delivering petitions relating to land titles to the same seven members of the governor's council), Jefferson was described as a formalist speaker "enumerating" arguments, quite in contrast to Henry, who "spoke powerfully from his heart."[4] And as president, more than a quarter century later, Jefferson not only delivered his first Inaugural address at such a whisper that most in attendance could not hear a word he said, but violated his predecessors' practice of addressing Congress in person by communicating his State of the Union messages in writing.[5] Throughout his two terms, "the early president known most for his democratic views, spoke the least to the public directly."[6]

But on June 28, 1776, as chairman of the drafting committee, Jefferson was expected to rise to the oratorical task of reading the text of the Declaration of Independence aloud to the assembled Continental Congress, a body that would dramatically alter his draft in ways Jefferson would later bitterly term "mutilations."[7] Whether he actually read it, or once again succeeded in passing the burden of public performance onto someone else, is unrecorded. There nevertheless is compelling evidence that he thought deeply about how it should be read and heard. Though the fact has received virtually no attention since Julian Boyd first noted it in 1976, a part of Jefferson's still-surviving rough draft of the Declaration (Figure 1), on which the now-missing final reading copy was based, is marked with what appear to be diacritical accents. Boyd speculated that the marks were used to assist Jefferson in his reading of the Declaration. They were, he suggested, comparable to those advised by John Rice in his 1765 *Introduction to the Art of Reading*

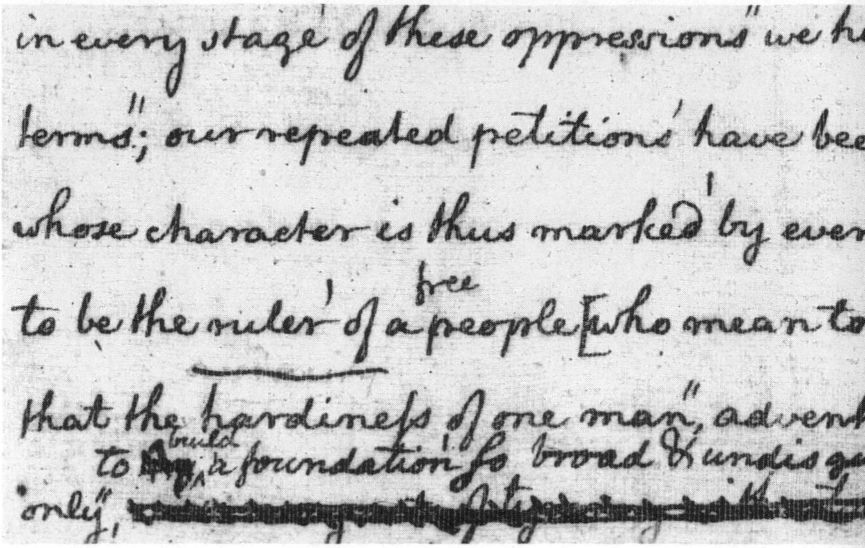
in every stage of these oppressions" we ha
terms"; our repeated petitions' have bee
whose character is thus marked' by ever
to be the ruler' of a free people [who mean to
that the hardiness of one man", advent
to build a foundation, so broad & undis gu
"only",

Figure 1. Marked passage from the rough draft of the Declaration, the draft prior to the fair copy presented to the Continental Congress. (Courtesy of the Library of Congress.)

with Energy and Propriety, one of several books Jefferson owned on the subject of effective public speaking, and to the accents Jefferson used to scan poetic meter in his essay "Thoughts on Prosody" (1786).[8]

Indeed, a unique proof copy of John Dunlap's official broadside printing of the Declaration, set hastily from Jefferson's original reading copy, which he had corrected with Congress's extensive revisions and deletions, is full of seemingly inexplicable quotation marks in the opening two paragraphs (Figure 2). Boyd ingeniously concluded that these quotation marks can only be explained as a printer's misreading of Jefferson's reading marks, marks that also appear in a surviving manuscript of the second Inaugural (Figure 3).[9]

An examination of both the one "marked" section of the rough draft of the Declaration and the relevant section of the second Inaugural manuscript clearly shows, however, that the marks Boyd understood to indicate emphasis make no sense as such. For exam-

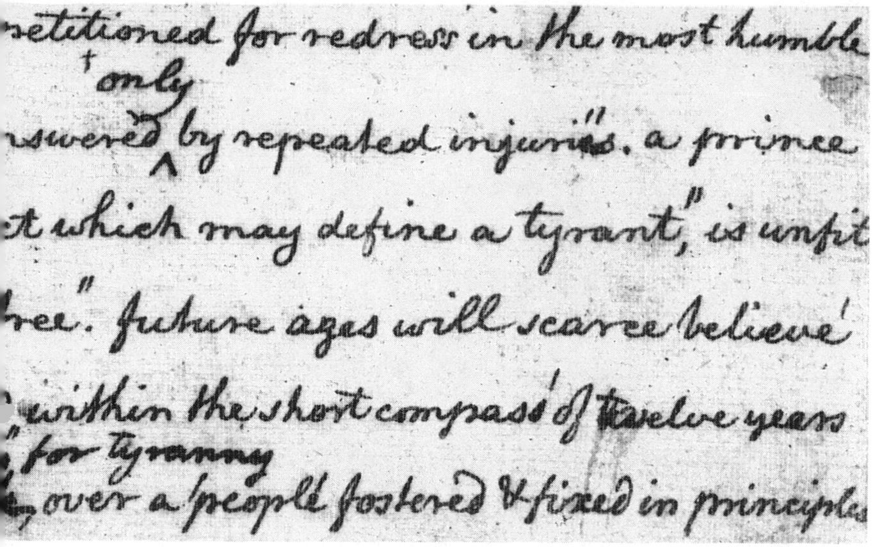

etitioned for redress in the most humble
only
nswered by repeated injuries. a prince
t which may define a tyrant, is unfit
ree. future ages will scarce believe
within the short compass of twelve years
for tyranny
over a people fostered & fixed in principles

ple, in the marked section of the Declaration, accents appear to fall on the last syllables of "oppressions," "injuries," and "compass," syllables that would in no reasonable reading ever be accented. A closer look indicates that in clear contrast to the metrical accents in "Thoughts on Prosody" (Figure 4), the marks in the printed and manuscript Declaration fall less on particular syllables of words than immediately before and immediately after words. All this suggests that the marks indicate not emphases but pauses.

In discussing the beauties of Homer's Greek in his "Thoughts on Prosody," Jefferson printed a verse passage from the *Iliad* as if it were prose and argued that the rhythms of the verse remain perfectly audible to the reader because Homer had "studied the human ear."

He has discovered that in any rhythmical composition the ear is pleased to find at certain regular intervals a pause where it may rest, by which it may divide the composition into parts, as a piece of music is divided into bars. He contrives to mark this division by a pause in the sense or at least

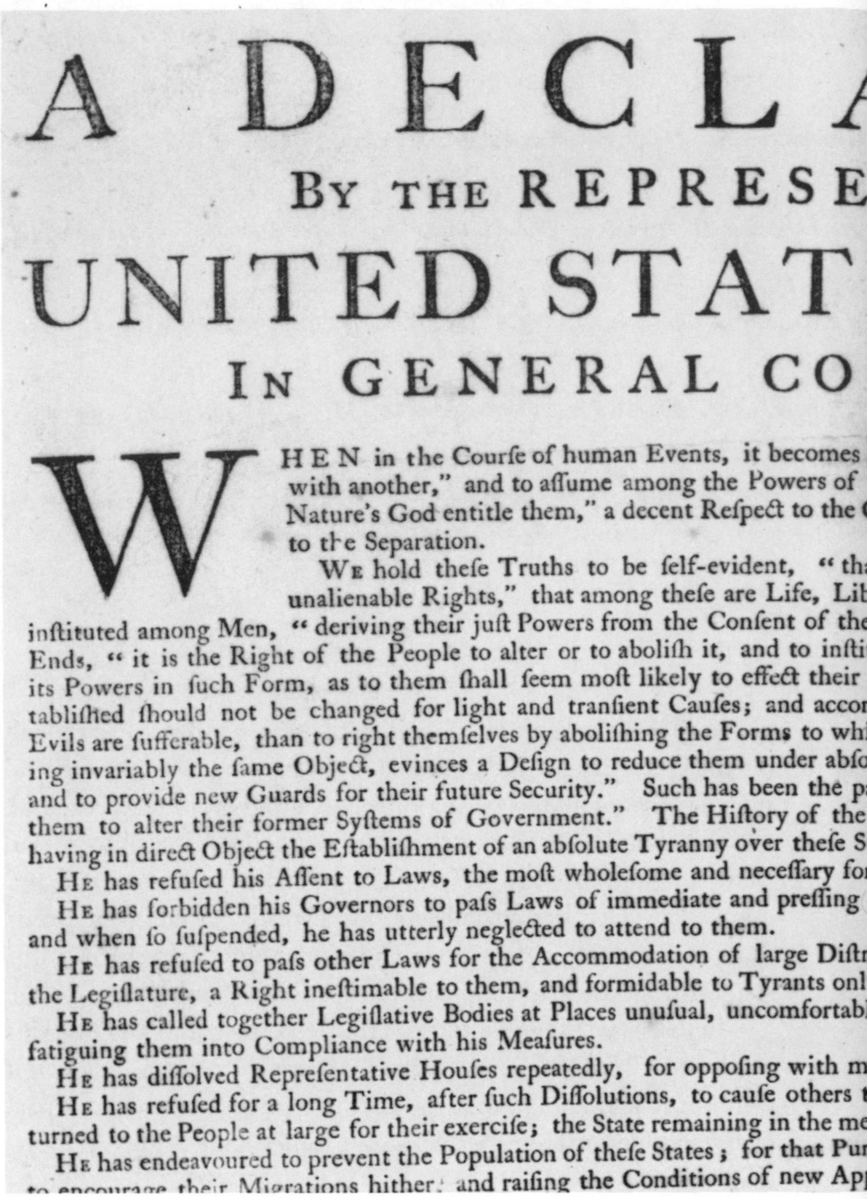
A DECLA

BY THE REPRESE

UNITED STAT

IN GENERAL CO

W HEN in the Courſe of human Events, it becomes
with another," and to aſſume among the Powers of
Nature's God entitle them," a decent Reſpect to the
to the Separation.

WE hold theſe Truths to be ſelf-evident, " th
unalienable Rights," that among theſe are Life, Lib
inſtituted among Men, " deriving their juſt Powers from the Conſent of the
Ends, " it is the Right of the People to alter or to aboliſh it, and to inſti
its Powers in ſuch Form, as to them ſhall ſeem moſt likely to effect their
tabliſhed ſhould not be changed for light and tranſient Cauſes; and accor
Evils are ſufferable, than to right themſelves by aboliſhing the Forms to wh
ing invariably the ſame Object, evinces a Deſign to reduce them under abſo
and to provide new Guards for their future Security." Such has been the p
them to alter their former Syſtems of Government." The Hiſtory of the
having in direct Object the Eſtabliſhment of an abſolute Tyranny over theſe S

HE has refuſed his Aſſent to Laws, the moſt wholeſome and neceſſary fo

HE has forbidden his Governors to paſs Laws of immediate and preſſing
and when ſo ſuſpended, he has utterly neglected to attend to them.

HE has refuſed to paſs other Laws for the Accommodation of large Diſtr
the Legiſlature, a Right ineſtimable to them, and formidable to Tyrants onl

HE has called together Legiſlative Bodies at Places unuſual, uncomfortab
fatiguing them into Compliance with his Meaſures.

HE has diſſolved Repreſentative Houſes repeatedly, for oppoſing with m

HE has refuſed for a long Time, after ſuch Diſſolutions, to cauſe others
turned to the People at large for their exerciſe; the State remaining in the me

HE has endeavoured to prevent the Population of theſe States; for that Pur
to encourage their Migrations hither, and raiſing the Conditions of new Ap

Figure 2. Opening paragraphs with erroneous quotation marks from the lone surviving proof copy of the Dunlap broadside. (Courtesy of The Historical Society of Pennsylvania.)

RATION

TATIVES OF THE

S OF AMERICA,

GRESS ASSEMBLED.

for one People " to diſſolve the Political Bands which have connected them
h, the ſeparate and equal Station " to which the Laws of Nature and of
of Mankind requires " that they ſhould declare the cauſes which impel them

en are created equal," " that they are endowed by their Creator with certain
d the Purſuit of Happineſs-—That to ſecure theſe Rights, Governments are
ed," that whenever any Form of Government becomes deſtructive of theſe
w Government, laying its Foundation on ſuch Principles, and organizing
d Happineſs." Prudence, indeed, will dictate that Governments long eſ-
ll Experience hath ſhewn, that Mankind are more diſpoſed to ſuffer, while
are accuſtomed. But when a long Train of Abuſes and Uſurpations, purſu-
potiſm, it is their Right, it is their Duty, to throw off ſuch Government,
fferance of theſe Colonies;" and ſuch is now the Neceſſity which conſtrains
King of Great-Britain is a Hiſtory of repeated Injuries and Uſurpations, all
To prove this, let Facts be ſubmitted to a candid World.
blic Good.
nce, unleſs ſuſpended in their Operation till his Aſſent ſhould be obtained;

eople, unleſs thoſe People would relinquiſh the Right of Repreſentation in

liſtant from the Depoſitory of their public Records, for the ſole Purpoſe of

mneſs his Invaſions on the Rights of the People.
ted; whereby the Legiſlative Powers, incapable of Annihilation, have re-
expoſed to all the Dangers of Invaſion from without, and Convulſions within.
tructing the Laws for Naturalization of Foreigners; refuſing to paſs oth..s
ons of Lands.

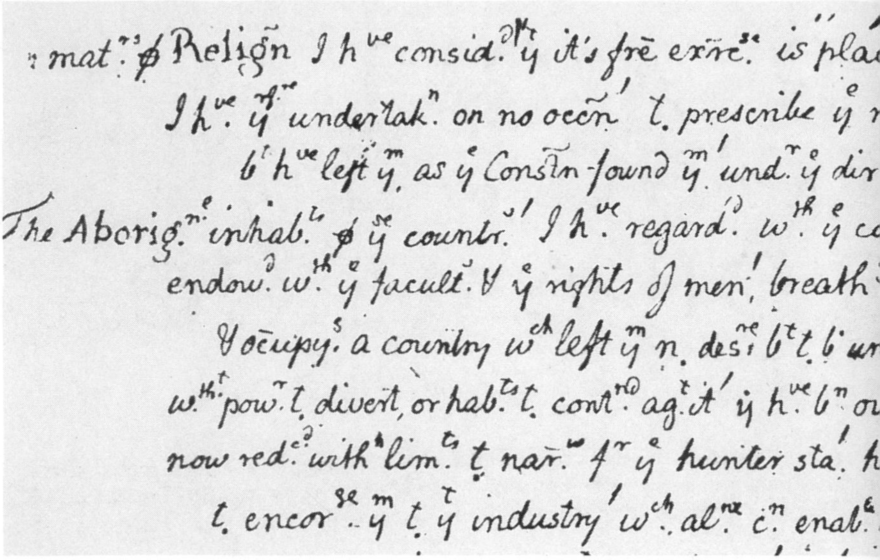

Figure 3. Section from the reading copy of Jefferson's second Inaugural, March 4, 1805. (Courtesy of the Library of Congress.)

by an emphatical word which may force the pause so that the ear may feel the regular return of the pause. The interval between these regular pauses constitutes a verse. . . . A well-organized ear makes the pause regularly whether it be printed as verse or as prose.[10]

The locations of the marks on the rough draft of the Declaration as well as the locations of the "quotation marks" on the proof copy of the Dunlap broadside represent not breath or punctuational pauses but precisely what Jefferson discusses: rhythmical pauses of emphatical stress that divide the piece into units comparable to musical bars or poetic lines. These marks are identical to ones suggested by the influential Irish rhetorician Thomas Sheridan in his *Lectures on the Art of Reading* (1775). Sheridan uses a "small inclined line, thus /," to indicate a short "pause marking an incomplete sense" and a double line, //, for a pause "double the time of the former." Thus, in Sheridan's example: "thy kingdom / come // thy will / be done //."[11]

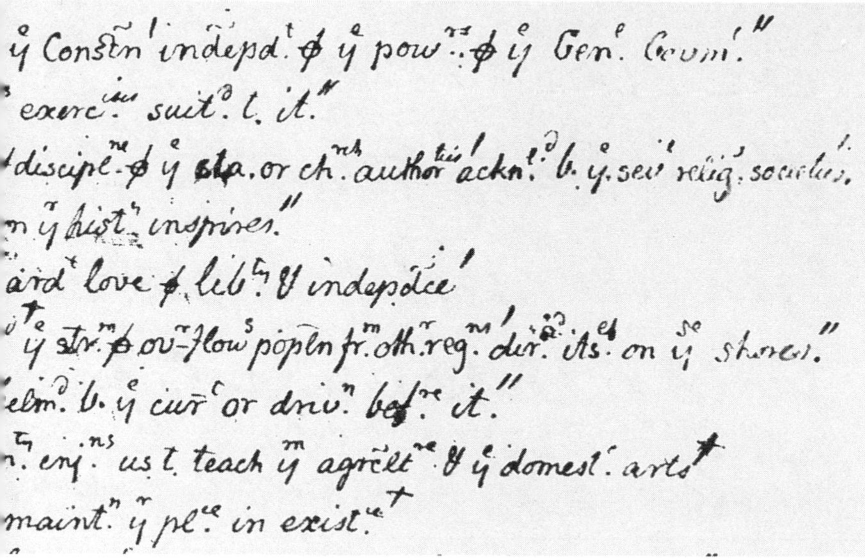

Below I have printed the one marked passage from the rough draft of the Declaration with single or short pauses (´ in the manuscript) indicated by diagonal lines and double or full pauses (´ ´ in the manuscript) indicated by new lines. The passage can now be read as Jefferson rhythmically set it forth:

in every stage / of these oppressions
we have petitioned for redress / in the most humble terms;
our repeated petitions / have been answered only by repeated
  injuries.
a prince whose character is thus marked / by every act which
  may define a tyrant,
is unfit to be the ruler / of a free people who mean to be free.
future ages will scarce believe / that the hardiness of one man
adventured within the short compass / of twelve years to build
a foundation / so broad and undisguised,
for tyranny

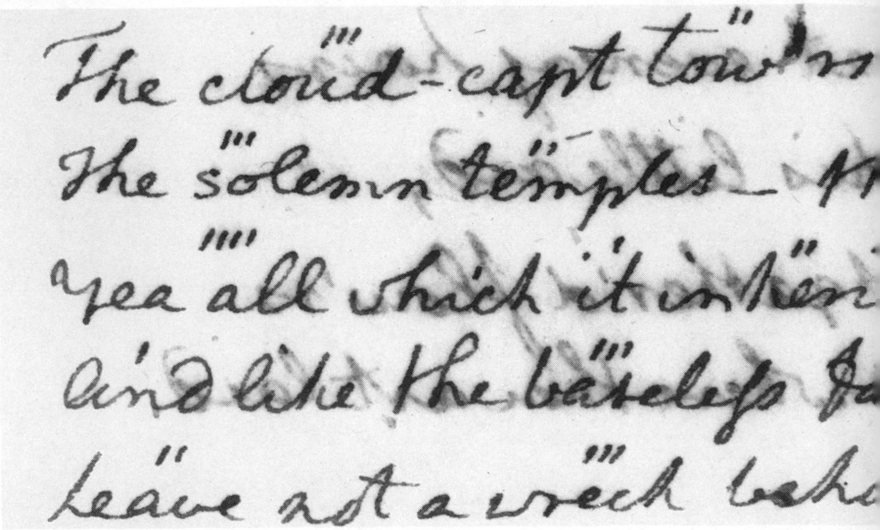

The cloud-capt tow'rs
The solemn temples
yea all which it inhe
And like the baseless
Leave not a wreck beh

Figure 4. Detail from "Thoughts on Prosody," 1786, with passages from Shakespeare accented. (Courtesy of the Library of Congress.)

Because the Dunlap "quotation" marks do not distinguish between single and double pauses, here is the opening paragraph of the broadside Declaration with each pause indicated by a new line:

> When in the Course of human Events, it becomes necessary for one People
> to dissolve the Political Bands which have connected them with another
> and to assume among the Powers of the Earth, the separate and equal Station
> to which the Laws of nature and of nature's God entitle them,
> a decent Respect to the Opinions of Mankind requires
> that they should declare the causes which impel them to the Separation.

In Sheridan's earlier, more theoretical work, *Lectures on Elocution* (1762), a book Jefferson purchased in the mid 1760's as part of his preparation for a career in law, the author argued that because

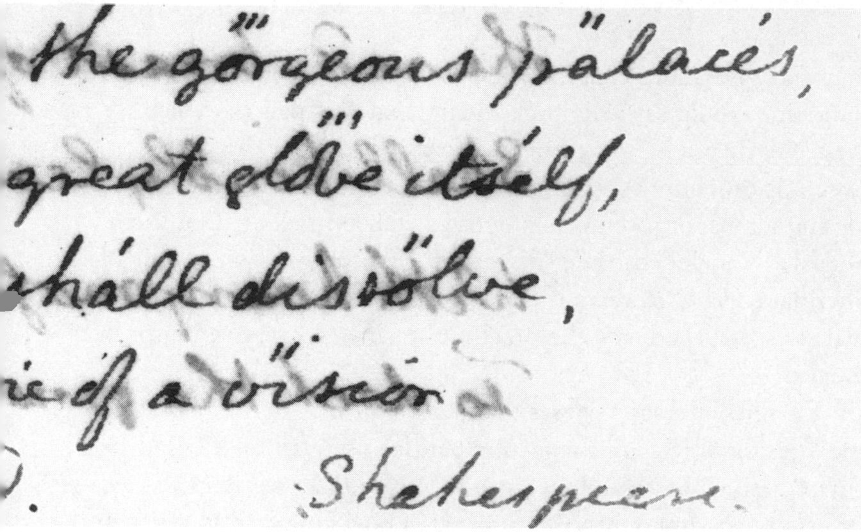
the gorgeous palaces,
great globe itself,
hall dissolve,
of a vision
Shakespeare.

of the false assumption that pauses correlate exclusively and merely with punctuation "there is no article in reading more difficult, than that of observing a due proportion of stops."[12] The "truth is that the modern art of punctuation was not taken from the art of speaking." Instead, punctuation was and is "in a great measure regulated by the rules of grammar; that is, certain parts of speech are kept together, and others divided by stops."[13]

In contrast to the formalism of punctuation, rhetorical pauses indicate the "matter of the discourse and the disposition of the mind of the speaker"—and thus express both text and speaker. They mark sense, create rhythm, are accompanied by infinitely various changes in tone that indicate "the kind of pause it is," and thereby "inform the mind what to expect from them," such as whether "the sense is still to be continued in the same sentence or not." They are also a mode of direct emphasis, and thus are part of a larger cultural code. If a proposition or sentiment is preceded "by a longer pause than usual," Sheridan argued, it will "rouze attention and give more weight when delivered."[14] Indeed, Edmund Randolph would say of Patrick Henry that "his pauses, which for their length might sometimes be feared to dispel the attention, riveted it the more by raising the expectation."[15] But if pauses are too numerous, or too much "liberty" is taken in elongating them, Sheridan concluded, they "disgust."[16] The entire second half of Sheridan's *Art of Reading* is printed with pause marks and accentual stresses to indicate the precise phrasing of every sentence in the text.

Finally, Jefferson's pauses make a crucial link between oratory and music, which according to Sheridan is "also distributed by phrase, demi-phrase and measures." Such a link clearly interested Jefferson, who not only was interested in how Homer rhythmically measured his language "as a piece of music is divided into bars," but who in a 1773 letter to a law student recommended John Mason's *Essay on the Power and Harmony of Prosaic Numbers*, a volume that described at length how prose, no less than poetry, could profit from being written "in measured Cadences." In addition, Jefferson, who devoted (in his words) "no less than *three hours* a day" to the practice of the violin (an instrument he brought with him to the Continental Congress), owned a number of books on musical theory that explicitly addressed the connections between oratory and music.[17]

One such volume, Francesco Geminiani's *The Art of Playing the Violin* (1751), not only defined "the perfect tone of the violin" as the one that rivals "the most perfect human Voice," but insisted that "all good music should be composed in imitation of a Discourse," with forte and pianissimo producing "the same Effects that an Orator does by raising and falling his Voice." Or, as John Holden put it in his *Essay Towards a Rational System of Music* (1770), another of the half dozen books on music theory listed in the earliest surviving catalogue of Jefferson's library, "the particular manners and modulations of the voice," which naturally obey "the custom of a particular country," and which "accompany the emotions . . . of common speech," are "the subject given to music." Irresistibly leading the listener "to distribute a tune into proper measure," music is the inflected and infinitely expressive speech and voice of a "particular country."[18]

Playing an instrument, like speaking, involved the expression of private feelings, yet at the same time demanded conformity to the social and musical etiquette of measured regularity and an articulation of the character and conventions of "common speech." Eighteenth-century public speaking, that is, involved a drama of competing understandings of orality. In one view orality was "an inner voice of emotion" and an expression of subjectivity. In another it was "public-oriented oratorical communication," a mode of expression in which national values and a common sensibility were to be articulated and reinforced or (if romanticized as preliterate) recovered.[19] Jefferson addressed such conflicting obligations toward self-expression and self-effacement by insisting that the document he authored constituted not an expression of his mind but "an expression of the American mind" and "the common sense of the subject."[20]

Let us now return to John Rice's *Art of Reading*, the book that served Jefferson as an early guide to the mechanics and character of public speaking, for another perspective on the significance of the Declaration's marks. In his long section on pauses (which along with cadence, tone, and gesture are treated as "natural" modes of emphasis), Rice argues, following his mentor Abbé Batteux, that their primary function is to allow

> the Objects of a Discourse . . . to be all represented distinct and without Confusion . . . separated by some Kind of Interval. Let us consider them as they are found in Nature, or in a Picture; not one but has its Line of Circumscription, which bounds it and separates it from every other Object . . . in the most exact and regular Manner. . . . Like a Painter, it draws

its Strokes one after another, whence they must necessarily be separated from one another by some Kind of Space or Interval.[21]

Like architectural columns or the geometrical grid Jefferson would later impose on the Western territories, the pauses (whether heard by an auditor or by "the well-organized ear" of the silent reader) are a mode of framing, of dividing a discourse into units that can be engaged and absorbed. In *Elements of Criticism*, a book Jefferson enthusiastically recommended to his nephew Robert Skipwith in 1771, the Scottish aesthetician, lawyer, and historian, Lord Kames, insisted that because "the eye is the best avenue to the heart," the successful poet must represent "every thing as passing before our sight; and from readers and hearers transform us . . . into spectators." In a related fashion, Thomas Paine declares in the first of his *Crisis Papers*, written in December of 1776, that he will "in language as plain as A, B, C, hold up truth to your eyes."[22] Because the visual is associated in the human mind with reality, and the will and passions operate largely in response to images, Kames argued, whatever serves to enhance the visual or material character of a spoken text, whatever transforms a text into a drama that one "beholds," both strengthens the illusion of an immediate engagement with truth and more effectively influences future behavior. By dividing a spoken text into what Rice called "multiple objects" of a discourse circumscribed and differentiated by painterly lines, by seeming to confer on the spoken text the palpable dramatic presence of the orator, Jefferson's pauses turn the text itself into units of self-evidence: we [be]hold these truths to be self-evident.

Jefferson's pause marks also suggest the degree to which music, which he called in 1778 "the favorite passion of my soul," was simultaneously an expression of personal sentiments and a mechanistic science.[23] A notational language based on precise mathematical relations, music was spirit and passion rooted not in transcendental feeling but in a materialist base, the actualization of fixed tonal relations. Thus, inscribing pauses in the Declaration that were like musical measures also manifested Jefferson's preoccupation with accounting, scientific measurement, and a lifetime habit of dividing virtually everything into mathematical units. For Jefferson, proportionality (as in his 1779 draft bill for "proportioning crimes and punishments") was a moral concept. Even in advising a new law student in 1773 on a course of reading, Jefferson divided the reading day into five distinct intervals, with different subjects appropriate to different times ("From Dark to Bed-time, Belles lettres, Criticism, Rhetoric, Oratory"), and with specific books given to be read in a specific order.[24]

While at the second Continental Congress, Jefferson purchased a thermometer to take and record the daily temperature, for in his view the precise recording of information not only permitted the past to be compared with the present but allowed patterns in nature and human nature to be seen and understood in a fashion that held out the seductive possibility of predictive value for the future. The keeping of records extended to the private sphere as well. For example, Jefferson recorded his Philadelphia purchases on the blank leaves of his *Timothy Telescope's Almanack for 1776*. On the page that records his accounts from June 20 to July 6, however, the anxious period of his writing and presenting the Declaration, Jefferson forgot that June has 30 rather than 31 days (Figure 5). He left out June 29 and entered purchases on a nonexistent June 31, making clear that the "scientific" record was always subject to the psychological preoccupation of the scientist.

Though, like many, he was, in his word, "charmed" by the new instrument of the pianoforte, with its full stroke-responsive capacity to express and interpret human emotions (he ordered a piano for his wife Martha in 1771), Jefferson's interest in music had as much to do with measure as with expression. As minister to Paris in the mid 1780's, Jefferson improved Renaudin's recent invention of a new mechanical metronome, further fixing the precise numerical relations between pendulum swings and vibrations for largo, adagio, and so on.[25] If playing, like public speaking, involved an

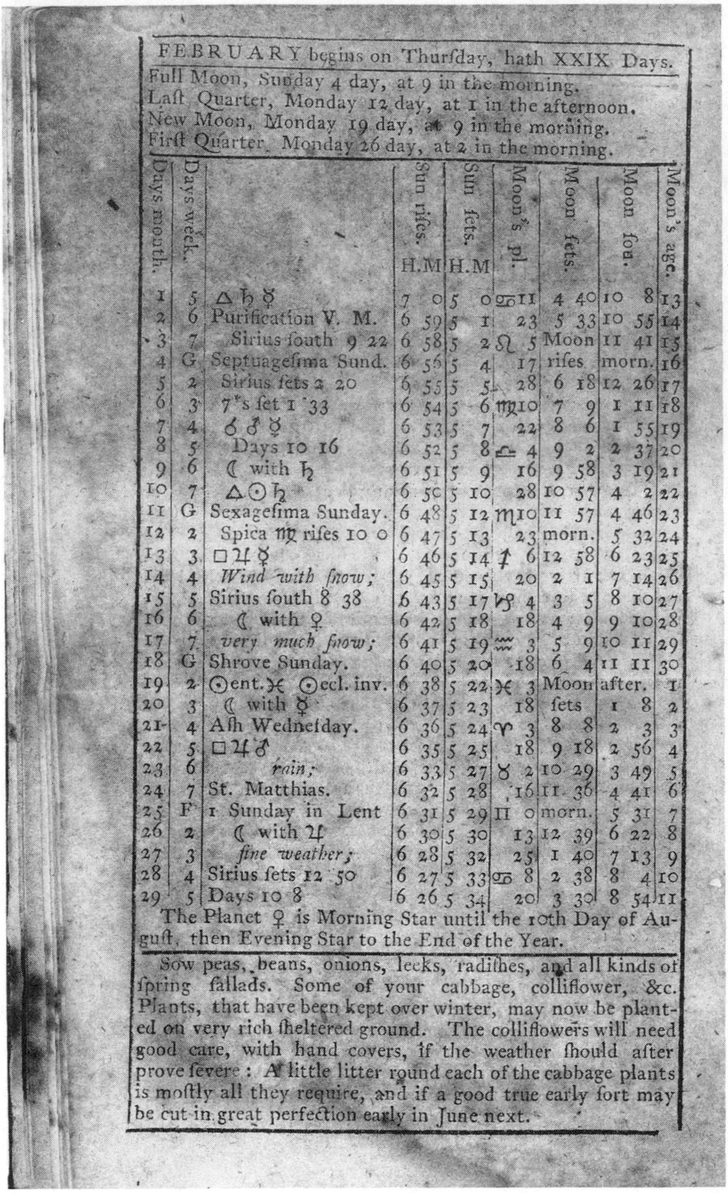

FEBRUARY begins on Thurſday, hath XXIX Days.

Full Moon, Sunday 4 day, at 9 in the morning.
Laſt Quarter, Monday 12 day, at 1 in the afternoon.
New Moon, Monday 19 day, at 9 in the morning.
Firſt Quarter, Monday 26 day, at 2 in the morning.

Days month.	Days week.		Sun riſes. H.M	Sun ſets. H.M	Moon's pl.	Moon ſets.	Moon ſou.	Moon's age.
1	5	△ ♄ ☿	7 0	5 0	♋ 11	4 40	10 8	13
2	6	Purification V. M.	6 59	5 1	23	5 33	10 55	14
3	7	Sirius ſouth 9 22	6 58	5 2	♌ 5	Moon	11 41	15
4	G	Septuageſima Sund.	6 56	5 4	17	riſes	morn.	16
5	2	Sirius ſets 2 20	6 55	5 5	28	6 18	12 26	17
6	3	7*s ſet 1 33	6 54	5 6	♍ 10	7 9	1 11	18
7	4	☌ ♂ ☿	6 53	5 7	22	8 6	1 55	19
8	5	Days 10 16	6 52	5 8	♎ 4	9 2	2 37	20
9	6	☾ with ♄	6 51	5 9	16	9 58	3 19	21
10	7	△ ☉ ♄	6 50	5 10	28	10 57	4 2	22
11	G	Sexageſima Sunday.	6 48	5 12	♏ 10	11 57	4 46	23
12	2	Spica ♍ riſes 10 0	6 47	5 13	23	morn.	5 32	24
13	3	□ ♃ ☿	6 46	5 14	♐ 6	12 58	6 23	25
14	4	*Wind with ſnow;*	6 45	5 15	20	2 1	7 14	26
15	5	Sirius ſouth 8 38	6 43	5 17	♑ 4	3 5	8 10	27
16	6	☾ with ♀	6 42	5 18	18	4 9	9 10	28
17	7	*very much ſnow;*	6 41	5 19	♒ 3	5 9	10 11	29
18	G	Shrove Sunday.	6 40	5 20	18	6 4	11 11	30
19	2	☉ ent. ♓ ☉ ecl. inv.	6 38	5 22	♓ 3	Moon	after.	1
20	3	☾ with ☿	6 37	5 23	18	ſets	1 8	2
21	4	Aſh Wedneſday.	6 36	5 24	♈ 3	8 8	2 3	3
22	5	□ ♃ ♂	6 35	5 25	18	9 18	2 56	4
23	6	*rain;*	6 33	5 27	♉ 2	10 29	3 49	5
24	7	St. Matthias.	6 32	5 28	16	11 36	4 41	6
25	F	1 Sunday in Lent	6 31	5 29	♊ 0	morn.	5 31	7
26	2	☾ with ♃	6 30	5 30	13	12 39	6 22	8
27	3	*fine weather;*	6 28	5 32	25	1 40	7 13	9
28	4	Sirius ſets 12 50	6 27	5 33	♋ 8	2 38	8 4	10
29	5	Days 10 8	6 26	5 34	20	3 30	8 54	11

The Planet ♀ is Morning Star until the 10th Day of Auguſt, then Evening Star to the End of the Year.

Sow peas, beans, onions, leeks, radiſhes, and all kinds of ſpring ſallads. Some of your cabbage, colliflower, &c. Plants, that have been kept over winter, may now be planted on very rich ſheltered ground. The colliflowers will need good care, with hand covers, if the weather ſhould after prove ſevere: A little litter round each of the cabbage plants is moſtly all they require, and if a good true early ſort may be cut in great perfection early in June next.

Figure 5. Leaf from Jefferson's copy of *Timothy Telescope's Almanack for 1776* with his June 31 account entry. (Courtesy of the Massachusetts Historical Society.)

11.

June 20. pd dinner at Smith's 7/
pd Hugh Walker for waggonage of sundries last winter to head of Elk 27/6
pd Aitkin for lining a map 5/
22 - pd dinner at Smith's 7/6
pd Sparhawk for pr spurs 25/
pd ferrge over Schuylkill &c. 10d.
23. pd Graaf 2. weeks lodging &c. £ 3 - 10.
24. pd Dinner at Smith's 5/6
25. pd for 2 pr stockings for Bob 15/
pd dinner at Smith's 5/
pd for a straw hat 10/
27. pd Byrne for 6 weeks shaving & dressing 30/
28. pd mrs Loremore washing in full 39/9
30. pd Sparhawk for a pencil 1/6 a map 7/6
pd Dinner at Smith's 8/6
31. pd expences riding 2/4
July 1. pd ferrge of horses 8d.
3. pd Towne for Doctor Gilmer 7/6
pd do. for myself 7/6
pd Smith in full 15/6
4. pd Sparhawk for a thermometer £ 3 - 15
pd for 7 pr women's gloves 27/
gave in charity 1/6
5. pd for a quire of paper 2/6
6. pd mr Braxton for 4 pr cotton cards 48/
pd for pamphlets 6/
pd for beer 1/

expression of character and personal feelings, in addition to the presentation of the character and arguments of a composition, the stress on regularity in music and speech suggested a complementary impulse to contain, restrain, and order that expression.

Discussing the difficulty of reading poetry out loud in his "Thoughts on Prosody," Jefferson concluded that "no two persons will accent the same passage alike. No person but a real adept would accent it twice alike." Even when cast in regular meters, poetic texts are fluid, and reading is an art not a science. "I suppose that in those passages of Shakespeare, for example, no man but Garrick ever drew their full tone out of them, if I may borrow an expression from music." Tone, for Jefferson, was both a feature of the speaker's voice and a feature of the printed text that sounded "an author's sentiments or revealed his character." Jefferson's mention of Garrick, the premier actor of the age, also suggests a new standard of professional theatrical performance by which anxious public speakers were to be judged by a public given a new franchise to be critical. Jefferson's defensive remark about his ability to accent poetry so as to elicit its full tone—"Let those who are disposed to criticise . . . try a few experiments themselves"—suggests his sensitivity to criticism. The mention of Garrick also extends to public speaking the theatrical problem of whether acting should involve the artful representation of feelings or the "natural" expression of those immediately felt. As we shall see, this was a major source of an oratorical anxiety shared by many more than Jefferson.[26]

When John Dunlap, the Declaration's printer, realized his error and removed the misread quotation marks that survive in the proof copy from the rest of the broadside's print run, the words in the opening paragraphs were only partially respaced, thereby leaving an awkward, unbalanced appearance (Figure 6). Thus, even after they were eliminated the markers of the Declaration's oral character left their trace presence in the deformation of the printed text. No subsequent printed transcription of Jefferson's original version of the Declaration—from the one Jefferson provided in his own *Autobiography* to the one in the Jefferson *Papers* to those available in textbooks and literary anthologies—reproduces those marks. But as part of the original text of the Declaration and as unique registers of the self-consciousness and protocols of public speaking that defined the conditions of its verbal production, those accents are crucial to its meaning.

In opposition to the spoken Declaration, whose speaker illuminated, elicited, and partially created its meaning in the context of a larger social interaction, the printed Declaration, experienced as it is today in the individualistic context of a silent reading largely untuned to the performative dimension of the text, is radically cut off from its original rhetorical context. It appears fixed in its visual field, and by the mystique of print is made to seem permanent and immutable, an analogue to what it calls the "perpetual" league sought by a people "fixed" in immutable principles of freedom. Its visual self-evidence is total—independent of a complex interpretive performance wherein a speaker's skill and sincerity are judged by a critical audience.

This separation of the printed document from its context of rhetorical performance has helped enable the cultural appropriation of the document as a primary text in America's civic religion. Though the famous painting by John Trumbull shows the Declaration's presentation to John Hancock, then president of Congress, the moment that has become culturally appropriated is the signatory moment (an event delayed until August, in part to avoid accountability for treason), in which the 56 members of the second Continental Congress are transformed into "the signers." That moment suggests authorization, consensus, and, by falsely equating the Declaration to formal legislation, legality and permanence.

In what probably is an early 1770's entry in his commonplace book, Jefferson, seeking to disprove the proposition that "Christianity is part of the Common Law," succeeded in tracing the

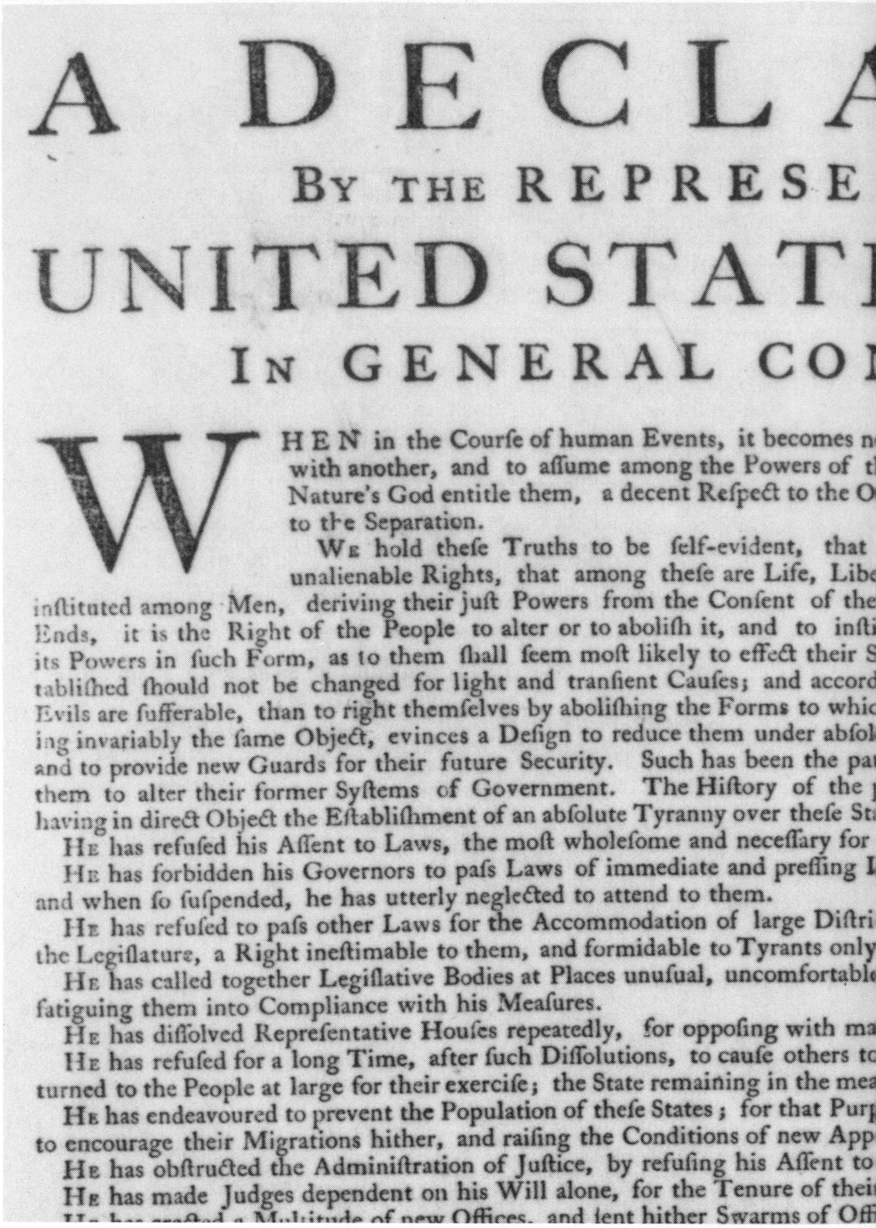

A DECLA

BY THE REPRESE

UNITED STAT

IN GENERAL CO

WHEN in the Courſe of human Events, it becomes n
with another, and to aſſume among the Powers of t
Nature's God entitle them, a decent Reſpect to the O
to the Separation.

WE hold theſe Truths to be ſelf-evident, that
unalienable Rights, that among theſe are Life, Lib
inſtituted among Men, deriving their juſt Powers from the Conſent of the
Ends, it is the Right of the People to alter or to aboliſh it, and to inſti
its Powers in ſuch Form, as to them ſhall ſeem moſt likely to effect their S
tabliſhed ſhould not be changed for light and tranſient Cauſes; and accord
Evils are ſufferable, than to right themſelves by aboliſhing the Forms to whic
ing invariably the ſame Object, evinces a Deſign to reduce them under abſol
and to provide new Guards for their future Security. Such has been the pa
them to alter their former Syſtems of Government. The Hiſtory of the
having in direct Object the Eſtabliſhment of an abſolute Tyranny over theſe St

HE has refuſed his Aſſent to Laws, the moſt wholeſome and neceſſary for

HE has forbidden his Governors to paſs Laws of immediate and preſſing L
and when ſo ſuſpended, he has utterly neglected to attend to them.

HE has refuſed to paſs other Laws for the Accommodation of large Diſtri
the Legiſlature, a Right ineſtimable to them, and formidable to Tyrants only

HE has called together Legiſlative Bodies at Places unuſual, uncomfortabl
fatiguing them into Compliance with his Meaſures.

HE has diſſolved Repreſentative Houſes repeatedly, for oppoſing with ma

HE has refuſed for a long Time, after ſuch Diſſolutions, to cauſe others t
turned to the People at large for their exerciſe; the State remaining in the mea

HE has endeavoured to prevent the Population of theſe States; for that Purp
to encourage their Migrations hither, and raiſing the Conditions of new App

HE has obſtructed the Adminiſtration of Juſtice, by refuſing his Aſſent to

HE has made Judges dependent on his Will alone, for the Tenure of thei

HE has erected a Multitude of new Offices, and ſent hither Swarms of Off

Figure 6. Opening paragraphs of the Dunlap broadside whose partial respacing still reveals sites of deleted quotation marks. (Courtesy of the Beinecke Rare Book and Manuscript Library, Yale University.)

RATION

TATIVES OF THE

S OF AMERICA,

GRESS ASSEMBLED.

for one People to diſſolve the Political Bands which have connected them
h, the ſeparate and equal Station to which the Laws of Nature and of
of Mankind requires that they ſhould declare the cauſes which impel them

en are created equal, that they are endowed by their Creator with certain
d the Purſuit of Happineſs—-That to ſecure theſe Rights, Governments are
ned, that whenever any Form of Government becomes deſtructive of theſe
ew Government, laying its Foundation on ſuch Principles, and organizing
d Happineſs. Prudence, indeed, will dictate that Governments long eſ-
ll Experience hath ſhewn, that Mankind are more diſpoſed to ſuffer, while
are accuſtomed. But when a long Train of Abuſes and Uſurpations, purſu-
potiſm, it is their Right, it is their Duty, to throw off ſuch Government,
fferance of theſe Colonies; and ſuch is now the Neceſſity which conſtrains
King of Great-Britain is a Hiſtory of repeated Injuries and Uſurpations, all
To prove this, let Facts be ſubmitted to a candid World.
lic Good.
nce, unleſs ſuſpended in their Operation till his Aſſent ſhould be obtained;

eople, unleſs thoſe People would relinquiſh the Right of Repreſentation in

diſtant from the Depoſitory of their public Records, for the ſole Purpoſe of

mneſs his Invaſions on the Rights of the People.
cted; whereby the Legiſlative Powers, incapable of Annihilation, have re-
expoſed to all the Dangers of Invaſion from without, and Convulſions within.
tructing the Laws for Naturalization of Foreigners; refuſing to paſs others
ons of Lands.
or eſtabliſhing Judiciary Powers.
s, and the Amount and Payment of their Salaries.
harraſs our People, and eat out their Subſtance.

absorption of ecclesiastical law into English common law (with what he saw as its heinous consequences) to a seventeenth-century English mistranslation of a French treatise on Anglo-Norman law. The phrase "en ancien scripture," he argued, had been falsely rendered as "holy Scripture" rather than laws in "ancient writing."[27] Once in print, the error was perpetuated by dozens of subsequent treatises, all relying on the translator's original codification. The close interplay between "holy Scripture" and "ancient writing" would, of course, come to characterize the status of the printed Declaration itself and speak to the dangers of the independent historical status and agency of print.

By viewing the Declaration as a text meant to be read silently rather than to be heard as performance we have lost sight of crucial mid-eighteenth-century assumptions about speakers and personal expression, about rhetoric and the art of reading (a phrase that, as in John Rice's title, still had the primary sense of reading aloud), assumptions necessary to a full understanding of Revolutionary American culture. Recovering those assumptions allows us to see the rhetoric of the Revolution as participating not only in a political revolution but in a revolution in the conceptualization of language, a revolution that sought to replace artificial language with natural language and to make writing over in the image of speaking. Once a decorous, rule-governed, and class-specific behavior that articulated the public virtues of civic humanism—the honor of the office and the public good—public speaking became reconceptualized in the mid eighteenth century as an occasion for the public revelation of a private self. Such a private self would then be judged by private rather than public virtues: prudence, temperance, self-control, honesty, and, most problematically, sincerity.[28] American independence occurred at a historical moment when the speaking voice was seen as a register of the speaker's subjectivity in ways that required a new set of rhetorical prescriptions and expectations in order to regulate the vagaries of that subjectivity. The narrative of America's "declaring independence" has hitherto emphasized the drama of the second term at the expense of the drama of the first, the drama suggested by the oratorical stresses felt as well as marked by Jefferson.

Jefferson's emphatical pauses call attention to the fact that the Declaration was written to be read aloud. Part of its own agenda as a "declaration" was to "publish and declare" (with the former verb carrying the contemporary sense of "to announce formally and publicly") that "these colonies . . . are free." On July 4 the Continental Congress ordered not only that "the declaration be authenticated and printed," but that "copies of the declaration be sent to the several assemblies, conventions and committees, or councils of safety, and to the several commanding officers [so] that it be proclaimed in each of the United States."[29] Massachusetts broadside printings included at the bottom of the text the legislative order: "That the *Declaration of Independence* be printed; and a Copy sent to the Ministers of each Parish, of every Denomination within this State; and that they severally be *required* to read the same to their respective Congregations."[30]

At the scene of the public readings in Philadelphia, John Adams reported: "The Declaration was yesterday published and proclaimed from that awfull Stage in the State house Yard. . . . These Cheers rended the Welkin. The Bells rung all Day and almost all night."[31] That "awfull" stage from which John Nixon of the Committee of Safety announced the consequences of "the course of human events" was the large balcony of the observatory David Rittenhouse had built in 1769 to witness the transit of Venus, the heavenly revolution that provided a conservative and naturalized metaphor for America's political revolution.

The public readings made the Declaration an event rather than a document. They gave it a voice, which like "the voice of the people [that] drove us to it," the delegates' "voices for it," and "the voice of justice & of consanguinity" to which "our British brethren" have been "deaf," was experienced emotionally and responded to vocally.[32] Read out loud, the document that denounced a false community would galvanize the bond of a true one. As Lord Kames insisted in his *Elements of Criticism* (1762), a volume taught in virtually every American college at the time, public speeches or spectacles "accessible to all ranks of people" were essential to offset the "separation of men into different classes, by birth, office, or occupation, however necessary," a separation that had severed "the connection that ought to be among all members of the same state."[33]

In his *Lectures on Elocution*, Thomas Sheridan dramatically extended Kames's point: one reason men have failed in social reform was "their extravagant idea entertained of the power of writing":

> Our greatest men have been trying to do that with the pen, which can only be performed by the tongue; to produce effects by the dead letter, which can never be produced but by the living voice, with its accompaniments. This is no longer a mere assertion; it is no longer problematical. It has been demonstrated to the entire satisfaction of some of the wisest heads in these realms.[34]

Obliged to accept the growing authority of print culture in the second half of the century (the *OED* indicates that "publish," not in the Declaration's oral sense, but in its now-current sense of "making public exclusively by means of print," first appeared in 1771), Sheridan and others fought the "dead letter" by articulating projects not only for improving public speaking but for preserving the special character of the spoken voice in written composition. Addressed to a wider audience than the literate gentry to whom the pamphlet literature of the period was largely directed, the properly delivered voice of the public speaker created consensus rather than fueling what Jefferson called "the morbid rage of debate."[35] It stimulated natural sociability rather than the disposition to quarrel.

In part as a response to a mass audience newly created by the immense diffusion of information by an enlarged print culture, public speaking was becoming precisely that, less addressed to specialized legal, political, or religious audiences with their own formalist codes than to a general public whose opinion Madison declared is the "real sovereign" in every free country.[36] Addressed with a "decent respect" by the Declaration, public opinion began to matter enough to be cultivated with a new model of speaking. It was crucial to the fate of public life, as Hugh Blair insisted in his widely read and taught *Lectures on Rhetoric*, that an "affected artificial manner of speaking" now "frigid and unpersuasive" give way to one in which "the tones of public speaking" were "formed upon" the "tones of sensible and animated conversation," in which prepared texts should always appear extemporaneous, and in which the public realm, in ways that problematically blurred the distinction between them, should be modeled more and more on the private.[37] The standard classical division of oratory, as Jefferson himself put it, had three styles: "the elevated," for which "Orators and Poets will furnish subjects," the "middling," the province of "historians," and the "familiar," appropriate to "epistolary and comic writers."[38] The "familiar" would eventually present itself as normative in a fashion that stigmatized the other two as unnatural affectations. The orator, like Wordsworth's poet later in the century, must be "a man speaking to men."[39]

Though the Continental Congress kept its meetings closed to maintain the secrecy of its proceedings, in 1768 the Massachusetts House of Representatives had constructed a public gallery for the viewing of its debates, thus obliging speakers in part to refashion speeches that before would have been composed largely for an audience of elite peers.[40] In a related instance of democratization, syllogistic disputations in Latin, the staple of mid-century American college classroom exercises and public exhibitions, increasingly disappeared by the 1770's, giving way to free-wheeling forensic debates unconstrained by formal logic or circumscribed subject matter. The College of New Jersey, which eliminated the syllogist form from its commencement in 1774, announced that it preferred declamations that "display the various passions, and exemplify the graces of utterance and gesture."[41] As public speaking became a moral spectacle for popular consumption, a new set of pressures descended on the speaker, pressures to speak in a new kind of language. To understand that language requires an understanding of developments in the history of rhetoric.

The Elocutionary Revolution

In his *Dialogues Concerning Eloquence in General* (1722), William Stevenson approvingly quotes François Fénelon, the Archbishop of Cambray, on the need to reinvigorate the study of rhetoric: "We must not judge so unfavourably of Eloquence as to reckon it only a frivolous Art that a Declaimer uses to impose on the weak Imagination of the Multitude, and to serve his own Ends. 'Tis a very serious Art; design'd to instruct People; suppress their Passions; and reform their Manners; to support the Laws; direct publick Councils; and to make Men good and happy."[1] Though rhetorics of trope and high style like Anthony Blackwell's *Essay on the Nature of those Emphatical and Beautiful Figures which give Strength and Ornament to Writing* (1733) continued to be popular to the end of the century, the eighteenth century witnessed the culmination of a movement away from a circumscribed, ceremonial view of rhetoric as but figures and tropes serving as handmaidens charged with the artful presentation of ideas determined by a master logic and expressed through the conventions of grammar. That movement toward rhetoric as "a very serious Art" can be traced back to the demands for new religious and political discourses in the wake of the Reformation and the maturation of parliamentary government. As logic became more strongly associated with the principles of scientific inquiry and "separated itself more and more from its ancient connection with the theory of learned exposition and debate," rhetoric began to be the "custodian of its own theory of exposition" with its own understanding of proof and evidence, its own theories of popular communication and of the character and function of belles lettres.[2] The new rhetoric of persuasion rather than trope sought to recover classical rhetoric, broadly understood as the active art of moving and influencing men, of galvanizing their passions, interests, biases, and temperament.

What was called the "new rhetoric" challenged the Aristotelian and Ciceronian assumption that rhetoric should limit itself to political, forensic, and ceremonial discourse (was not persuasion the essence of all discourse?). It also challenged the Aristotelian "bondage" to highly stylized and artificial rhetorical forms. In the spirit of Baconian empiricism, the new rhetoric enjoined that arguments should be made from the facts of the case under debate rather than drawn from set topics or commonplaces. Indeed, in the course of the eighteenth century the very meaning of the word "commonplace" would undergo its telling transformation from a necessary, authoritative locus to a hackneyed expression devoid of originality.

In lectures on rhetoric delivered in the 1760's at the University of Glasgow, Adam Smith used Cicero's famous defense of Milo, a speech whose power and rhetorical figures had enchanted the young John Adams, to demonstrate the sterility of the "artistic" or ceremonial arguments central to the old rhetoric. Smith berated Cicero for engaging in an act of empty bravura by slavishly following the Aristotelian topics ("*De Causa, Effectu, Tempore*") in order to argue that Milo "had no motive to kill Clodius; that it was unsuitable to his character, that he had no opportunity," even though the facts of the case (the "nonartistic" arguments) were that Milo "declared his intention to kill Clodius . . . that he had killed 20 men before . . . and that we know he did kill him." Formalist arguments and commonplaces, Smith insisted, must give way to "natural" persuasion.[3]

Writing in the 1750's and 1760's, a host of rhetoricians, all of whom were widely read in America—James Burgh, Thomas Sheridan, and John Rice among them—proposed a redefinition of the very function and nature of rhetoric, of oratory, and of language itself. They heatedly rejected the narrow conception of rhetoric as stylistic ornaments, as Aristotelian topics, and as topically generated arguments in the service of proving or disproving a point against opposition. In its stead they favored a purified rhetoric of persuasion broadly understood as the active art of moving and influencing the passions.[4] Crucial to this definition was the elevation of the performative aspect of speech over the argumentative. Tonal and gestural delivery, which in classical rhetoric had been the minor element of *pronunciatio*, was given a new position of centrality. If in classical rhetoric *elocutio* meant style, the choice and arrangement of words, by the mid eighteenth century it signified oral delivery. Indeed, one scholar has identified the first use of the word "elocution" in the sense of oral delivery as appearing in George Fisher's *The American Instructor*, a book that Jefferson owned as a young man and that went through a dozen editions before 1775.[5]

The shared mission of all those works was to teach their readers that meaning does not so much depend upon the words spoken as on "the *manner*," as James Burgh put it in 1764, "of speaking them."[6] Thomas Sheridan elaborated the point: "All writers seem to be under the influence of one common delusion, that by the help of words alone, they can communicate. . . . They forget that the passions and fancy, . . . all that is noble and praise worthy . . . in man considered as a social being" depends "upon having a language of their own utterly independent of words." Elocution, the physical performance of language, articulates this "other language."[7] Speaking thus becomes less a form of argumentative or expository communication than a revelation of "internal moral dispositions" and passions registered by vocal tones, physical "exertions," and facial expressions that are received in unmediated form by the sympathetic "social" nature of the auditor.

Burgh's *The Art of Speaking . . . in which are given Rules for expressing properly the principal passions and Humours, which occur in*

Reading or Public Speaking (1764), reprinted in Philadelphia in 1775, was the most influential account of that crucial but "too much neglected" part of the art: delivery. Burgh's volume is nothing less than a theatrical text committed to the physiognomy and tonal semiotics of over 75 passions. Or as John Moore, who adapted Burgh's work for his school text, *The Young Gentleman and Lady's Monitor*, described Burgh's agenda, it was to teach a "system of the passions" and "the exact adaptation of the action to the word" so that one would know how "to appear in the countenance and operate on the body" when expressing any emotion. Even Noah Webster's *American Selection of Lessons in Reading* (1785) opens with Burgh.[8]

Burgh's choreography of countenances and his confidence that "nature has given to every emotion of the mind its proper outward expression" anticipates and complements Johann Caspar Lavater's vastly influential effort in his *Essays on Physiognomy* (1775) to offer a "definitive" taxonomy of facial expressions as infallible registers of personal character, his version of the transparency of natural expressive language.[9] At the moment a speaker wishes to project a particular emotion, he must not paint it but become a portrait of it.

The appropriate tone for "simple persuasion," for example, as Burgh advised speakers, is "moderate love":

> *Love*, (successful) lights up the *countenance* into *smiles*. The *forehead* is *smoothed*, and enlarged; the *eyebrows* are *arched*; the *mouth* a little *open*, and *smiling*; the *eyes languishing*, and *half shut*. . . . *The countenance* assumes the *eager* and *wishful* look of *desire*. The *accents* are *soft* and *winning* . . . both *hands pressed* to the *bosom*. *Love* unsuccessful, adds an air of *anxiety*, and *melancholy*. See Perplexity and Melancholy.[10]

For Burgh (whose *Political Disquisitions*, published in 1774, defended the colonies against monarchical oppression), "true eloquence" translated the sublimity of kingship into a power consistent with republicanism; it made the "tongue of the orator" equivalent to "the *sceptre* of a monarch."[11] It sought to find a rhetorical equivalent to the power of beauty to trigger involuntary desire, or more precisely, in gender terms, a male equivalent to the power of female beauty to solicit an involuntary sexual response. The creation of desire, that "internal act, which, by influencing the will, makes one proceed to action," was in the view of virtually all the period's rhetoricians the ultimate purpose of all oratory.

> Like irresistible *beauty*, it *transports*, it *ravishes*, it *commands* the *admiration* of all, who are within its reach. If it allows us time to *criticize*, it is not *genuine*. The hearer finds himself as *unable* to resist it as to *stop* the flow of a river with his *hand*. . . . His *passions* are no longer *his own*. The *orator* has taken *possession* of them: and with superior power, *works* them to whatever he *pleases*.[12]

The orator makes the will of the auditor the instrument of the latter's own surrender. But this seduction, the elocutionists ingenuously and ingeniously protested, must not be confused with the seduction effected by the dazzling figures and ornaments of an *ars oratoria* which, as Kant famously put it in his *Critique of Judgment*, was but a "beautiful show . . . a treacherous art which means to move men in important matters like machines to a judgment that must lose all weight upon reflection."[13] It was to this dangerous "show"—conventionally gendered as a woman's seduction of a man—that John Adams was alluding when in 1776 he proposed a design for a national seal depicting Hercules choosing between "Virtue beckoning [him] to labor" and Sloth "wantonly reclining on the Ground, displaying the Charms both of her Eloquence and person, to seduce him into Vice."[14] Because it subordinated argument to the tonal register of feelings, the new eloquence, in contrast, was the nakedness of truth, a true beauty, a self-evidence that required no judgment, the ultimate Protestant plain style. It presented or promised to present not arguments but the spectacle of a speaker stripped of what Paine called the "plumage" of office, station, and birth, a speaker revealed in the fullness of his natural feelings who announced the passing of an age of political supersti-

Figure 7. John Singleton Copley, *Paul Revere*, 1768–70. (Gift of Joseph W., William B., and Edward H. R. Revere. Courtesy of Museum of Fine Arts, Boston.)

tion.[15] If "government, like dress, is the badge of lost innocence," and monarchy is "something kept behind a curtain, about which there is a great deal of bustle and fuss," naked eloquence promised a new kind of governance, a governance appropriate to a republic in which, as David Ramsay put it, "mankind appear as they really are without any false colouring."[16]

John Singleton Copley's portrait of Paul Revere (1768–1770)—so different from the later portraits of his English period—is perhaps the best-known American icon of the new ideal of the unadorned private man (Figure 7). Depicted at his workplace without his wig, his hair unpowdered, in violation of portrait conventions of the period, Revere is conspicuously not dressed for public display. The viewer thus is placed in a position of unusual familiarity. The silver teapot is also unadorned, a tabula rasa awaiting the application of the engraving tools that lie on the bench. The masterful reflection of the hand in the unmarked surface of the teapot, like the reflection of Revere's smock in the painted surface of the bench, suggests that the larger painting is itself a simple mirror held up to the sitter. In contrast to Gilbert Stuart's distinctive use of visibly applied "broken" paint, Copley's glassy concealment of his brushstrokes, like Revere's "reflective" pose, reinforces the illusion of reflection, of naked truth unmediated and undisguised by artistry. Like the artificial "Fore-teeth" Revere made in his capacity as dentist and advertised as not only improving "looks" but facilitating "speaking both in Public and Private," Copley's portrait theatrically conceals the art used self-consciously to construct a natural man within society.[17]

Eight years before becoming the only clerical signer of the Declaration, John Witherspoon, then President of the College of New Jersey (later Princeton) and the first important American teacher of rhetoric, inaugurated an annual series of college lectures on eloquence in which he too addressed the antiornamental ideal. Attended by a number of students, including Madison, who would later become leading figures of the Revolutionary generation, those lectures helped bring about, by their stress on speaking in public deliberative assemblies, what Edmund Morgan has called the intellectual agenda of the Revolution: "the substitution of political for clerical leadership and of politics for religion as the most challenging arena of human thought and endeavor."[18]

In his opening lecture, Witherspoon cited the second chapter of Paul's first epistle to the Corinthians to remind his audience of the apostle's distinction between "artful divisive eloquence, such as the sophists . . . made use of to varnish over their foolish sentiments" and Paul's insistence that "he came not to show his skill in speaking for and against anything . . . but to communicate truth that needed no ornament."[19] Perfect eloquence, as Paul put it, effaced "the enticing words of man's wisdom" (1 Cor. 2.4) to become a self-evident demonstration of divine and, as Witherspoon extended it to the secular sphere, moral truth. Oratory at its most naked and transcendent became a kind of manifested spirit, an instrument and embodiment of a new Anglo-American republican authority.

The assumption that, to invoke a common trope of the period, language is but the dress of thought, its guise and disguise, problematically implies not only that the same thought can be variously expressed but that expression and thought are fully distinguishable, that thought has a pure, embodied, and naked existence separate from its articulation. Though the trope of rhetorical nakedness, key to the new eloquence, implies a "body" of pure thought, Blair concludes: "It is a very erroneous idea which many have of the ornaments of Style, as if they are things detached from the subject, and that could be stuck to it, like lace upon a coat . . . the real and proper ornaments of Style are wrought into the substance of it. They flow in the same stream with the current of thought."[20] If style has no separate existence, the call for a natural or naked language that embodies rather than represents thought turns language into something that is simultaneously body and dress. The illusion is like the trompe l'oeil effect of Copley's portraits of women whose dresses are overlaid with such perfectly rendered lace work that the viewer feels the lace might easily be lifted off or, more extremely, is made to feel there is a painted body beneath the painted clothes.[21] Though the expressive body is rendered paramount in the new performative elocution, it is also dematerialized into a trope itself, a trope for the undressed "body" of thought and feeling.

Soft Compulsion

No longer conceived of as the stigmatized power to coerce, political authority became redefined in a republican setting as the ability to secure consent, "to command," in Jefferson's phrase describing the Declaration, not individuals as subordinates, but "their assent."[1] Increasingly it signified an oratorical ability, not merely to persuade by rational argumentation, but to excite, animate, motivate, and impress. Those verbs must be understood according to the period's sensationalist view of knowledge as a set of extrapolations from sense events, of action as produced by the power of the single strongest motive, and of the human mind and heart as impressionable instruments whose psychological natures, once understood, could best be played upon by sound, looks, and gestures.

Those verbs also register the period's antirationalist preoccupation with ruling passions, desire, and an involuntary moral sense, all of which are more effectively excited by powerful delivery than by rational argumentation. Franklin's sentiment, "so convenient a thing it is to be a *reasonable Creature*, since it enables one to find or make a Reason for every thing one has a mind to do," was a cultural commonplace.[2] Speaking as the heart in the famous Head and Heart dialogue he sent to Maria Cosway in 1786, Jefferson put it in these terms: "Those who want [lack] the dispositions to give, easily find reasons why they ought not to give."[3] In 1818 Adams regaled Jefferson with an anecdote about "the Gods" talking about mankind. Responding to the proposition that man is rational, one of the Gods finally declares: "'Man a rational creature! How could any rational being ever dream that man was a rational creature?'"[4] If reason is, as Hume put it, "a species of sentiment"[5] or, as these passages suggest, a rationalizing faculty in the service of the passions (a faculty whose "logic" is a strategically useful determinism), rhetoric must turn from convincing the reason or impressing the intellect with casuistic or legalistic maneuvers to the more crucial project of reaching the informing heart.

An age preoccupied with efficacious persuasion and with uncovering hidden designs behind the masquerade of deceptive action and misleading speech translated a growing distrust of reason and rational persuasion into a wishful faith in an irresistible discourse of feelings. Such wishfulness is apparent in Lavater's *Physiognomy*, the text that provided pseudoscientific support for the belief in the transparency of natural expressive language. Responding to critics who argued that the promulgation of a "natural" code that correlated expression, feeling, and character encouraged rather than exposed dissimulation, Lavater skillfully begged the question: "The act of dissimulation itself, which is adduced as so insuperable an objection to the truth of physiognomy, is founded upon physiognomy. Why does the hypocrite assume the appearance of an honest man, but because that he is convinced, that all eyes are acquainted with the characteristic marks of honesty."[6]

In his criminal *Memoirs*, the notorious eighteenth-century American forger Stephen Burroughs describes a conversation he had with a physician who knew him in his youth. Not recognizing Burroughs, who had disguised himself to avoid capture, the physician insists that, because physiognomy is an excellent index to "natural disposition," he can confidently assert: "I never saw a more striking contrast, than between the designing, deceitful countenance of Burroughs, and your open, frank, and candid countenance."[7] The irony of the passage, an irony perversely confirming Lavater, is that the honest, open countenance *is* the countenance of deceit.

One reason novels of seduction on the model of Richardson's *Clarissa* had such popularity in Revolutionary America was that they spoke to the larger preoccupation not only with deception, but more specifically with the seductive power of the potent word to convince others to surrender themselves freely to one's will. Much as divine suasion avoided compelling an independent human will to act against its own inclination by transforming the character of that inclination (or as Jonathan Edwards put it in his *Freedom of the Will*, by its power to determine the pleasures of those who then are free to do as they please), such persuasion manipulated the passionate springs of human motivation in such a way as to avoid violating human freedom. With its blurring or fusion of idea and emotion, implicit in the word "sentiment," such antirationalism was in part derived from a secular reformulation of the lesson of evangelical religion: conviction is a matter of the heart as much as of the mind. The rejection of ornamental Ciceronian rhetoric for one of heartfelt persuasion thus stemmed from a culture at once republican and evangelical.

Indeed, as Alan Heimert has argued, what lay behind much of the rhetoric of the Revolution was a cultural appropriation of the enormously successful techniques of the evangelical rhetoric of sensation. That rhetoric was epitomized by the oratory of men like George Whitefield, whose voice, according to Franklin, provided the same kind of pleasure "as an excellent piece of Musick" and could turn an auditor "out of thy right senses" with a desire to fill the collection plate. According to other witnesses, Whitefield could bring an audience to tears merely by his affecting pronunciation of "Mesopotamia." Though some praised him as "an unaffected and natural orator," others damned him for his "*theatrical gestures*."[8]

During the first great religious awakenings of the 1730's and 1740's, and later during the Baptist and Methodist revivals of the 1770's, revivalist oratory was excoriated for its emotional manipulativeness and theatricality, but its techniques were simultaneously appropriated by many of the ministry at large. Similarly, the silver-tongued seducer of the sentimental novel was censured at the same time that he served as a silent model for the republican orator wooing voters. The thematic relations between the public and private dramas of "courtship" are further underscored by the fact that the figure of the coquette, the eighteenth-century novel's female version of the seducer, derives her name from the older male figure of the coquet, a political flatterer at court.

In one of his earliest surviving letters, the twenty-year-old Jefferson describes to his friend John Page what may be the inaugurating instance of his anxiety over public speaking. Having escorted Rebecca Burwell to a dance (Jefferson calls her Belinda in the letter, invoking the wronged heroine of Pope's *Rape of the Lock*), the young suitor narrates what happened next:

> I never could have thought that the succeeding sun would have seen me so wretched as I now am! I was prepared to say a great deal: I had dressed up in my own mind, such thoughts as occurred to me, in as moving language as I knew how, and expected to have performed in a tolerably credible manner. But, good God! When I had an opportunity of venting them, a few broken sentences, uttered in great disorder, and interrupted with pauses of uncommon length, were the too visible marks of my strange confusion![9]

Conceiving speaking as a performance and language as the costume of thought, Jefferson experiences a form of stage fright. His "few" sentences "interrupted with pauses of uncommon length" become markers not of his plaint, but of his confusion.

In 1816 John Quincy Adams suggested a new seal for the "federal association of American States." Drawing on Horace's commentary on Orpheus in *De Arte Poetica*, the proposal provides a coda to Adams's *Lectures on Rhetoric and Oratory* (1810), lectures he had delivered as holder of Harvard's first endowed chair in rhetoric:

> Orpheus was a legislator whose eloquence charmed the rude and savage men of his age to associate together in the state of civil society, to submit to the salutary restraints of law. . . . It was the lyre of Orpheus that civilized savage man. It was only in harmony that the first human political institutions could be founded. . . . After the death of Orpheus, his lyre was placed among the constellations, and there, according to the Astronomics of Manilius possesses its original charm.

The seal would depict the American eagle with thirteen stars around it projected into the heavens in the midst of the constellation of the Lyre. The "moral application of the emblem" is that the "same power of harmony which originally produced the institutions of civil government to regulate the association of individual men, now presides" as "the soul" of the young federated nation. The harmony Adams was talking about is not that of multiple voices formed into a single chorus, but the harmonizing power of an eloquence that draws forth the indwelling moral and social nature of its auditors, compelling them to submit to law in charmed silence.[10]

The lyre's mesmeric power to induce receptivity or conductivity was a symbol, Adams suggested, of a new hegemony that derived authority from the power of "soft compulsion" to "charm" consent. (Connecting the response to song with the dynamics of sexual attraction, Jefferson's greatest compliment to his adolescent love, Jenny Taliaferro, was that he could hear in her spinet playing "the charm of Orpheus's music all in thee.") Figured as the furrow-browed, slightly open-mouthed countenance depicted in John Trumbull's 1778 physiognomic sketch entitled *Attention* (Figure 8), silent, heart-felt listening became a new model of political submission, a submission that represented not rational assent but a new mesmerist mixture of voluntarism and involuntarism. Such a mixture, which dominated the rhetoric of the entire period, was characteristically captured by Charles Brockden Brown in the opening line of *Wieland*, the eighteenth-century American novel about a ventriloquist that makes the new mesmeric voice its principal subject. "I feel little reluctance in complying with your request," declares the heroine Clara. Such compliance, as a feeling of diminished reluctance, was the new affective version of the consent of the governed.[11]

Affective consent was, itself, a version of the operations of sympathy, the faculty that puts individuals beyond themselves and their own self-interest into the realm of a mutuality of feelings. According to the social theory that, in part, underlies the elocutionary revolution, the essence of attention was sympathetic identification rather than judgmental detachment. As implied by Adam

Figure 8. John Trumbull, *Attention*, a physiognomic sketch, c. 1778, copied from Charles Le Brun's *Methode pour apprendre à dessiner les passions* (1698). (Courtesy of the Beinecke Rare Book and Manuscript Library, Yale University.)

Smith's high-wire image for sympathy—what is felt by those who "gaze at a dance on the slack rope" and naturally "writhe and twist and balance their own bodies . . . as they feel that they themselves must do if in his situation"—the spectator/auditor was neither judge nor impassive witness.[12] Though it is a copy of a seventeenth-century physiognomic illustration by Charles Le Brun, Trumbull's attentive face suggests the infectious dynamics of eighteenth-century sympathy, which both depended on and was recorded in the intelligibility of countenances as emotional registers. Prescriptive as well as descriptive of the expression of attention, the sketch also suggests the degree to which the new eloquence was preoccupied, as Terry Eagleton has described the agenda of much eighteenth-century aesthetic thought, with "refashioning the human subject from the inside, informing its subtlest affections and bodily responses," transforming "structures of power" into "structures of feeling."[13] Oratory not only addressed an audience, it sought, like pedagogy, to create within that audience a particular subjectivity.

God, John Quincy Adams reminded his rhetoric students, raised Moses up as his people's "deliverer," but because Moses was a stutterer, "Aaron, the Levite, thy brother," an "ELOQUENT SPEAKER," was also appointed by God as a now-forgotten second "deliverer," not of a nation but, as importantly, of "the divine will" to the twin audiences of the oppressor and the oppressed.[14] In 1758, the year before Harvard mandated public exhibitions of oratory on each Visiting Day, and a half century before Quincy Adams made the above remarks, his father, deeply engaged in the study of Cicero's forensic oratory, came to a conclusion essential to preparing him to be a future political Aaron: "Sound is I apprehend a more powerful Instrument of moving the Passions than Sense. . . . Every Passion has its distinct particular sound. . . . An orator to gain the

Art of moving the passions must attend to nature . . . [and] adapt his own voice to the passion he would move."[15]

John Adams's striking insistence on the primacy of sound over sense in the moving of passions (what virtually all mid-century rhetoricians described as the primary function of speech) was rooted in what had become a fundamental assumption of the new rhetorical theory emerging in the 1750's and 1760's: "What speech primarily does is communicate and what it chiefly communicates are [not ideas or information but] feelings and intentions." The virtuosity of manipulating arguments gives way to the aural and moral spectacle of sincerity; the credibility of the speaker and not the credibility of the argument becomes paramount. Whereas *pathos* (emotion) is set in opposition to *ethos* (character) in classical rhetoric, here the former becomes the revelation of the latter. If the obligation of the speaker was to make the auditor feel as he feels, to be moved as he is moved, speaker and auditor ideally become doubles of one another. When John Adams later insisted that a representative assembly should be "in miniature, an exact portrait of the people" it represents and "should think, feel, reason, and act like them," he was describing representation as the political operation of sympathy. This would be especially the case after 1787. Unlike the Articles of Confederation, the Constitution acted directly on the people and not on the states; consequently it became all the more crucial, cautioned the anti-Federalist George Mason, that "representatives should sympathize with their constituents; should think, as they think and feel as they feel; and for these purposes should be resident among them."[16]

By insisting that the universality of language lay less in the features of language than in the features of delivery and countenance, the body of the speaker and its attitudes, not the body and attitudes of the text, become the site and text of meaning. The very word "attitude"—central to all these texts—connects the disposition of mind and body. Indeed, Thomas Sheridan opens his *Lec-*

tures on Elocution by comparing his agenda to the liberation of the body. "Any stranger in China, observing the uncommon smallness of feet in all the women," he writes, would "conclude that they were the defects and blemishes of nature" because of the unimaginability that "a people driven by a mistaken idea of beauty would purposely persevere in such customs." Yet "far more fatal is the English custom of binding up and contracting from early childhood, and moulding into unnatural forms, the faculties of speech." Teaching students to speak in public "in a different way, with different tones and cadences from the propriety and force of private conversation" required a liberation of the expressive body. "Conversational freedom" was the Addisonian essence not only of good prose, but of good speech.[17]

The presumption that intimate conversation and correspondence were more frank than public utterance, that to tell the truth was to speak in private, meant that the private sphere could no longer remain private. It is not surprising that perhaps the most successful propaganda strategy of the Revolutionary period—one that provided voyeuristic pleasures popularized by epistolary fiction—was intercepting private correspondence (most famously in Franklin's acquisition of Thomas Hutchinson's private letters and in the Tory fabrication of Washington letters) and publishing it as evidence of hypocrisy. But one could not always rely on the discovery of discrepancies between public and private utterance to discern hypocrisy; there had to be another instrument of knowing. Scottish Common Sense philosophy, the great challenge to Lockean sensationalism, grandly and influentially obliged.

In a chapter on natural language in his *Inquiry into the Human Mind* (1764), a book Jefferson much admired and recommended to his nephew, Robert Skipwith, in 1771, Thomas Reid, the founder of the Common Sense school and a major influence on Witherspoon's lectures, distinguished between artificial language "whose meaning is affixed . . . by compact and agreement" and natural language whose modulations of the voice, gesture, and features "every man understands by the principles of his nature."[18] Reid's concept of a natural language, like the oratorical revolution itself, rested on the assumption that moral truths cannot be known, discovered, or proved by traditional reasoning. Reid's self-evident truths were intuitively known by a communitarian rather than individualistic or subjective epistemology, which in turn rested on the assumption of a shared universal social nature. Humanity's social nature entailed the expectation that others—betters—will by means of public oratory and education intervene in the development of these basic, universal abilities.

True oratory represented and reiterated shared beliefs in an effort to maintain a shared cultural world, one that provided a circumscribed scene for human action and created consensus by calling forth the universal nature of man, whose moral dictates would then ensure that sociability would rule individual behavior. Before that nature (and it is this universal sensibility that Paine intended by his phrase "common sense" and Joel Barlow in his *Vision of Columbus* called "the God conceal'd"), all differences of interest and condition would at least momentarily disappear.[19] "However our eyes may be dazzled with show, or our ears deceived by sound; however prejudice may warp our wills, or interest darken our understanding, the simple voice of nature and of reason" will oracularly say "it is right" or it is wrong, Paine declared in *Common Sense*.[20] That simple voice was implicitly antiaristocratic. Indeed, in the view of some, common sense was a characteristic of artisans rather than a universal faculty. Isaiah Thomas, for example, would defend the plain speaking of his Revolutionary newspaper *The Massachusetts Spy* (explicitly written for those "whose labour" leaves them little time to read) by insisting that "common sense in common language is necessary to influence one class of citizens, as much as learning and elegance of compositions are to produce an effect upon another."[21]

Paine and Thomas were following out the democratic tendencies implicit in Reid's account of natural language by challenging an earlier, very different class-specific understanding of common speech as that spoken by a gentleman, "the only member of society who spoke a language universally intelligible; his usage was 'common' in the sense of observing neither a local dialect nor inflected by the terms of any particular art." Paine and Reid take the abstracted antiprovincial common speech of the gentleman (which Noah Webster would later reformulate as a classless uniformity of language essential to banish the "dissocial spirit" of "local standards") and extend the abstraction into oracular universality and natural language.[22] Speech animated by "the tones of nature," insisted John Herries in his *Elements of Speech and Vocal Music on a New Plan* (1773), would be infallibly recognized and identically read by the indwelling passions of every auditor. Such speech would achieve the semiotic clarity contemporaneously ascribed to music, every auditor instinctively knowing, for example, that a major key suggests happiness, a minor, sadness.[23]

The wish for an infallible and irresistible language of sound was rooted in a growing conviction that, in the formulation of the political theorist Jeremy Bentham, "the ambiguity of words" ensured that "political discussions may be carried on continually, without profit and without end." Indeed, believing in 1775 that the abuse and devastating corruption of language was the fundamental cause of England's political strife with its colonies, Bentham rushed to complete his dictionary of moral and jurisprudential terms. He confidently believed that with everyone understanding key words identically, a war might be avoided—a war that would be caused in part by conflict over what Paine, thinking of George III's seductive use of the "Pretended title of *Father*," later called the "Bastille of a Word."[24]

Tone must also be absolutely controlled because, argued John Rice, audiences listen to tone and not to sense for the true meaning of a speech. "The Orator, Actor and Reader," he concluded, will invariably "be understood to *say*, what they appear to *mean* [what the tone of their speech signifies], rather than what they literally utter."[25] As suggested by the question Samuel Keimer tremblingly posed to his verbally intimidating employee Benjamin Franklin—*What do you intend to infer from that?*—the need was to fix the relationship not only between intention and statement, but also between statement and inference.[26] The language of natural sound and gesture sought to satisfy those needs for precision and control, and in addition, to counteract and undermine the dangers of eloquence, the dangers, that is, of calculating language empty of real feeling. "Abolish the use of articulate sounds and writing among mankind for a century," said Thomas Reid, "and every man would be a painter, an actor, and an orator." By this remark Reid made clear that, at least in his view, an "orator" is a speaker not merely of words, but of "natural language," defined as an exercise "not of the voice and lungs only, but of all the muscles of the body. It is a language "like that of dumb people and savages" that, "as it has more of nature, is more expressive and is more easily learned."[27]

In his *Essai sur l'origine des connaissances humaines* (1746), the French philosopher Condillac provided the larger primitivist argument that underlay Reid's position. Condillac traced the origin of language to early man's involuntary and instinctual way of expressing thoughts, not only through bodily gestures, but through "the gestures they produced by the voice, the 'cris naturels'—or interjections—which gave expression to some inward passion—desire, want, hunger, fear." These distinct cries, each stimulated by a particular situation, ultimately took the form of particular recallable words, words whose autonomy distinguished them from the original involuntary cries or signs from which they derived. After citing Condillac in his lecture, "The Rise and Progress of Language," Hugh Blair brings the primitivist argument to the present: "In like manner, among the Northern American tribes, certain motions and actions were found to be much used as explanatory of their meaning." Thus, as the philologist Horne Tooke put it in 1786, "the Dominion of Speech is erected upon the downfall of Interjections." The elocutionists' efforts to recover a natural language of gesture paralleled the quest of eighteenth-century philologists to discover, through the science of etymology, an original universal language.[28]

Because real meaning lay in the speaker's feelings and intentions and not in the words themselves, the "uncomplicated and evocative" discourse of sounds, tones, and facial expressions promised to replace the "complex and argumentative" rhetoric of ornament, which was used to conceal rather than reveal intentions.[29] Thus would the problematic gulf between intention and statement at last be closed. And with that closure would come relief from the obsessive anxieties over the adequacy of linguistic representation. The Scottish Common Sense insistence that the world is immediately perceived as it is, rather than mediately through the agency of ideas, would in some sense be given concrete demonstration; an epistemological transparency would be achieved.

Reid's concept of natural language quickly became identified as the language of the heart in opposition to purely rational discourse, the language of the head. In what is traditionally cited as the first American novel, William Hill Brown's *The Power of Sympathy* (1789), the hero, Harrington, the would-be seducer of Harriot, approached "his beloved," with a head full of "ready-made arguments," he tells his correspondent Worthy. Speaking in "a tone something between sighing and tears," he articulated "the violence of my passion" and "concluded by largely answering objections."[30] Having related at length the precise words of their conversation, Harrington then denies to Worthy that he and Harriot ever spoke. He offers the following extraordinary explanation of the paradox of their unspoken conversation:

> There is a language of the eyes and we conversed in that language; and though I said not a word with my tongue, she seemed perfectly to understand my meaning—for she *looked*—(and I comprehended it as well as if she had *said*)—"Is the crime of dependence to be expiated by the sacrifice of virtue?" "No my love," answered I passionately, "it shall not."
>
> Of all those undescribable things which influence the mind, and which are most apt to persuade—none is so powerful an orator—so feelingly

eloquent as beauty—I bow to the all conquering force of Harriot's eloquence—and what is the consequence?—I am now determined to continue my addresses on a principle the most just, and the most honourable.[31]

Because feelings and the arguments of the heart are "undescribable," they must have their own language. Here the language of the eyes (like Reid's natural language or the performative language of gesture) seems able to reform the rake and silence his dangerous eloquence. But equally it allows the seducer to project his choice of meaning into those eyes: insisting on the inadequacy of spoken language is a way of scripting silence.

In his *Theory of Agency or, An Essay on the Nature, Source and Extent of Moral Freedom* (1771), John Perkins of Boston compared the effect of rhetoricians who used language to avoid "manly reflection" to "that of the serpent's enchantment of small animals which is said to be done by a bewitching appearance round the serpent's head, when his eyes are fixed on the creature; drawing it, by admiration, to still nearer views of the thing, till it is brought within his reach, so weaken'd that he becomes an easy prey." The rattlesnake's power of "fascination," which is frequently commented upon in late eighteenth-century natural history, was a natural instance of the threat and fantasy of silent hypnotic control represented in the contemporary debate over mesmerism and romanticized in the sentimental "language of the eyes."[32] The monitorial Mrs. Holmes of *The Power of Sympathy* warned women against seducers who, like "some species of American serpents," lock eyes with their prey until "the fascinated bird . . . unable any longer to extend its wings . . . falls into the voracious jaws of its enemy."[33] The rattlesnake was literally the serpent in the American garden.

An unselfconscious or natural language, a nonrhetorical rhetoric, allowed the orator to avoid, or give the appearance of avoiding, both rational argumentation, with its failure to address the heart and its risk of precipitating rancorous debate, and rhetoric's radical suspension of logic, with its attendant risks of misrepresentation and emotional manipulation. The quest for such a language ironically led to rhetoric's cloaking its agenda, the conciliating and galvanizing of passions, in the agenda of logic: "assent, upon a just view of things fairly represented to the mind."[34] It led back, that is, to the most excoriated part of Aristotelianism: the syllogism.

In his *Sketches of the History of Man*, first published in 1774 and reissued in Philadelphia in 1776, Lord Kames insisted, on the subject of syllogisms, that the "despotism of Aristotle with respect to reason was no less complete, than that of the Bishop of Rome with respect to religion." The syllogism, pronounced Thomas Reid in an attack on Aristotle printed as a supplement to Kames's work, led to nothing but numberless disputes. Unlike "the Art of Induction . . . which forced nature to confess many of her secrets," syllogisms were mere circularities, deductively proving only that what is true in the general case is true in the particular.[35]

At the heart of this attack (and one should not underestimate the radicalizing effect on the Revolutionary generation of the Baconian revolution against artificial authority) was a radical rejection of the central assumption governing British works on logic in the seventeenth and early eighteenth centuries. That larger assumption was that truth is a quality that a proposition has by virtue of its precise consistency with a proposition already known to be true, rather than the quality of being consistent with the particular facts of a particular case. Such a view of truth denied the emergence of novel truths newly discovered. In addition, as George Campbell argued in a widely influential treatise of 1776, it denied "the acquisition of knowledge in the things themselves."[36]

The syllogism, however, had its modern defense, turning not on logic but on the matter of persuasion. In his *Elements of Logick* (1758), a book Jefferson studied at William and Mary with William Small (who introduced the modern lecture course to American universities), William Duncan argued that the highest order of proof is a syllogism with a self-evident truth serving as its major premise.[37] A self-evident premise ironically (given Reid's objections) anticipated what James Wilson, a signer of the Declaration from Pennsylvania and a disciple of Reid's, described as Common Sense philosophy's major tenet: "first principles are in themselves apparent," and "to make nothing self-evident is to take away all possibility of knowing anything."[38] Such a syllogism, that is, would command conviction as a matter of "intuitive" consent and immediate recognition rather than producing mere intellectual conviction, a lower order of certainty. Though an element of logic, it would function as would natural language addressed to the heart, with the added benefit of seeming to be free of any possible taint of rhetorical dissimulation. Wilbur Samuel Howell has suggested that the Declaration followed precisely that form. The major premise was, in Howell's reformulation, that "all governments denying that men are created equal and have inalienable rights may be altered or abolished"; the minor premise was "that the history of his present Majesty's is precisely such a government"; and the conclusion "that all allegiance and subjection to that government is renounced" naturally followed.[39]

Like the authority of an oracular voice and the tonal, measured language of musical speech, syllogisms grounded on self-evident truths furnished their own eloquence, required no argumentation, and freed the Declaration from the charge of innovation or individualistic utterance. They represented the ultimate interior of rhetoric, in which a speaker suggests that he has transcended rhetoric and arrived at a nonrhetorical form of persuasion, a natural language that doesn't threaten self-exposure—the unconscious condition of the "naive" poet. In this liminal historical period in which the neoclassical aspirations for a universal deductive and inductive logic coexisted with emerging expressivist protocols, both logic and affective rhetoric could be made to serve similar rather than opposite ends. The redefinition of logic from a basis in Aristotelian commonplaces to a basis in self-evident truths paralleled the simultaneous sanctioning and containing of nonrational appeals effected by the concept of a natural language.

Of three modes of persuasion described by Aristotle in his *Rhetoric*—"the first depending on the personal character of the speaker; the second on putting the audience in a certain frame of mind; and the third on the proof, or apparent proof, provided by the words of a speech itself"—the "spoken" or affective Declaration may be said to be most closely attached to the second. The "written," syllogistic, or philosophical Declaration conforms to the third. Indeed, it was the paradoxical rhetorical agenda of much philosophical writing in the eighteenth century to suppress the first two forms of persuasion and to embrace the ideal or pose of a nonrhetorical presentation that does not persuade, one that places "before mankind the common sense of the subject in terms so plain and firm as to command their assent," as Jefferson described his mission in writing the Declaration.[40]

When Jefferson declared in his July 1774 *Summary View of the Rights of British America* that "the great principles of right and wrong are legible to every reader," a legibility threatened by George III, whose name might prove "a blot in the page of history," he was not only making over the moral law in the image of the materiality of a text, but recasting democratic self-evidence as a visual rather than an intuitive phenomenon—much in the same way that his measured pauses turned the larger Declaration into a sequence of visualizable units.[41] If tyranny achieved its ends by coercive force, or as Jefferson argued in his *Notes on the State of Virginia*, by the "power of eloquence . . . to take any hypothesis whatever, or its reverse" and furnish "explanations equally specious [in its older sense of "attractive"] and persuasive," the discourse of wise government, in contrast, must abjure sophistry and submit "facts" to a reasonable mind or "candid world," which then is permitted to draw its own conclusions freely.[42] And if "the whole art of government consists in the art of being honest," the distinction between legitimate and false governments rests on a distinction between presenting facts, setting them forth in such a way that they will be distinct, and prejudicially dressing them. Yet in practice, the Declaration repeatedly violates that distinction. To invoke the biblical narrative of the plagues, by saying that George III has "sent hither swarms of new officers to harass our people and eat out their substance," is of course to do more than set forth a fact.[43]

Jefferson's reverence for Bacon, which bordered on idolatry, was informed by a deep desire to believe in Bacon's inductive dream, his scientific ideal. That ideal, though the opposite of syllogistic deduction, offered its own version of self-evidence by insisting that the assembling of facts can neutrally precede and be unprescribed by any prior theorizing. Distant and alienated "observing" (rather than a familiar and engaged "looking at") contains the subjectivity of the scientist and advances the larger agenda of self-control and self-effacement. Like the word "candid," which meant at that time "without prejudice or bias" (significantly displaced in the Declaration from speaker to an idealized inscribed audience), or the preoccupation with disinterestedness as the essence of true virtue, Baconianism was part of a larger cultural project of denying or transcending the filter of personalized interest, subjectivity, and unconscious motivation.[44]

Part of the internal drama of the rough draft of the Declaration is how its Baconianism is undone by being protested too much. Phrases excised by Congress from Jefferson's original draft, such as "for the truth of which we pledge a faith yet unsullied by falsehood" and "future ages will scarcely believe," betrayed too much of a confessional anxiety about credibility and disinterestedness. Others, including "if history may be credited," called into question the authority of "all experience hath shewn" and the complacency of "these facts." By urging orators to make use of the biases, prejudices, and passions of their audiences, which if secured would, as John Adams cynically put it, convert "one's plain common sense into profound wisdom, nay wretched doggerel into sublime heroic," the new rhetoric denied that there was such a thing as a "candid world."[45] At the same time, however, it promulgated the notion of a disinterested audience capable of dispassionate judgment.

The ideal of natural language also paralleled the deistical ideal of natural rather than revealed religion. Creation and not Scripture was, as Paine would later put it, the "ever existing original" word of God, which "cannot be forged . . . cannot be counterfeited . . . cannot be lost . . . cannot be altered . . . cannot be suppressed." It speaks a universal language, independently of human speech or human language, "multiplied and various as they be." If the "public visibility" of the resurrection was limited to but "eight or nine" problematic witnesses, here that visibility of revelation was available to all.[46] What natural religion was to revealed religion, speech was to print. With its immediacy, tones, gestures, and the countenance of a visible speaker, speech, the new oratory implied, presented truth better than the flat, derivative printed word, which ultimately had to be spoken and brought to life by the reader. If, as the young Alexander Hamilton put it in his essay *The Farmer Refuted* (1775), "the sacred rights of mankind are not to be rummaged for among old parchments or musty records" but "are written, as with a sunbeam, in the whole *volume* of human nature," the book of nature had a companion volume in the book of human nature. In contrast to parchments, here was the living textuality of speech.[47]

The multiple proposals for "normalizing" spelling so that it would follow sound (orthoepy dictating orthography) and the effort of Burgh and others to return printing to a period "when the emphaticall word, or words, in every sentence, were printed in Italics," were both part of a project to make spoken language the archetype of written language.[48] Such a project would compensate for the anonymity (the absence of a physical speaker) of written prose, and for whatever ambiguity was occasioned by that anonymity. But it would also have an additional benefit that Sheridan chose not to mention. Because the human voice speaking accessibly and sincerely appears to be speaking truthfully, a prose that registers that voice is potentially much more manipulatively powerful than either traditional eloquence or elevated language. That is precisely why the plain style, which sought to redress rhetoric (in both senses of the verb), ultimately came to dominate both fiction and journalism.

And yet in 1777 the English grammarian, scientist, dissenter, and future political radical Joseph Priestley (who after emigrating to America would advise Jefferson on curricular matters for the projected University of Virginia) could argue that the "natural voice" inhered not in plain, but in figurative speech:

> Figurative speech . . . is indicative of a person's real feelings and state of mind, not by means of the words it consists of, considered as *signs of separate ideas* . . . but as circumstances naturally attending those feelings which compose any state of mind. Those figurative expressions, therefore, are scarcely considered and attended to as *words*, but are viewed in the same light as attitudes, *gestures*, and *looks*, which are infinitely more expressive of sentiments and feelings than words can possibly be.[49]

In Priestley's formulation, figures of speech are no longer self-conscious, conventional formulas or strategies (like personification), consigned to the status of ornament as a way of containing the dangers of their irrational appeal. Rather, they constitute the natural and unselfconsciously expressive dimension of language itself. They inscribe the gesturing body on the printed page and thus serve as print culture's compensation for the loss of an expressive oral mode, a compensation for the inadequacy of print culture to rise to the challenge of demonstrating rather than merely representing the affective.[50]

The suggestion by Francis Hopkinson that verbal arguments be printed in progressively "wrathful types, like ranters on the stage" (Figure 9), the proposal by William Thornton to introduce into American English "a mark of irony," and Franklin's suggestion that question marks be placed at the beginnings of sentences so

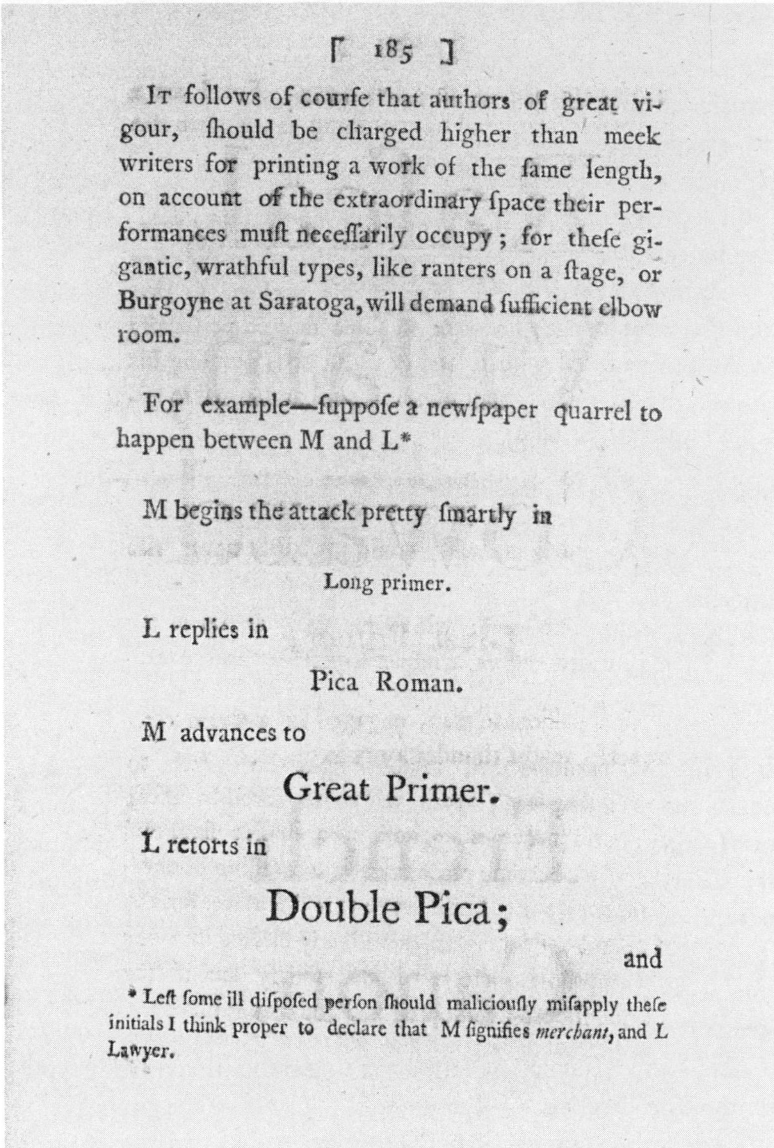
[185]

It follows of courſe that authors of great vigour, ſhould be charged higher than meek writers for printing a work of the ſame length, on account of the extraordinary ſpace their performances muſt neceſſarily occupy; for theſe gigantic, wrathful types, like ranters on a ſtage, or Burgoyne at Saratoga, will demand ſufficient elbow room.

For example—ſuppoſe a newſpaper quarrel to happen between M and L*

M begins the attack pretty ſmartly in

Long primer.

L replies in

Pica Roman.

M advances to

Great Primer.

L retorts in

Double Pica;

and

* Leſt ſome ill diſpoſed perſon ſhould maliciouſly miſapply theſe initials I think proper to declare that M ſignifies *merchant*, and L Lawyer.

Figure 9. Pages from Francis Hopkinson's "Plan for the Improvement of the Art of Paper War," proposing a printing device to render "the temper and the vivacity of [an author's] feelings," *The Miscellaneous Essays* (Philadelphia, 1792). (From the library of the author.)

[186]

and at laſt the conteſt ſwells up to

Raſcal,

Villain,

Coward,

in five line pica; which indeed is as far as the art of printing or a modern quarrel can conveniently go.

A philoſophical reaſon might be given to prove that large types will more forcibly affect the optic nerve than thoſe of a ſmaller ſize, and therefore become mechanically expreſſive of energy and vigour; but I leave this diſcuſſion for the amuſement of the gentlemen lately elected into our philoſophical ſociety. It will ſatisfy me if my ſcheme ſhould be adopted and found uſeful.

I recol-

that the reader would not discover too late that "he had improperly modulated his voice" were playful but ultimately serious.[51] So was Boswell's desire that Dr. Johnson's conversation "be preserved as musick . . . according to the very ingenious method of Mr. Steele, who has shown how the recitation of Mr. Garrick . . . might be transmitted to posterity *in score*."[52] Joshua Steele's *An Essay toward Establishing the Melody and Measure of Speech* (1775), like Abraham Tucker's *Vocal Sounds* (1773) and John Walker's *The Melody of Speaking Delineated: or, Elocution taught like Music, by Visible Signs* (1787), provided notational systems indicating how, as Walker put it, "vocal sounds" are, in reality, a "species of chromatic music."[53] These texts and projects reflect a desire to find a notation for pronunciation so that printed texts could indicate, as in song, the precise affective accent intended by the author for each word—an effort to turn oratory, in this age that revered Handel, into oratorio, to somehow empower language so that, like music or a species of theatrical singing, it could communicate pure emotion from one heart to another.

Robert Darnton has argued that the identical mission—the desire to make writing what Rousseau called the "art of speaking to those who are absent . . . communicating without any meditation our feelings, wills, desires"—was central to the unprecedented international success that greeted *Emile* and *La Nouvelle Héloïse* following their publication in the 1760's.[54] In the new genre of the psychological novel of bourgeois life, as well as through fictionalized works of pedagogy (both usually cast as a series of private letters, and thus direct communications), Rousseau, like Richardson before him, was preoccupied with nothing less than redefining the nature of reading. In a post-Lockean milieu that believed the self to be the sum total of its experiences and reflections upon those experiences, reading would become not a substitute for experience but a primary emotional experience itself, a constituent of identity, a way of understanding and making one's self.

The fiction of fiction was that novels (told in letters, or through an engaging narrator's voice, or by transcribed dialogue) were not books, as books had been traditionally experienced. "Books are cold," declared Arthur Mervyn, the eponymous hero of Charles Brockden Brown's novel of 1799, implicitly exempting his own text. They "allow no questions, offer no explanations. . . . They talk to us behind a screen. Their tone is lifeless and monotonous. They charm not our attention by mute significances of gesture and look."[55] The anonymous author of *The Adventures of Jonathan Corncob* (1787), one of the earliest fictionalizations of the Revolution, was even more specific: books lacked a physiognomy. *The Adventures* opens with the importunate fellow traveler of the narrator pressing him for an account of his adventures: "I am sure you tell a story admirably, for I have not, since the death of my friend Stern, seen a quainter phiz." The narrator then directly addresses his readers: "I do not know whether I shall amuse anybody else: my quaint phiz will be wanting, and in that perhaps lay the principal merit of my tale."[56]

In his 1789 autobiographical account of his life as a slave in pre-Revolutionary Virginia and in the Caribbean, the West African Olaudah Equiano describes his early effort to imitate what he understands to be the reading process: "I have often taken up a book, and talked to it, and then put my ears to it, when alone, in hopes it would answer me; and I have been very much concerned when I found it remaining silent." Equiano's "talking book" is not just a "preliterate" construct, but as the savvy author probably knew, a writerly ideal. An early reviewer attributed the fact that Equiano's own "narrative wears an honest face" to its "artless" voice—a voice conventionally mandated of non-white authors.[57]

The conversational ideal would quickly be impressed into the service of the revolutionary project of defining the distinctiveness of American letters. James, the protagonist of Crèvecoeur's *Letters from an American Farmer* (1782), agrees to provide his unnamed European correspondent with epistles on the social conditions of America only after he is convinced that "writing letters is nothing more than talking on paper." For to engage seriously and consistently in the act of writing is, in the words of James's wife, "a heinous crime" unworthy of a "plain dealing honest man" with a farm to cultivate and debts to pay. By associating the act of self-conscious composition with class-specific leisure and artful and formalist European culture, Crèvecoeur locates the Americanness of James's letters in their character as untextual conversational "effusions." The new model of writing required a new model of reading. When Bell's Circulating Library of Philadelphia, located three blocks from where the Continental Congress met, opened in 1774, it advertised itself on its bookplates as a place "where *SENTIMENTALISTS*, whether Ladies or Gentlemen, may become Readers" (Figure 10). Bell meant by that capitalized and italicized word something very much akin to Rousseau's conception of the reader as immediately addressed and emotionally engaged by the speaking voice of the text.[58]

In his 1771 letter advising the young Robert Skipwith on a general course of study, Jefferson himself addressed the character of the "new" reading in his moral defense of the entertainments of fiction as offering an "exercise of our . . . moral feelings":

> We never reflect whether the story we read be truth or fiction. If the painting be lively, and a tolerable picture of nature, we are thrown into a reverie, from which if we awaken it is the fault of the writer. I appeal to every reader of feeling and sentiment whether the fictitious murther of Duncan by Macbeth in Shakespeare does not excite in him as great horror of the villain, as the real one of Henry IV by Ravaillac?

Because history offers "few incidents . . . attended with such circumstances as to excite in any high degree this sympathetic emotion of virtue," man has been "wisely framed to be as warmly interested for a fictitious as for a real personage." A new model of representation that defines truth as truthfulness to feelings rather than to facts subordinates history to the word pictures of romance. What happens within the text is judged by what happens within

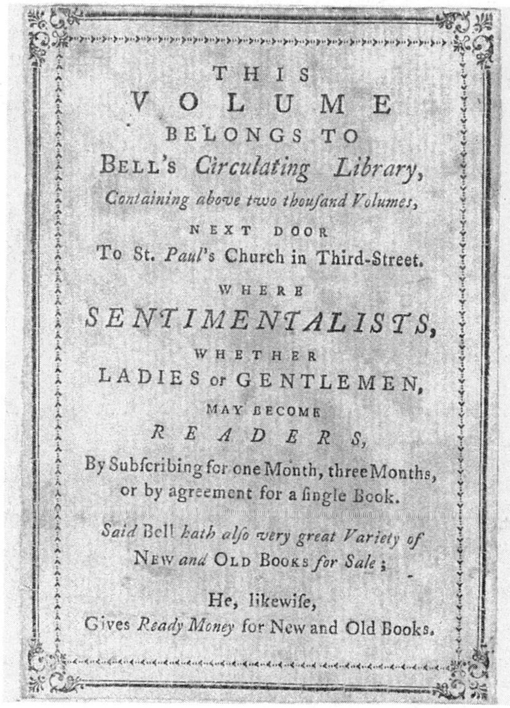

THIS
VOLUME
BELONGS TO
BELL's *Circulating Library*,
Containing above two thouſand Volumes,
NEXT DOOR
To St. *Paul's* Church in Third-Street.
WHERE
SENTIMENTALISTS,
WHETHER
LADIES or GENTLEMEN,
MAY BECOME
READERS,
By Subſcribing for one Month, three Months,
or by agreement for a ſingle Book.
Said Bell *hath alſo very great Variety of*
NEW *and* OLD BOOKS *for Sale*;
He, likewiſe,
Gives *Ready Money* for New and Old Books.

Figure 10. Bookplate from Bell's Circulating Library, in a copy of Bell's own 1775 Philadelphia edition of James Burgh's *Political Disquisitions.* (From the library of the author.)

the reader. When confronted with an instance of extraordinary behavior, sentimental readers either commit themselves to future emulation or "secretly resolve *we* will never do so." Jefferson's emphasized pronoun makes clear that this account of reading "cloathed in the warmest expressions of sincerity" describes his own reading.[59]

The twenty-year-old John Trumbull, who would go on to write some of the most significant poetry of the Revolutionary period, set forth in a speech to the Yale graduating class of 1770 what Leon Howard fifty years ago called the substance of "an intellectual revolution"—the claim that sentimental readers constituted (or should constitute) a new moral elite. Speaking to an audience trained "in the self-abnegation of [Yale President] Clap's ethics, the predestinarianism of Edwards theology, and the empiricism of Locke's philosophy," the young poet "advocated belletristic study on the grounds of self-interest, self-determination, and innate aesthetic taste."[60] Aestheticizing morality, Trumbull called on the graduating students to become part of a new social order—not the elite of God's chosen, but one that consisted of "persons of judgment" who feel "an openness of heart and an elevation of mind" and become "more sensible of the dignity of human nature" after "reading a fine Poem, viewing any masterly work of genius, or hearing an harmonious concert of Music."[61] Three years later in his long poem, *The Progress of Dulness*, Trumbull made fun of an empty classical education and extended his call for what his German contemporary Schiller would call "an aesthetic education."

Indeed, what ultimately made possible the Declaration's opening rhetorical act of independence—its simple introductory assertion that Americans are "one people" connected only by "political bands" with another, a people fundamentally different and distinguishable from what are later called "our British brethren"—was the insistence that, according to the aestheticized politics of sentiment and pathos, those "British brethren," unlike the Americans, were "deaf to the voice of justice & of consanguinity." As Jefferson would later say about one who could not appreciate the "numbers" of Homer's verse, who was "insensible to the charm of music," or "insensible to love or gratitude," such a British brother was "an unfavored son of nature to whom she has given a faculty fewer than to others of her children." Insensibility to what Trumbull called "the dignity of human nature" provided the test differentiating one people from another.[62]

Harmonies: Homer, Fugues, and Chairs

The writer who many in late eighteenth-century America—Jefferson enthusiastically among them—believed most successfully kept alive the oratorical and musical ideal on the page was Homer. Homer's language represented a crucial ideal: it transcended merely personal expression. Pope, who declared, "Homer is nature," put the point succinctly: "Homer makes us Hearers, and Virgil leaves us Readers." Virgil's style has the refinement and complexity appropriate to a written text that can be paused over and contemplated. Homer's poetry, in contrast, is like a "painting in outline which produces its effect only at a distance." It is stripped of the complex argumentation and false refinement that would be lost to a listening audience and yet it is sufficiently "ductile," as Jefferson put it, to accommodate and marry the "variety of dialects" that constitute "the riches" of Greek. Homer's language represented a lost verbal purity, unrefined and of the people.[1]

Like Ossian's poetry, the Anglo-Saxon language, and Chief Logan's oratory, three other preoccupations of Jefferson's, the pure Homeric voice was still audible even on the page, a rare survival from a period before political deceit and corruption had become universal. It is to that Orphic age that Franklin alludes when he fancifully imagines that the folk ballads his brother Peter has composed will permit him "in the spirit of some ancient legislators" to "influence the manners of your country by the united powers of poetry and music." In a 1762 letter to his friend Lord Kames, Franklin praised Scottish folk ballads, "simple tunes sung by a single voice," because their every note harmonized with the vibration of the preceding note, thus translating the simultaneity of harmony into the sequentiality of melody. In isolating the fact that their "melody was harmony," he was articulating a paradox used to praise Homer: a single voice singing in harmony.[2]

In the view of Thomas Blackwell and Robert Wood, the English scholars central to the eighteenth-century revolution in Homeric scholarship, Homer's poems were written less by a self-conscious or even literate artist than by "the voice of the people."[3] His poetry was popular eloquence uncontaminated by the individuated expression of a particular personality striving for singularity. It thus represented corporate rather than individual consciousness, or at least the merger of the two. Homer's poetry in this regard had the character of a silhouette, a popular art form practiced in the 1770's by everyone from Charles Willson Peale to Goethe. In a silhouette, personal identity is not represented by the painterly specifics of facial features, but, as in the pure, emptied-out line drawings of Flaxman, by the equally revealing precision of outline. Like Homer's style, a silhouette both effaces and identifies; it generalizes (Lavater used them to indicate physiognomic types) and specifies.[4]

Here was one of the paradoxes of the elocutionary revolution. The living voice must be both particular, referring back to the sincerity of a specific speaker, and general, articulating the auditors' feelings to themselves. Its power was essential to inspiriting the killing letter of the text, to making communication, defined as the expression and recognition of feeling, possible, and to articulating the sentiments of the community through that communication. Like the voice of the ideal political representative, its accents must also be those of the constituency. In his *Introduction to the Art of Thinking*, a collection of aphorisms on which Franklin drew heavily, Lord Kames put the point even more simply: "We make so disagreeable and ridiculous a figure with the monosyllable I, I did, I said, that it were better to forswear it altogether."[5]

Jefferson warmly approved Franklin's dictum "never to contradict anybody," given how "cheap a price" it was to secure "the good will of another," not because it provided a means of escaping confrontation or a cynical method of securing power but because it articulated the larger cultural value behind the injunction to control the self: the necessity of cultivating the art of pleasing.[6] In a cultural context that defined both beauty and virtue as species of "the agreeable," harmonizing and not dialectical dispute or confrontation was perceived to be the road to truth. Indeed, one rule of Jefferson's *Manual of Parliamentary Practice* was that "no person in speaking, is to mention a member then present by his name." Another rule insisted that "the consequence of a measure may be reprobated . . . but to arraign the motives of those who propose or advise it, is a personality, and against order." Being sociable and polite was not only the mark of civilized man but the essence of the civilizing process. "Personality" was against order.[7]

Like the infallible sources referred to in three popular phrases of the period, "the oracle of reason," the "oracle of history," or the "vox populi" articulating the "vox dei," "the voice" of the ideal text is harmonious, vatic, and by implication "true." Part of the agenda of such a voice was to blot out authorial innovation, to ventriloquize common sense and sensibility, and to "harmonize" the wisdom of previous texts and voices, as Jefferson said he did in the Declaration. Unlike the French Declaration of Rights, which because it identified popular "ignorance, forgetting, and neglect of the rights of man" as "the universal cause of public misfortune and the corruption of the regime" was written to inform the popular mind, the American Declaration was intended to be "an expression" of it, as Jefferson would later say.[8] The title of the original rough draft, "A Declaration of the representatives . . . in General Congress assembled," identified real speakers. The printed title of the engrossed copy that was finally signed, "The Unanimous Declaration of the thirteen united States of America" (a formulation made possible by the delegates from New York finally receiving authorization to vote for the document), eliminated them. Without mediation the states spoke their "unanimous" chorus.

No treatment of the dilemmas and idealization of the speaking voice can ignore the history of the singing voice. The harmonizing of voices, especially because it involved the absorption of a distinctive single voice into a choral consensus, was a much-contested ideal in the musical culture of Revolutionary America. That contest came to a head in the controversy over psalmody, church singing, and musical literacy. What in the 1760's and 1770's was called the "old style" of church singing derived from oral and ballad traditions. Though a line reader would read out each psalm line in advance of its being sung (so as to assist the illiterate and those without books), each line would then be sung according to melodies remembered and interpreted by individual singers. Hostile to the obligation to obey the "rules of singing" and thus to the idea of printed musical notation (which the rhetoricians of the period so envied), old style church singing was individualistic and highly ornamented with turnings and flourishes. According to two of its early opponents, it encouraged individual singers to "take the Liberty of raising every Note of the tune or lowering it as it best pleas'd his Ear" or to hold notes until they caused "Tittering" among the congregation.[9] In a diary entry for August 1774, John Adams voiced what had become a common complaint: "psalm-singing in New York is in the Old Way, as we call it—all the drawling, quavering Discord in the World."[10]

By the 1770's, a campaign to enforce musical literacy, reflected in the rise of singing schools, had in a great many congregations succeeded in replacing an ideal of individual expression and virtuosity practiced in a corporate setting with the more communitarian and aestheticized ideal of beauty and harmony achieved by the rule of print. One advocate of the harmonious ideal was the premier political agitator, Samuel Adams, whose appreciation for the powers of the human voice extended to an enthusiasm for teaching psalm singing. Indeed, the Tory judge Peter Oliver accused him of mixing music and politics: "He had a good Voice, & was a master in vocal Musick. This Genius he improved, by instituting singing Societys of Mechanicks, where he presided; and embraced such Opportunities to [be] inculcating Sedition."[11]

Oliver was right in recognizing that with the new harmonics one had the power, as it were, to call the tune, to gather the voices of many into one. This was especially true given the political character of the larger musical culture beyond psalm singing. Indeed, *Common Sense* itself built on sentiments Paine expressed earlier in "The Liberty Tree," an extremely popular political song that he wrote and published with musical score in the July 1775 issue of *Pennsylvania Magazine*.[12] What Oliver failed to fully appreciate was the social and republican ideal implicit in Adams's teaching.

In 1756, the year of his famous son's birth, Leopold Mozart set forth that ideal in an essay written to teach young violinists (not unlike Jefferson) the art of "good delivery." In it he explained why the orchestral player should be "prized far more highly than the mere soloist" even though "today everyone wants to be the soloist":

> The soloist can play everything as he pleases and adjust its delivery to his own ideas . . . the orchestral player must have the ability to grasp at once and to deliver properly the taste, the ideas, and the expression of different composers. The soloist, to bring things out cleanly, has only to practice at home—others must adapt themselves to him; the orchestral player must read everything at sight—often, indeed, passages such as run counter to the natural arrangement of the measure—he must adapt himself to others.[13]

Rather than identifying the orchestral mode with submission or conformity and solo performance with distinctiveness or self-assertion, Mozart undercut the distinction by defining virtuosity as, in fact, adaptability. The essence of virtuosity was, in other words, the social instinct. Mozart's discussion makes clear the ideological position that underlay, for example, what Mitchell Breitwieser has described as Franklin's commitment to being agreeably neutral, his unwillingness to exhaustively identify the self with any particular position and so rob it of its boundless potential for growth. If, to use John Holden's 1770 definition, the musical term "temperament" meant "adjusting the fixed sounds" of an instrument "to answer equally well in all kinds of passages," Franklin made sure he was well-tempered.[14]

The valorizing of virtuosity as social adaptability (though often in uneasy dialogue with an irrepressible appreciation of individual genius) was central to the agenda of the numerous volumes describing "the state of music" published in the 1760's and 1770's. One of the most popular was Charles Burney's *The Present State of Music in France and Italy* (1771), a volume Jefferson purchased and knew well. (Having become friendly with Burney in the 1780's, Jefferson actually supervised the building of a harpsichord for Burney's daughter, Patsy, the sister of novelist Fanny Burney.) Burney praised the Italians as more musical than the French because they learned from an early age not only their native tongue but the full gestural and vocal range of "true Italian expression." That expressive language was, of course, central to the eighteenth-century opera, whose contemporary popularity derived in large part from its literal embodiment of the new elocutionary ideal. As opera musicalized drama and dramatized music, it rendered specific emotion self-evident, at least in the ideal, through the universally recognizable languages of musical tone and performative gesture. In addition, as the classical and formalist operatic tradition represented in France by Gluck became challenged by the "opera comique" of men like Piccini, opera became increasingly anticlassical and popular. Enchanted by the new opera that forsook kings and queens in order to dramatize the emotions of common folk, Jefferson, while in Paris after the Revolution, befriended Piccini and regularly attended the Opéra Buffon.[15]

As a register of a growing American musical literacy brought about by a greater appreciation of music in general, magazines and newspapers in the 1770's began routinely printing the musical text of new songs. Increased literacy, in turn, created a demand for novelty and sophistication in church music. That demand was addressed by the introduction of complex church music like the fuguing tune, music whose very complexity, ironically, violated the antiornamental ideal of the reformers who had championed musical literacy in the first place.

The first book-length compilation of music composed by an American to be published in the colonies was William Billings's *The New England Psalm Singer* (1770), written exclusively for the voice, the only instrument capable of awakening "every passion of which the heart is capable."[16] Billings chose as his dominant musical vehicle the fuguing tune, an overlapping four-part harmony in which the variation of the second part would, as he later put it, "briefly engage in Musical warfare" and then "sweetly coincide." He went on to explain what he called the fugue's "paradox of contentious harmony": each part "seems determined by dint of harmony and strength of accent, to drown his competitor in an ocean of harmony, and while each part is thus mutually striving for mastery, and sweetly contending for victory, the audience are delighted, suprizingly agitated, and extremely fluctuated; sometimes declaring in favour of one part, and sometimes another."[17] The paradox of the fugue was that each accent, each voice (both within the music and within the agitated audience), contended for mastery in the quality and character of its eventual agreement.

Consensus and harmony became the ground for individual victory. Billings concluded: "Push on, push on ye sons of harmony, and Discharge your deepmouth'd canon, full fraught with Diapasons."[18] The pun on "canon"—the musical form in which one voice repeats precisely a figure of melody previously heard in another voice—reconceives the weapon of oppositional violence as a form of musical imitation. Discharged by the sons of harmony rather than by the sons of liberty, the canon's diapasons, a term for chords that include all tones, defeat dissent by prior absorption. The political version of this strategy insists on conceiving dissent as loyal opposition rather than as treason, as a disagreement over means rather than ends. It proposes all measures—musical or otherwise—as the recovery of a conformity with principles on which all are in a priori agreement. Or as Jefferson, responding to the bitter partisanship of the late 1790's, put it in his first Inaugural: "every difference of opinion is not a difference of principle. We have called by different names brethren of the same principles. We are all republicans—we are all federalists."[19]

While deliberating in the Assembly Room of the State House, members of the Continental Congress sat on Windsor chairs that addressed the principle of self-effacing unity in a very different context (Figure 11). The chairs were so named, according to traditional anecdote, because George II, having sought refuge during a thunderstorm in a peasant's cottage near Windsor Castle, discovered a chair whose comfort and simplicity of design so impressed him that he had his cabinetmakers copy it. More than a royally sanctioned product of the cult of rusticity, the Windsor, which mid-century chairmakers from Boston, Philadelphia, and New York turned into a distinctively American product, was the most popular chair in eighteenth-century America. Originating in a reaction against the unsturdiness of earlier rush-bottom chairs, the uncomfortableness of uncontoured slat-back or banister-back chairs, and the ponderous weight of baroque furniture, the Windsor's utilitarian and aesthetic appearance derived from its extraordinarily light and functional mix of "beautifully turned maple legs and arm supports . . . thick seats, made of easily worked soft wood, usually tulip, poplar or white pine, modeled and contoured," and "thin spindles, which formed the backs and the bent crest and arm rails . . . generally made from oak or hickory—strong woods that become pliable with the application of heat and moisture."[20] The Windsors were then painted green, red, or black to disguise the variety of woods used in their construction. The mass scale of the Windsor's sectional construction (eighteenth-century chairmakers would stock hundreds of separate seat rounds and backs for easy assembly) and the interchangeability of component parts clearly constituted an artisan version of mass production. As such, the

Figure 11. Edward Savage, *Congress Voting Independence*, unfinished stipple engraving after a painting by Robert Edge Pine, after 1796. (Courtesy of The National Portrait Gallery, Smithsonian Institution.)

Windsor both participated in and helped create a mass market whose ultimate tendencies were to nationalize and standardize taste. In addition, because political resistance in the wake of the Non-Importation Agreements took the form of boycotting British goods, buying "American" became a language of revolutionary protest.[21] Like the Continental Congress, which sat on them, the chair was a material culture version of *e pluribus unum*, it was a whole not only greater than the sum of its parts but one whose heterogeneous materials and connections (like spindles driven deep into the seat rather than attached to it) could often no longer be discerned in that whole.

Because its rounded back accommodated the body's form (rather than imposing a "rectitude" on it), the Windsor not only offered comfort without luxury and republican simplicity without the sacrifice of style but it sustained the primacy of the craftsman and the visible purity of design against the obliterative talents of the upholsterer. In contrast to heavier furniture whose fixed positions prescribed fixed seating and thus social relations, Windsors (and "stick" furniture in general) could be endlessly reconfigured. Capable of being used indoors or out, Windsors were ordered by Washington for his Mount Vernon porch, by Franklin for his home, and by Jefferson for Monticello (he ordered four dozen, though he really preferred French furniture). Equally fashionable in wealthy and humble homes, Windsors suggested in the "symbolic universe of commonplace 'things'" a more fluid and open vision of social relations.[22]

The ideal of self-effacement was part and parcel of another eighteenth-century project, the wishful quest to escape the narrow corridor of the perspectival and subjective by attaining to a prospect point that permitted a comprehensive, transcendent, or universalist view. After visiting Jefferson's hilltop Monticello, the Marquis de Chastellux commented that Jefferson had placed his house as he had his mind, "on an elevated situation from which he might contemplate the universe." The impulse to attain such a view is everywhere in Jefferson's work. Just before the convening of the Continental Congress, he commissioned the building of a swivel chair (his invention) that turned on the coil of venetian blind cord he had taken from his own window dressing. The chair, in which he most probably drafted the Declaration, permitted him, in the fashion of a speaker in an eighteenth-century "prospect poem," to have from one spot a 360-degree panoramic view (Figure 12). But such a position did not necessarily make possible a greater and less self-interested epistemological clarity. From the site of cen-

Figure 12. Jefferson's swivel chair with center spindle and rollers, commissioned in Philadelphia, in which he probably sat while writing the Declaration. The writing arm was added subsequently. (Courtesy of the American Philosophical Society.)

trality one could either achieve a larger, distinctive perspective or, as with Bentham's Panopticon, impose oneself and one's vision over all that one surveys. As the following sentence used to define "comprehend" in Noah Webster's first folio dictionary so pointedly suggests, the comprehensive gaze contains without necessarily understanding: "The empire of Great Britain comprehends England, Scotland and Ireland with their dependencies."[23]

The title *A Summary View*, given to Jefferson's 1774 pamphlet on the rights of British America by his associates, who published it without his authorization, is a common eighteenth-century one; it speaks to the period's effort to resolve the tension between the perspectival and self-interested (view) and the comprehensive and disinterested (summary). That effort is rooted in the belief that there is a larger perspective (a greater good) that comprehends the interests of all parties and that can be articulated by a natural rhetoric of consensus.

Such a resolution was the subject of the powerful final chapter of Lord Kames's *Elements of Criticism*, a book Jefferson owned in the early 1770's and recommended several times thereafter. The chapter was devoted to disproving the "dangerous" maxim "There is no disputing about taste." If "every man's taste is to himself an ultimate standard without appeal," then "there is no ground of censure against any one, if such a one there be, who prefers Blackmore to Homer, selfishness to benevolence." And yet, Kames pointed out, by invariably speaking of "a right and a wrong taste," "a good and a bad taste," all individuals at one point or another concede a standard of taste. That concession, he argued, derives from a universal "sense or conviction of a common nature, not only in our own species but in every species." Because "this common nature is conceived to be a model or standard for each individual that belongs to the kind," the speaker, critic, or statesman devoted to articulating that standard is not imposing his taste or views on his audience, but rather articulating the standard of their nature. By effecting an end run around subjectivism in a fashion anticipating Kant's *Critique of Judgment*, Kames strategically reformulated the very maxim that he sought to undermine. To dispute about taste is to deviate from the standard of nature, which "disgusts" both the deviator and society.[24] There really is "no disputing about taste."

Yet might not the appeal to the higher standard of nature, to the common sense and sensibility of the people, be viewed as sanctioning a lowest-common-denominator populism that enfranchised a new vulgarity? To those committed to a rhetoric of decorum and to addressing their literate peers, not the public in general, the answer too often seemed obvious. When Joseph Warren commemorated the Boston Massacre in 1775 by warning "ye orphan babes [beware], lest, whilst your streaming eyes are fixed upon the ghastly corpse, *your feet slide on the stones bespattered with your father's brains*"; or when Josiah Quincy declared (on the subject of Tories), "A rank adulterer riots in thy incestuous bed, a brutal ravisher deflowers thy only daughter, a barbarous villain, now lifts his murtherous hand and stabs thy tender infant to the heart—see the sapphire current trickling from the wound," was this the outraged voice of human nature, or that of a vulgar, rabble-rousing, and artfully heightened rhetoric? How was one to distinguish between calculated and theatrical attempts to arouse passion and the power of the spontaneous and wounded "voice of justice & of consanguinity"?[25]

In a privately printed burlesque of Warren's Boston Massacre address, the Tory Thomas Bolton rejected such "flourishes of rhetoric . . . these will I leave to the SONS OF LIBERTY of this degenerate age." The "turgid bombast" and "frothy food" of Warren and other "*modern heroes*" mark them as "*Indian chiefs*," savages whose "*Os frontis*," according to "the observation of a learned physiognomist," is "uncommonly flat." In addition, having "sapsculls" neither "square, oval nor round" is proof "that their judgments can never be found." But worse than their innate inferiority, which is evident in their "countenance," is their conceit. Dr. Warren is described as giving up "Quack" medicine upon realizing it is "a profession too grovelling for so sublime a genius. For such a genius only one profession is suitable: *Orator*."[26] Bolton's real worry was that a new elite of populist orators ("Whorators," as one musical attack on Patriot leaders called them) would supplant a traditional elite of their social superiors.[27]

In 1773 the Loyalist historian Jonathan Boucher attributed the power of the rebel leadership to their particular brand of oratory: "As though there were some irrefutable charm in all extemporaneous speaking, however rude, the orators of our committees and sub-committees, like those in higher spheres, prevail with their tongues. To public speakers alone is the government of our country now completely committed. . . . An empire is thus completely established within an empire."[28] In the Tory view, the rule of law and thus of print had given way to the rule of the tongue. Mocking those who sought political and social elevation through the offices of eloquence and the new "profession" of orator, a Tory broadside of 1775 addressed the rebel chairman of a New York committee in charge of appointing deputies. Its title carries its message: *To the Very Learned, Loquacious, Rhetorical, Oratorical, Disputative, Flexible, Incomprehensible, Impenetrable, Pathetic and Irresistible Eloquent Chairman.* Clearly there is jealousy in the condescension.[29]

The Tory attack on Whig oratory as merely demagogical social climbing and inflammatory propaganda failed to recognize that such propaganda rested, in part, on what may be seen as a new emotive theory of representation, one consistent with the objectives of the new oratory. For example, Paul Revere's famous engraving of the Boston Massacre, which shows British soldiers ordered to fire on helpless citizens under the sign of "Butcher's Hall," may be described as a propagandistic misrepresentation of an incident in which, in fact, British soldiers were sorely provoked and no clear order to fire was issued (Figure 13). Or it may be said that what the engraving depicts is less the "outrage" committed by British troops than the "outrage" felt by patriots in response to it. It depicts and gives voice to what the poem printed below it calls "speechless sorrows lab'ring for a tongue," the kind of sorrow expressed in the countenance of the shawled woman behind the action on the left, who is the inscribed surrogate for the viewer of the print. In other words, the misrepresentation of the event serves to make possible the accurate representation of an emotion or emotions that otherwise could not be represented. Mimetic pictorialism gives way to psychological representation. If oratory, and, by extension, all the rhetorical arts, were defined as provocations to action, made possible, in the new mode, by making an audience

Figure 13. Paul Revere, *The Bloody Massacre perpetrated in King-Street, Boston, on March 5th 1770 by a party of the 29th Regiment*, 1770. (Courtesy of the American Antiquarian Society.)

feel what the speaker or artist feels, then the representation of a targeted feeling displayed for sympathetic experiencing becomes both the primary subject and primary objective of those arts. When John Allen, in his *Oration on the Beauties of Liberty* (1773), asks in a Gothic mode: "has not the voice of your father's blood cry'd yet loud enough in your ears?" he is, in effect, dramatizing, externalizing, and pictorializing the operations of conscience.[30]

In short, both the distortions of Revere's engraving and the hyperbole of Warren's oration are efforts to find, in the theatricality of (spoken and visual) language, a way of representing as well as communicating natural emotions, the outraged voices of human nature. The neoclassical linearity of the firing squad is stigmatized as an insane rationality in contrast to the emotional energies of the victims. Revere's engraving displaces its own agenda of provoking (its viewers) to act onto the libeled Captain Preston, who did not, as shown, stand behind his troops and order the "Massacre." At the same time, the bayonetted muskets of the British, with their stocks and triggers effaced by smoke, visually suggest Revere's own engraving tools, and thus the symbolic appropriation of British "fire power" by the rebel artist and propagandist.[31]

It is the nature of politics, however, that the self-exculpating defense of one camp's propaganda not be extended to the propaganda of one's opponents. A generation after Revere's engraving, Paine, in his *Rights of Man*, attacked Burke's *Reflections on the Revolution in France* as a verbal collection of "tragic paintings by which Mr. Burke has outraged his own imagination," paintings "very well calculated for theatrical representations, where facts are manufactured for the sake of show, and accommodated to produce, through the weakness of sympathy, a weeping effect." Burke had divided the temporal and narrative character of language into a series of framed visual moments so as "to exhibit consequences without causes." Whether in prose or paint, propaganda, Paine suggests, is always visual and dramatic. Indeed, Paine himself had declared that the project of his *Crisis Papers* was to have his readers "look on this picture and weep over it."[32] The rhetorical figure of speech, the moving motif, unsubdued by the plain style, has its analogue in the dangerous drama of the image. The fact that Paine's attack could serve as a critical appraisal of both Revere's engraving and, indeed, of his own prose makes clear that one man's theatricality was another's voice of nature.

Natural Theatricality

Though Quintilian's maxim that "only the good man can speak well" was widely subscribed to, the distinction between theatrical *ethos* and natural character was in fact being blurred by the oxymoronic project of discovering a natural rhetoric.[1] That the distinction between calculated rabble-rousing and heartfelt discourse was finally highly problematic, if not deceptive, had, however, to be repeatedly denied lest it compromise the agenda of the rhetorical revolution. For example, by accusing George III in the rough draft of the Declaration of "exciting those very people [American slaves] to rise in arms among us, and to purchase that liberty of which he has deprived them," Jefferson was carefully trying to differentiate between the supposedly noninflammatory language of the Declaration and George's "heinous" and unnatural call to revolutionary arms.[2] But precisely such a call to arms and such an incitement to revolution are as implicit in the Declaration as they are explicit in Jefferson's "Declaration of the Causes and Necessity of Taking up Arms," written with John Dickinson the year before.

The tension between the natural and the theatrical was the central problem posed by the popular oratorical texts of the period. Though, as Hugh Blair put the commonplace, a public speaker must never "vitiate" his delivery by laying "aside the voice with which he expresses himself in private; [in order] to assume a new, studied tone, and a cadence altogether foreign to his natural manner"—"his gestures and motions ought all to carry that kind of expression which nature has dictated to him"—there was, providentially, "room in this matter for some study and art." Every emotion of the mind naturally has its own countenance, sound, and gesture, but those countenances, sounds, and gestures still must be taught if they are to be effectively displayed.[3] Thus there is no sense of paradox in John Herries providing in his *Elements of Speech* rules and charts to teach the "universal untaught language of nature" as a "mechanical art."[4] For all the insistence that eloquence was an art of magnifying feelings actually experienced and not of deceptively fabricating feelings, to teach the code of voice and gesture—to elide the distinction between the production of natural sounds and the reproduction of them made possible through a descriptive taxonomy in the service of a mechanical science—was to equip all men to deceive, to act a role. The contradiction is apparent in this introductory passage in Burgh's *Art of Speaking*:

> Supposing a person to be ever so sincere and zealous a lover of *virtue*, and of his *country*; without a competent skill and address in *speaking*, he can only sit still, and see them wronged, without having it in his *power* to prevent or redress the evil. Let an artful and eloquent statesman harangue the house of commons upon a point of the utmost consequence to the publick good. He has it greatly in his power to *mislead* the *judgment* of the house. And he, who sees through the delusion, if he be awkward in delivering himself, can do nothing toward *preventing* the ruinous schemes.[5]

As Burgh's passage ironically makes clear, the same eloquence, whether informed by truth or not, serves both the "artful" demagogue and the "sincere" patriot who saves his nation. Distinctions between "sincere" and "artful" to the contrary, "the art of speaking" was always artful, the show of naturalness was still a show. The function of speech was not so much to express feelings as to elicit particular responses. Even John Adams understood in 1759 that the point was to adapt one's voice not to the passion he felt but "to the passion he would move." Or to the emotion he wished to feel; for, at least in the view of painter Charles Willson Peale, by putting an expression on one's face one could through "sweet contagion" call forth the emotion to which it corresponded, thus generating natural feeling through theatrical imitation. Indeed, it was Peale's hope that practiced facial expressions, by conforming the interior to the exterior, could serve as a means of curing mental disorders.[6]

Deeply influenced by the new naturalistic acting style introduced on the English stage by Garrick, which displaced the grand style onto opera and offered further testimony to the disturbing but useful psychological fact that a costumed actor playing a beggar could pluck the heart strings and elicit tears as readily as, if not more readily than, a real beggar, the oratorical manuals of the period were often indistinguishable from acting manuals. The oft-quoted advice of the former to readers of other people's prose—reading should be "nothing but *speaking* what one sees in a book, as if he were expressing his *own* sentiments as they rise in his mind"—in the larger world beyond the stage had the consequence of confounding "by like signs two things so very different as a copy and an original," as William Cockin put it in his 1775 critique of Burgh.[7] The line between expressing emotion and counterfeiting it, between delivering one's own sentiments and another's, was blurred, and with it the line between theatrical performance and natural behavior. Burgh enviously informed his readers that "the ancients used to procure for their youth, masters of pronunciation from the theatres."[8]

Indeed, Rousseau would go so far as to say of the new eighteenth-century "man of the world" who inhabited a deceptive, competitive, and less rigidly demarcated society that not only is he "entirely covered with a mask," but "he is so accustomed to disguise, that if, at any time he is obliged for a moment to assume his natural character his uneasiness and constraint are palpably obvious."[9] Unlike the eighteenth-century Iroquois "false face" masks worn to invoke the curative power of nature, the Rousseauian mask is worn to hide the natural beneath the social. If the self was no more than an endless sequence of self-presentations structured for different audiences without an overarching and definable core self (a view with which Franklin teases the readers of his *Autobiography*), theatricality was the essence of natural behavior. And if acting was ultimately an act of self-possession and personal expression rather than of emotional identification or self-effacing alienation (a position Diderot would argue in his posthumous *The Paradox of Acting*), then, to reverse the formula, natural behavior was the essence of theatricality. The title character of Charles Brockden Brown's *Ormond*, Brown tells us, had an acting skill that, because it was the acting of real life, made the performance of professional actors appear nothing more than "the sport of children": "He blended in his own person the functions of poet and actor and his dramas were not fictitious but real. The end that he proposed was not the amusement of a playhouse mob. His were scenes in which hope and fear exercised a genuine influence, and in which was maintained that resemblance to truth so audaciously and grossly violated on the stage."[10] At the heart of the antitheatrical prejudice first articulated by Plato and reinvigorated and recontextualized by figures as different as William Prynne, Rousseau, and John Witherspoon was a fear that the actor, especially if playing a villain, would take on the character of the role he played. A protean understanding of self, in Rousseau's words, "the art of putting on another character than his own, of appearing different than he is, of becoming passionate in cold blood, of saying what he does not think as naturally as if he really did think it . . . would lead to forgetting his own place by dint of taking another's."[11] In this sense the antitheatrical prejudice is an effort to challenge the understanding of the self as an ongoing circumstantial and protean process.

Charles Stearns's *Dramatic Dialogues for the Use of Schools* (1798), the first American text to teach theatrical performance, is less concerned with the power of a role to corrupt or transform than with its power to mislead an audience into identifying the actor with his role. Stearns offers a theory of casting opposites as a way of resolving the problem:

> Scholars uniformly perform best in the character which is natural to them, or that which is directly opposite. . . . The character of a rogue is best performed by an honest person, provided he understands the business of taking off characters well. The honest man's aversion to a rogue causes him to observe the peculiar features of the character from which cause he will strike it off in a lively manner and feel no kind of fear lest it should be applied to himself.[12]

"The business of taking off characters" or "striking [a character] off" refers simultaneously to the contradictory obligations to enact and to differentiate. Although defining successful theatrical impersonation, the phrase also, idiomatically, reinforces the moral insistence that neither the actor nor his audience confuse a player with his role. Stearns goes to great lengths to reassure his readers that good acting is based on identification only when the role is virtuous; when the role is that of a rogue, good acting is accomplished through minute observation, observation that he wishfully insists has its source in natural aversion rather than fascination.

When Jefferson in 1786 went to sit for his earliest known likeness at the London studio of American painter Mather Brown, the artist had just completed a series of theatrical engravings for *Bell's Edition of Shakespeare* showing English actresses and actors (*Mr. Kemble as King Richard*) in their most famous roles. Brown had also just finished a separate full-scale oil painting, *Miss Burnton and Mr. Holman in Romeo and Juliet*. Brown's biographer suggests that these theatrical pieces "opened up a whole new range of possibilities for him," a liberated vision of portraiture that seems to have borne fruit in the portrait of Jefferson as romantic visionary (Figure 14), so much more theatrical than Brown's earlier portraits. A coquettish figure of liberty serves as muse.[13]

In *Absorption and Theatricality*, Michael Fried has argued that a new moral seriousness in eighteenth-century French art took the form of representing scenes in which the attention of all the participants was turned upon a central figure. In their concentration,

Figure 14. Mather Brown, *Thomas Jefferson*, 1786. (Courtesy of Charles F. Adams.)

they ignored the beholder of the painting, instead of implicitly playing to him or her. Although this new "absorption" spoke to an ideal of unselfconscious engagement, it simultaneously articulated a yet more artful theatricality in which acts of attention within the paintings (like that of the woman with the clenched hands and the shawl in the Revere engraving) in effect destroyed the viewer's self-conscious distance and brought the viewer into the painting itself. Such theatricality had considerable implications for the relationship of art and nature.

Take, for example, the case of Patience Wright, a remarkably talented Quaker woman who in 1772 moved from New York to

London to pursue what *The London Magazine*, dubbing her on her arrival "the Promethean Modeller," called a "new style of picturing superior to statuary and peculiar to herself and the honour of America," a style that "the hand of nature" had designated her "to provide." This new American style was utterly realistic, fully in-the-round, life-size wax portraiture modeled from life. "Remarkable for expressing the exact likeness of the human face and passions of the soul," as another London newspaper put it, the wax models, whose sitters included George Whitefield, John Dickinson, Garrick, Franklin, and Pitt, were finished with "delicate skin texture and coloring, glass eyes characterized by lids, lashes and brows, and veins introduced under the waxen skin of face and hands." So realistic were they that Wright took pleasure in describing herself as "the Witch of Endor," able to "raise the dead."[14]

Keeping the wax warm and soft by holding it between her thighs, Wright did all her sculpting beneath her apron, in a simulacrum of birthing. She enjoyed shocking visitors by drawing "busto" heads from beneath her apron. A contemporary engraving shows her holding (her hands significantly are unseen) a fully dressed and bewigged busto of a man as if he had just issued from her body (Figure 15). Here was "Promethean" artistic creation whose realism left the viewer, even the informed viewer, uncertain whether what was seen was alive or not. Wright's "invisible hand" archly and actively competed with "the hand" of nature. It also competed with the hand of nurture, for the medium itself seemed a literalization of the Lockean insistence on the impressionability and malleability of the individual, formed and reformed by the determinant press of experience and environment. Wright was not alone in blurring the distinction between wax and flesh. Garrick was praised for the "astounding plasticity of his facial expressions. His exquisite feeling was likened to wax, ready to receive any impression."[15]

Like the trompe l'oeil painting of her contemporary Charles Willson Peale and the fiction Jefferson defends in his 1771 letter to Robert Skipwith, Wright's witching art did not seek so much to

Mrs. WRIGHT.
Publish'd as the Act directs Decr. 1. 1775.

Figure 15. Mrs. Wright Finishing a "Busto," The London Magazine, 1775. (Courtesy of the American Antiquarian Society.)

represent reality as to partake of it, to provide the viewer with the experience and consumption of a reality objectified in order to become consumable. Like the contemporary oratory mired in the paradox of natural theatricality (simultaneously imitating and realizing nature), this was art that was simultaneously intensely naturalistic and intensely theatrical: surreally mimetic. Like the Constitution's "We the People," this was representation masquerading as embodiment, the problematic relationship of signifier and signified resolved by the sleight of hand of a third term that was neither one nor the other.

Seeking, if only momentarily, to blur the distinction between art and nature, Wright's bustos, which turned public figures into public art, were a kind of confidence game. At one point, as Wright's biographer tells the story, the fully dressed model of Franklin was seated at a desk in the study of a private home where specially invited guests, honored to be in the presence of the great man, were told, when they peered in on him, that he was deep in reverie. Moments later they became outraged witnesses when the host "boxed the ears" of Franklin. When finally told of the fraud (which, in effect, punished them for their desire to gaze at Franklin, to feel the *frisson* of proximity to celebrity), they became outraged yet again.[16]

If Wright's work in her own way turned private people into objects for scrutiny, her secret life as an American spy extended her own desire to penetrate and expose. Outspoken about her American sympathies, Wright pumped her well-placed visitors, who included the king and queen, for information that she then would pass on—sometimes buried in bustos—to Franklin at Passy, and after the war to Jefferson himself, then minister to France. A 1780 portrait of her by her son shows her "taking the head" of a figure with exactly the features—as one contemporary reviewer put it—"of that *incorrigible tyrant, Charles I*," a symbolic stand-in, as another reviewer immediately recognized, for George III: "Wright on her lap sustains a trunkless head / And looks a wish—the King's was in its stead."[17] A year before the painting, after Wright warned Lord North during a sitting that he might lose his head "if he did not make atonement for the blood he shed" in America, North replied that "if they should cut my head off, 'tis in your power to make me another."[18] Both anecdotes point to the intensely aggressive and political character of an art so natural that it threatens to replace the natural (that is, political) order, rather than to represent it.

One index of that threat is suggested by the history of the word *unnatural*. According to the *OED*, it carried a variety of senses in the eighteenth century: "not in accordance with the physical nature of persons or animals" (in his *Natural History* Goldsmith described the appetite of the black rat as "unnatural" because of the disproportion of appetite and animal size); "not in accordance with the usual course of nature" (period almanacs would describe unseasonable weather as "unnatural"); and, when applied to human nature, "at variance with or devoid of natural feelings or moral standards." (The linkage of "natural feelings" and "moral standards" points to a hidden agenda of the oratorical revolution: to make private feelings over in the image of public expectations.) The *OED*, however, cites a new definition of *unnatural* emerging in the 1740's: "artificial or devoid of natural qualities"—the artistic disguising or transforming of nature.

The *OED*'s earliest example of this meaning is a poetic reference to inexpensive woods painted with the graining of higher grade woods (a common practice in eighteenth-century decorative arts): "rich with various dyes, / Unnatural Woods with awkward Art arise." In his 1775 *Journals*, the itinerant Quaker John Woolman describes a crisis of conscience that sheds light on the new definition of "unnatural," a crisis occasioned by wearing "garments dyed with a dye hurtful to them." Risking being perceived as "one affecting singularity" by not wearing a modish white-dyed hat, Woolman gives testimony to the purity of his faith by "wearing a hat of the natural color of the fur."[19] In this episode sin itself becomes the act of denaturing things so that they can no longer be seen for what they are. Detached from a Christian metaphysics that defined the natural as fallen, purity becomes identified with the natural. In the days following July 4, 1776, Jefferson sent to several friends copies of his original Declaration as well as the version finally agreed upon and asked them to "judge whether it is the better or worse for the Critics."[20] Responding on July 21, Richard Henry Lee consoled the author by saying that "the Thing is in its nature so good, that no Cookery could spoil the Dish for the palettes of Freemen."[21] The raw state was to be preferred to the cooked.

The elocutionary movement in America that helped destabilize the distinction between the natural and theatrical was exactly contemporaneous with the beginnings of the professional American theater. There had been makeshift theater companies occasionally touring the major cities as early as 1750. Jefferson, for example, had attended a number of theatrical entertainments in Williamsburg in his youth. But it was not until 1766 and against Quaker objections that the Southwark Theatre in Philadelphia was built, the first permanent theater in America. It was in this structure, whose Palladian windows and cupola seemed impiously reminiscent of a meeting house, that Samuel Greville, America's first professional actor, debuted in Rowe's *Tamerlane* in 1767, the same year that saw the production of the *Prince of Parthia*, usually considered the first American play. Within five years permanent theaters were in every major city except Boston. Yet even there the theatricality of the Boston Tea Party in 1773, an event described in one contemporary broadside as "The Grand Indian Opera," suggests the powerful impact of costume drama.[22] Significantly, the Tea Party was staged by men who for the most part were Freemasons, members of a society that started with gentlemen in craftsmen's aprons impersonating artisans and ended with on-the-make artisans challenging the gentry's monopoly on status and social position, a society in which secret rituals were enacted with "full costumes, wigs, pancake makeup, sets, and theatrical lighting."[23]

From the period of the Stamp Act on, in an effort to focus a still widespread antitheatrical prejudice onto Britain, the popular press had repeatedly identified Britain with the artifice, dissimulation, effeminacy, and luxury popularly associated with the theater. One New York newspaper, for example, characterized Lord North (whose Tea Act was intended to salvage the failing East India Company) as "the author of the curious East-Indian farce, lately prepared in England to be played . . . on the American stage." Another referred to the Boston Massacre as Britain's "Theatre of Blood."[24]

The fact that General Burgoyne not only wrote plays while occupying Boston but turned Faneuil Hall into a theater for his soldiers' theatrical performances, that Howe did the same in occupied Philadelphia, and that Sir Henry Clinton did them one better by turning his soldiers' theatricals into a large moneymaking operation in New York, seemed to clinch the connection. In October 1778, Samuel Adams, an arch-opponent of the theater, reported to the Continental Congress the fact that some of Washington's men had "condescended to act on the stage" in "humble imitation as it would seem, of the Example of the British Army" and thus stood in "Contempt of the Sense of Congress," that is, in contempt of their earlier resolution to "discourage and discountenance . . . the exhibition of all shews, plays and other expensive diversions."[25] In response, the Continental Congress passed on October 16 an even more stringent resolution.

At the heart of professional theatricality lay what the rhetorician/signer John Witherspoon in his *Serious Enquiry into the Nature and Effects of the Stage* called the dangerous subordination of one's real character to the unnatural impersonations of often "vicious men."[26] If such impersonations were associated with British vice, American virtue was, in contrast, rooted in the consumer end of theatricality, in a concept related to impersonation, but whose threat to the stability of self had positive rather than destructive moral consequences: the operations of sympathy and identification, the experience of being moved. Those operations that permitted one, in Pope's popular phrase, "to feel another's Woe," were routinely described in the eighteenth century with reference to what happens to a spectator in a theater.[27]

In turn, American republicanism was associated with the "real" theatricality of history. In the wake of the anti–Stamp Act agitation, John Adams described what he saw to be a common but prideful view that "America was designed by Providence for the Theatre, on which Man was to make his true figure."[28] In a similar vein, Francis Hopkinson described America in 1776 as "a scene of desolation and distress; a theatre whereon is acted a real tragedy."[29] The dramatic conception of America as acting out a providential national role, as the locus of the fifth act of a divinely scripted historical drama that in Bishop Berkeley's famous words would "close the drama" of "the course of empire," required the naturalization rather than the wholesale rejection of the theatrical.[30]

In his history of the American theater, the early American playwright William Dunlap describes a performance of Burgoyne's farce, *The Blockade of Boston*, put on while the general's troops were confined "to a narrow neck of land" surrounding Boston:

> While the officers were performing Burgoyne's farce, an alarm was given that the rebels had assaulted the lines, and when a sergeant entered and announced the fact, the audience supposing his words "The rebels have attacked the lines on the Neck," belonged to the farce, applauded the very natural acting of the man, and were not disturbed until successive encores convinced them that it was not to the play that the words, however apropos, belonged.

The confusions between history and theater brought on here by "very natural acting" lead to applauding a sentiment that in reality should terrify. In interrupting the play, the rebels have "attacked the lines" in a punning second sense that Dunlap's passage clearly encourages, thereby forcing the British play to give way to the real drama of military engagement. Shortly after the Battle of Yorktown and before an audience that included Washington, Philip Freneau took the occasion to announce, in a dramatic prologue performed at the Southwark Theatre, that a nation in wartime "Constrain'd to shun the bold theatric show, / to Act long tragedies of real woe," now in victory could and should allow itself to enjoy a different and more diverting kind of "theatric show." One kind of theater could now give way to another.[31]

Yet the distinctions between historical and professional theatricality were slippery indeed. When asked to repeat his eloquent defense of the necessity of declaring independence for the benefit of three new delegates from New Jersey who had just arrived for the crucial July 2, 1776 vote, John Adams expressed his hesitation that "it had so much the Air of exhibiting like an Actor or Gladiator, for the Entertainment of the Audience, that I was ashamed to repeat what I had said twenty times before."[32] Without the context of immediate debate, bald repetition seemed too theatrical. As Franklin implied by identifying the ability to repeat sermons as the great advantage itinerant ministers had over their pulpited brethren, repetition turned speeches into scripts.[33]

And yet Adams himself traced his choice of law to the pleasure he felt at having his reading voice praised at the newly established Harvard play-reading groups of 1750 and 1751: "I was as often requested to read as any other," he recalled proudly.[34] Despite some lingering Puritan ambivalence about the stage, Adams records that while in France in 1778 he often went to the theater (a generic term that subsumed musical and operatic performances) and enjoyed it.[35] Many years later, John Quincy Adams, who attended some of those performances with his father, would conclude his *Lectures on Rhetoric and Oratory* by tracing the history of the word "actor." From its classical meaning as a public accuser (having no application at all to the stage), the word eventually enlarged so as to mean a speaker of any kind ("the speaker was called the actor"), whether that speaker is a lawyer (whom Adams calls "an actor of truth") or a stage actor (whom Adams calls "an imitator" of truth). Finally it takes on its modern, circumscribed sense whereby it refers primarily to those who work in the theater, so that "a lawyer, a divine, a legislator, would at this day deem it an insult to be called an actor." Significantly, Adams identifies the modern shift as occurring in the decade before the Revolution and in the context of Whig-Tory politics: "Dr. Johnson doubtless meant it an insult upon Lord Chatham, when he described him as 'the great actor of patriotism.'"[36] Though Johnson in all probability intended the word as an insult, the insult had the protective masking of a word that still ambiguously suggested both an actor on stage and an actor in history.

Long after the war, Adams asserted that "The Declaration of Independence I always considered as a theatrical show . . . [in which] Jefferson ran away with all the stage effect . . . and all the glory of it."[37] In Adams's eyes, Jefferson had not cut a "true figure" in the history of the American Revolution but instead had finessed his standing with the American people through what Adams, in an 1805 letter to Benjamin Rush, called a "coup de theatre."[38] Indeed Adams sought to one-up Jefferson on the matter of their relative importance as historical actors by insisting that "the most essential documents" of the Revolution were the "debates and deliberations in Congress," debates and speeches that, never having been committed to writing, were "lost forever." Insisting that what Jefferson called "the life and soul of history" resided only in the unrecoverable congressional debates in which Adams was a key figure, Adams demoted published documents like the Declaration and *Common Sense* from their position as central embodiments or legible registers of history.[39] In an 1811 letter to Benjamin Rush, Adams asserted that in "point of republicanism" the essential difference between Adams and Jefferson was "the difference between speeches and [written] messages. I was a monarchist because I thought a speech more manly, more respectful to Congress and the nation. Jefferson . . . preferred messages."[40] In implying the ontological superiority of the oral over the written, Adams asserted his priority over Jefferson. For Adams presidential addresses did not revisit the stagecraft of monarchy, but opened a dialogue with Congress. It was the representational world of texts that was fundamentally theatrical; the supposed originary moments of "manly" oral performance constituted a participation within real history.

Adams's jealousy of Jefferson's "coup de theatre" was, however, compounded by his grudging awareness of the impossibility of separating the doing of things for effect from the doing of things to effect, the doubleness, that is, of being an effectual historical "actor" in both the general sense of agent and the specific sense of performer. Indeed, though he had attacked Governor Hutchinson a generation earlier for ostentatiously introducing what he called "scenery . . . so theatrical and ecclesiastical" into the courts, it was Adams who argued that Washington should be given the title of "Majesty" and perhaps a throne because the European powers with whom he would deal had long understood politics to be theater.[41]

The Figure of Patrick Henry

If there were such oxymoronic entities as natural theatricality and natural language, there was one Revolutionary orator who virtually all agreed embodied the former and articulated the latter: Patrick Henry, a figure about whom Jefferson was deeply and revealingly conflicted. Long after the war, Jefferson offered this description of Henry to Daniel Webster, who set it down:

> His eloquence was peculiar, if indeed it should be called eloquence; for it was impressive and sublime, beyond what can be imagined. Although it was difficult when he had spoken to tell what he had said, yet, while he was speaking, it always seemed directly to the point. When he had spo-

ken in opposition to my opinion, had produced a great effect, and I myself been [sic] highly delighted and moved, I have asked myself when he ceased: "what the devil has he said?" I could never answer the inquiry. . . . His pronunciation was vulgar and vicious, but it was forgotten while he was speaking.[1]

Henry both impressed and disturbed Jefferson. Though he was, in Jefferson's words, "the laziest man in reading I ever knew," a man who had "read nothing and had no books," a man who "wrote almost nothing" and "could not write," Henry could speak in a mesmerizing way.[2] Indeed, Jefferson seems to suggest (perhaps because the reverse formulation applied to himself) that Henry's astonishing command of spoken language was a function of his lack of learning and written skills; his speech was unmediated by the writerly mind. Because of the pure, untextual character of his speaking, "Henry spoke," Jefferson concluded, conferring his greatest compliment, "as Homer wrote."[3] Yet for Jefferson, torn between the norms of naturalness and of decorum, the virtues of common and of elevated speech, and the conflicting claims of passion and reason, a style that did not seem to rely on logical argumentation, charmed even its opponents, and could not be paraphrased cut both ways, as his telling phrase "what the devil" suggests.

The Ciceronian orator Edmund Randolph, indulging a class bias Henry repeatedly inspired, patronizingly described Henry's speaking success as resting on the "discovery" that "a pronunciation which might disgust in a drawing room may yet find access to the hearts of a popular assembly."[4] Unlike Jefferson, who during his career at the bar "drew copiously from the depths of the law," Henry drew from the "recesses of the human heart." More specifically, Randolph continued, his power lay not only in his voice but in the power of his countenance to mold the hearts of his auditors in its own image: he "transfused into the breast of others the earnestness depicted in his own features, which ever forbade a doubt of sincerity."[5] Here was a homegrown version of Franz Anton Mesmer's claims (reported in the *Pennsylvania Gazette* in April of 1777) that his "magnetic" gaze could produce an artificial tide within the bodies of his Viennese patients.[6] In contrast to Socratic dialectic, which involved one-to-one communication, rhetoric involved addressing the "multitudes," a fact that stimulated in Randolph, as it had in Plato, fears of democracy. Unlike Randolph, Jefferson was less certain whether a public discourse that fell below drawing-room standards condemned "the people" as vicious or condemned elite, decorous discourse as unnatural.

Some light is thrown on Jefferson's fascination with Henry by understanding the tradition of national orator/poet in which Jefferson albeit somewhat reluctantly located Henry. In 1773, Jefferson wrote a particularly revealing letter to Charles MacPherson, a former Virginia merchant and brother of James MacPherson, the ventriloquizing "translator" of the poems of Ossian, that ancient Gaelic bard ecstatically believed by the thousands that devoured MacPherson's translations of a largely nonexistent original to be the newly discovered Homer of the British Isles. Jefferson requested that his correspondent ask James MacPherson, "to whom the world is so much indebted for the collection, arrangement and elegant translation, of Ossian's poems," for a copy of the manuscript of the originals. Because "these peices have been, and will I think during my life continue to be to me, the source of daily and exalted pleasure," and because "I am not ashamed to own that I think this rude bard of the North the greatest Poet that has ever existed," Jefferson rapturously declared, he was "desirous of learning the language" in which the poet "sung."[7]

For this he requested a Gaelic dictionary and to be "possessed of [a manuscript copy of] the songs in their original form," transcribed, he specified, in a "fair, round, hand on fine paper." Because "the glow of one warm thought is to me worth more than money," Jefferson made his request without regard to "the cost" and without the skepticism that accompanied Dr. Johnson's request for a copy of the originals.[8] In addition to expressing his sentimental pleasure in the warm thoughts of Ossian, Jefferson's neoprimitivism, like his fascination with the geometrical orderliness and republican simplicity of neoclassical architecture, was part of an effort to free America from its immediate British derivativeness by providing it with an alternative past. Ossian and the entire primordial past of warrior/orators was a strategically invented tradition. Indeed, Jefferson proposed in 1776 that the Saxon chiefs Hengist and Horsa be represented on the verso of the national seal.[9] Whether it was an invented past or not, Patrick Henry was in Jefferson's mind the closest approximation to a figure from that preliterate era—the closest white approximation.

In the year after Jefferson's correspondence with MacPherson, Lord Dunmore, then governor of Virginia, having recently returned from an expedition against the Indians, brought with him the text of a speech delivered to him by a Shawnee Indian chief named Logan. The speech was "so affecting," as Jefferson later reported, "so fine a morsel of eloquence, that it became the theme of every conversation in Williamsburg." Himself smitten by it, Jefferson duly entered the "translation" of it he had been given in "my pocket-book of 1774," a translation whose diction suggests that the speech had been heard through the filter of both Ossian and the Gospel of John.[10] The stir occasioned by the speech is partially explained by its unintended political resonance. Lord Dunmore had in 1773 dissolved the House of Burgesses for proposing a committee to address colonial grievances. The Indian "war" he undertook allowed him to distract attention from worsening political matters. Addressed to Dunmore, Logan's speech, with its mixture of conciliation and anger, offered a displaced articulation of colonial grievances.

Though earlier he had devoted himself to avenging the murder of his family by colonial soldiers, Logan opens his brief speech with the Gospel-echoing insistence that no "white man . . . ever entered Logan's cabin hungry and he gave him not meat" or entered "cold and naked, and he clothed him not." Claiming to have "fully glutted my vengeance," the sole survivor of his family closes with the elegiac Ossianic note: "Who is there to mourn for Logan—No one."[11] Insisting that in the "whole orations of Demosthenes and Cicero and indeed in all of European oratory" one could not "produce a single passage superior to the speech of Logan," Jefferson later quoted the speech in *Notes on the State of Virginia* as refutation of the "contumelious" theory of Buffon that the combined effects of the American soil and climate degenerated animal nature and ultimately the moral faculties of its human inhabitants—a degeneration supposedly evident in the American Indians (whose "small organs of generation" result in their having "no love for their fellow men") and soon to appear in white Americans.[12]

Several years after the publication of *Notes*, when Jefferson was falsely accused of having invented the eloquent speech to make his point, he responded: "But wherefore the forgery? Whether Logan's or mine it would still have been American. . . . He would have a just right to be proud who could with truth claim that composition."[13] Jefferson's insistence on the interchangeability of himself and Logan as "Americans" may be seen to carry the silent but proud suggestion that in writing the Declaration he too assumed the role of a national poet by producing a text that realized, animated, and invented his people. In that national text he had wielded the native genius of oratory that he so revered in Logan and Homer, joyfully discovered in Anglo-Saxon literature, and later attributed to the naturalized Christ in his private, scissor-edited version of the Gospels, and that, though disconcertingly atavistic and stripped of a comforting moral and elegiac tonality, he found in Patrick Henry.

In one of the extremely rare references to his father, Peter Jefferson, who died when his son was 14, Jefferson recalled in an 1812 letter to Adams that:

> the great Outassete, the warrior and orator of the Cherokees, . . . was always a guest of my father, on his journeys to and from Williamsburg. I was in his camp when he made his great farewell oration to his people . . . before his departure for England [where he would be received by the king] . . . his sounding voice, distinct articulation, animated action, and the solemn silence of his people at their several fires filled me with awe and veneration, altho' I did not understand a word he uttered.[14]

In retrospect, the memory of the Cherokee orator's departure speech seems to have served Jefferson as a way of addressing, mourning, and ennobling the death of his father, a deeply traumatic event that left him "at 14 years of age" head of the family with "the whole care and direction of myself . . . thrown on my self entirely, without a relative or friend qualified to advise or guide me."[15]

It was one thing to conceive of Logan's oratorical power as a racial primordialism, a register of stoic dignity, or to project onto Outassete's speech a regressive nostalgia for a mystified paternalism that inspired (words that the anticlerical Jefferson seldom used) "awe and veneration" detached from any rational understanding. It was quite another to see that power transmuted in the case of Patrick Henry into an indecorous class-specific energy with an undisplaced political agenda, especially in the midst of a nation being born, rather than a nation disappearing into what Ossian popularized as "the Celtic twilight." MacPherson addressed a nostalgia for older hierarchies and charismatic authority in poems whose publication was subsidized by the British government, in gratitude for which he later attacked the colonies in a 1776 pamphlet, *The Rights of Great Britain Asserted against the Claims of America*. In contrast to Ossian or the contemporary anthologists of German lieder, Henry revealed the revolutionary potential for a national poet to galvanize a people into revolutionary action, and in so doing to effect a degree of social leveling that even the democrat Jefferson felt to be frighteningly disruptive.

Figure 16. Gilbert Stuart, *The Skater* (Portrait of William Grant), 1782. (Courtesy of The National Gallery of Art.)

But the disruption of decorum was precisely what made Henry's oratory so powerful. Judge Spencer Roane, Henry's son-in-law, invoked the Burkean distinction between the sublime and the beautiful to indicate the essential difference between Henry's oratorical style and that of Richard Henry Lee, the Virginian who moved the resolution for independence in Congress. Lee's style was "always chaste." He "did not ravish your senses nore carry away your judgment by storm. . . . He was like a beautiful river meandering through a flowery mead, but which never overflowed its banks." In contrast, "it was Henry who was the mountain torrent that swept away everything before it. It was he alone who thundered and lightened."[16] The aestheticized contrast here between the two models of oratory is ultimately the standard contrast between the stasis, fixity, and ordered regularity signified by the beautiful, and the revolutionary process, uprooting change, and irresistible power signified by the sublime. In a revolutionary context, Henry's sublimity had to be given priority, but only if there was an attendant certainty that the dangers of its excess had been reined in by an admixture of the beautiful. Like the famous Natural Bridge of Virginia that Jefferson describes in *Notes on the State of Virginia* as offering from its top a vertiginous view that was "painful and intolerable," and from below an elevating view "delightful in an equal extreme," Henry offered a double spectacle, fearful or ennobling according to the perspective of the viewer.[17]

Roane's preference for Henry's sublimity over, but not to the exclusion of, Lee's regularity speaks to a larger cultural and political effort to reconceive the "beautifully regular" in terms consistent with the energies of the sublime. The form this most often took was to reconceive order as a fluid rather than fixed state. For example, Gilbert Stuart's first major success, *The Skater* (1782), takes the classical (architectural) ideal of balance and makes it dependent on movement rather than threatened by movement (Figure 16). No longer associated with the increasingly illusory stability of social class, the upright grace of the gentleman skater can only be maintained as long as he is moving, etching Hogarthian curves on London's Serpentine. To stand still on skates is to lose one's balance. In a similar vein, rather than fearing factionalism as a source of political instability, Madison, in his famous *Federalist* 10, would champion the dynamic tension among competing factions as the very essence of political stability. Passions would serve reasonable ends. Like the boundless power simultaneously produced and harnessed by James Watt's condensing steam engine, first demonstrated in March 1776, revolutionary energy was a constituent part of a new model of political and social stability.

What had traditionally been called "moderation" is revealed after 1776 for what it usually was—not the rational insistence on a middle ground, but an exhausting and nondialectical alternation between conflicting and often equally compelling extremes. In the quintessential moderate text of the pre-Revolutionary period, John Dickinson's *Letters from a Farmer in Pennsylvania*, the author (who, preferring conciliation, voted against the Declaration) defined a patriot as one who makes it "impossible to determine whether an *American's* character is most distinguishable, for his loyalty to his Sovereign, his duty to his mother country, his love of freedom, or his affection for his native soil."[18] And as late as 1775, John Adams could declare: "An Absolute independence on parliament . . . is very compatible with an absolute dependence on it."[19] These are not expressions of moderation, but the rhetorical denial of internal and external conflicts, a denial that paradoxically sets forth the conflicting terms. As Stuart's *Skater* and Madison's *Federalist* 10 suggested by example, the dynamics of those and other conflicts needed to be cast in the form of productive dialectics rather than in self-contradictory and self-canceling formulas.

In 1795, Friedrich Schiller described the "sentimental" in literature as the self-conscious re-creation of that "naive" and unselfconscious relation to the natural that for most individuals has been forever lost.[20] The sentimental mode was the means whereby the reflective faculty preserved the essential value of the intuitive. Schiller would undoubtedly have labeled Patrick Henry a "naive" artist, who like Homer, Shakespeare, and Goethe wrote intuitively rather than reflectively. However, Silas Deane's description of Henry's oratorical style as "high-wrought yet natural," as yoking art and nature, suggests Henry was equally implicated in the agenda of the sentimental: to re-create the natural, to preserve it even in the state of alienated and self-conscious artfulness.[21] Like eighteenth-century landscape painting, which found nature most interesting when, as in the case of the Natural Bridge, it seemed to be imitating or recalling art *picture*squely, Henry brought art and nature together in a way that dramatically blurred their difference. Though offering a theoretical resolution to a fundamental cultural opposition, such an effort at yoking self-consciousness and naturalness was inevitably suspect as leading to the worst kind of wolf-in-sheep's-clothing deceptions, such as Britain's "artful" insistence on its "natural" parental love of the colonies. But once again Henry seemed the exception.

In a late character sketch of the Virginian, Jefferson suggested that the real secret of Henry's oratorical power lay in a juxtaposition of the sublime and beautiful within Henry's own nature: he was a man "whose anger was terrible" and yet whose "temper was excellent," who, though a man of passion, was at least in his own view always "yielding and practicable and not disposed to differ."[22] In this regard he represented not just the ideal of self-control, what elocutionist John Mason called "the right Management of the voice," but, like the self-regulating Newtonian universe itself, the spectacle of self-control.[23] He demonstrated what the rhetorician Hugh Blair insisted contributes most to "please and persuade": the spectacle of self-command whereby the auditor can hear and witness "the effect of reason in the midst of passion," a representation in miniature of the inner dynamic of energy and its containment at the heart of the period's still largely dominant cyclical vision of history. The oratorical moment for which he was most famous was precisely one of almost theatrical self-control. In the version reconstructed by Henry's biographer, William Wirt, with the help of Jefferson himself, who was in attendance, Henry concluded an attack on the Stamp Act with these words: "Tarquin and Caesar each had his Brutus—Charles the First his Cromwell and—George the Third. . . ." At that point Henry was interrupted with boos and cries of "Treason." He recovered with the self-censoring euphemism: "may profit by their example." The systole of that line permitted him the diastole of the next line: "If this be treason, make the most of it."[24] Here once again was the oscillation between self-assertion and submission to the judgments of others that operated beneath the deceptively static label of moderation.

In describing the trials of Revolutionary leadership, Robert Wiebe has suggested that Jefferson's "periodic headaches so severe that they incapacitated him for weeks," which only departed when he left office, Madison's "reticent, mumbling public style," which served as a "buffer against his gentry judges" and against his "epileptoid hysteria," Elbridge Gerry's stammer, Rufus King's frequent freezing before a suspicious audience, and Patrick Henry's "geyser of rage" beneath an "impressively smooth manner" were all manifestations of "the pressures of an incessant control," a tyrannical ethic of self-command.[25] If Wiebe is right, oratory itself became in the Revolutionary period not only an act of communication in the service of creating community, but also a ritualized forum for demonstrating self-control. It was a forum in which aggressive self-expression was unleashed in order to be contained, in which ruling passions were disciplined into polite sentiments by the "rules" of expression, and in which the private individual was ultimately socialized as the public servant.

The act of public speaking was a continual war between modesty and the ambition to excel, or as Douglass Adair put it in his essay, "Fame and the Founding Fathers," clearly favoring the second term, between the "static, complacent urge in the human heart to merely *be*" and "the strenuous effort to *become*"—to become a persona and force in history.[26] This self-canceling character is what made speaking so difficult for so many; it is in part what turned Madison into a mumbler and Jefferson into a whisperer. Public speaking was a local instance of the larger internal drama of republicanism, in which the citizen's double identity as sovereign (part of the authorizing People) and as subject (one of the governed) endlessly contend.

The *Pennsylvania Magazine*, which at the time was edited by Thomas Paine, featured in its June 1775 issue an article by "Epaminondas" on the prerequisites of successful public speaking. Chief among these is "what is called presence of mind, to be entirely free, and to seem to be free from any embarrassment, hurry or disorder"—the seeming is as important as the being. "The least degree of this confusion . . . shows that he was not wholly master of himself." This loss of self-mastery has as its primary cause "bashfulness or modesty," the consequence of being in respectful awe of the "greatness of the occasion . . . or those assembled." The cure for modesty (as well as for the "prideful desire to shine"—the other destroyer of presence of mind) is "composure"; the speaker must be stoically "indifferent" to "what the audience think of his performance . . . indifferent as to reputation and constrained by a sense of duty." And yet, paradoxically, modesty, which is "the greatest hindrance in the world to a man arriving at eminence in public speaking," is simultaneously the very thing that "recommends a man more than almost anything else to the favour of the public." Hence, self-control must not be so in evidence as to violate Cicero's rule of the art: to "appear a little embarrassed in entering upon a discourse" without having "one grain of it in the heart."[27] One must not only be composed, but one must compose oneself in public. One must serve as one's own editor and censor, inflicting on oneself

Figure 17. Plate from William Scott's *Lessons in Elocution . . . and Elements of Gesture* (New York, 1799). (From the library of the author.)

cuts of the sort Jefferson so bitterly insisted the Congress had inflicted on the first draft of the Declaration. Silence was far less exhausting.

In his 1779 *Lessons in Elocution*, a volume often reprinted in late eighteenth-century America, William Scott extended Burgh's disciplining of the voice and countenance to the rest of the body. A speaker must begin, he declares, "by resting the entire weight of his body on the right leg; the other just touching the ground . . . the right arm must be held out with the palm open in a 45 degree angle."[28] He goes on to position every finger and every joint so that the entire body finally traces a three-dimensional trapezoid that

Scott illustrates in one plate as a kind of cage—the rule of geometry—for the speaker (Figure 17). Appropriate gestures are essential, but "violent convulsions," a phrase used to describe the war itself, necessitated a literal straitjacket.[29] The wild, irrational gestures of James Otis during his breakdown, or of George III during those periods in which he was in the care of "a keeper," or of Shaker founder Ann Lee before she was nearly dragged to death behind a team of horses in punishment for ecstatic dancing and speaking in tongues, would be considered convulsive. Even the so-called long hair on the liberty figure featured on the first American silver dollar was judged to be too convulsive. In 1795, a draped-bust design sketched by Gilbert Stuart tied liberty's hair with a bow. Stuart is said to have commented: "Liberty on the other coins had run mad. . . . We will bind it up and thus render her a steady matron."[30]

No less than the act of speaking, the act of writing also offered a setting for the exercise of self-control. Referring to the late 1760's and early 1770's, the editor of Jefferson's *Literary Commonplace Book* comments that the "most conspicuous feature of Jefferson's handwriting in this period is the rigorous suppression of the long *s* [which had gone out of favor, in part, because of its visual similarity to an *f*] and the regular substitution of an open or serpentine character."[31] Despite such "rigorous suppression" Jefferson was unable to rid himself fully of the habit even after a decade of self-conscious effort. In the rough draft of the Declaration the long *s* reappears in the "hardiness" ascribed to George III as plotter of tyranny, a hardiness that, like the long *s*, must also be suppressed.[32]

Social Leveling and Stage Fright

It must be remembered that self-control is not only a self-disciplining, it is also a holding back, a strategy of saving oneself from being used up by a scrutinizing audience, from being repeatedly taken the measure of by those farmers and landowners well-skilled in the art of surveying. The protection of the private self was a drama analogous to the protection of the colonies from prying Customs officers, appointed officials, and occupying armies. The demystifying agenda of Enlightenment science had been appropriated by the propaganda of the American Revolution as a desire to see men, not in the false garments of their office, but, like Horatio Greenough's 1841 undraped statue of Washington, in their nakedness as men. That desire to see "things as they are" had the secondary consequence of obliging the demystifiers themselves to stand forth naked and leveled. For Jefferson, who was himself both class-conscious and deeply committed to destroying certain of the instruments of class perpetuation, notably primogeniture and entail, some kinds of leveling were essential, but others made him feel especially vulnerable.

The impulse toward social leveling in the period was literalized in the widespread mid-century rendering of previously capitalized nouns in lower case. *The American Instructor, or The Young Man's Best Companion*, Jefferson's first grammar book, announced (using capitalization to illustrate the old style) that "the Custom of beginning all Substantives with Capital Letters is not followed, at present by polite Authors." Not only did Jefferson follow suit by choosing to put in lower case what the *Companion* called "the more eminent Words in a Sentence," he took this license a step further.[1] In his private letters throughout his career, and indeed in the draft of the Declaration, Jefferson insisted on putting the first word of every sentence in lower case, thereby both minimizing or disguising the assertiveness of new beginnings and delivering a beheading blow to the artificial primogeniture of first letters.[2] In dramatic visual contrast, the printed Declaration capitalizes *all* of Jefferson's nouns, treating them as a special class of words.

What Jefferson's lowercasing did on the page, political electioneering did in practice. It brought the ruling gentry down to the level of the general population. As evidence of their liberality, the classic gentry virtue, candidates for local office in Jefferson's Virginia were expected to woo voters with rum and pork. Jefferson disdained such electioneering, especially because voting was done orally and in the presence of the assembled candidates. Such face-to-face elections, in Daniel Boorstin's summary, "differed from a modern American election mainly in the publicity given to every voter's choice and in the resulting opportunity for gratitude or resentment between the candidate and his constituents."[3] Reacting to his son's being turned out of office by an ungrateful electorate, Landon Carter, Jefferson's fellow Virginian, wrote George Washington in October 1776 that he believed "popularity" to be a greater "enemy to freedom" than even the British ministry. Or as he had gendered the issue in his diary several months earlier: "She [popularity] I long ago discovered to be an adulteress of the first order; for at any time let her be most sacredly wedded to one man she will even be grogged by her gallant over his shoulder."[4]

The contemporary anxiety about "courting" the electorate suggests another reason why the one classical oration that received the most attention in the rhetorics and political texts of the period was Cicero's oration for Milo. As Hugh Blair records it in his *Lectures on Rhetoric*, Cicero defended his client, a candidate for Consul who was accused of killing Clodius a few days before the election, by asking if "any one could believe that Milo would be mad enough, at such a critical time, by a most odious assassination, to alienate from himself the favor of the people whose suffrages he was so anxiously courting." Cicero goes on to describe the power of public opinion in terms especially resonant for his eighteenth-century readers: "we are afraid not only of what we may openly be reproached with, but of what others may think of us in secret. The slightest rumours, the most improbable tale that can be devised to our prejudice, alarms and disconcerts us. We study the countenance, and the looks, of all around us. For nothing is so delicate, so frail, and uncertain, as the public favour."[5] The passage makes clear that the anxieties of political life are but an intensification of the anxieties of social life in general: being the object of the public gaze becomes the subject of one's constant thoughts, the essence of self-consciousness. The jury system (*Juris dictio*: they speak the law), which in Revolutionary America was not compromised by the antidemocratic controls put on the English system by Lord Chief Justice William Murray, stood as a metaphor for the operations of society in general.

If, as Jefferson warned those who preferred commerce to agriculture, "corruption of morals . . . is the mark set on those, who, not looking . . . to their own soil and industry . . . for their subsistence, depend for it on casualities and caprice of customers," then the candidate (and public speaker) was precisely in such a marketplace situation of dependence on the irrationality of others' desires.[6] Though, as Jefferson insisted in *A Summary View*, flattery "is not an American art," the degrading submission of self to the "caprice of customers"—the corrupting heart of slavery and the marketplace—hastened the cultivation of such an art.[7] Because "the first secretion of them [the people] is generally crude and heterogeneous," Jefferson wrote in 1776, using a virulent antipopulist idiom in which he seldom indulged, the secondary judgment of popularly chosen electors is to be much preferred.[8]

The following letter submitted by an artisan reader to *The Pennsylvania Evening Post* on April 27, 1776, offers a revealing account of how electioneering literally and radically altered the physical distance between social classes, occasioning a unique social drama:

A poor man has rarely the honor of speaking to a gentleman on any terms, and never with familiarity but for a few weeks before the election. How many poor men, common men, and mechanics have been made happy within this fortnight by a shake of the hand, a pleasing smile and a little familiar chat with gentlemen; who have not for these seven years past condescended to look at them. Blessed state which brings all so nearly on a level! What a clever man is Mr. —— says my neighbour, how agreeable and familiar! He has no pride at all! He talked as freely to me for half an hour as if he were neighbour—there! I wish it were election time always! Thursday next he will lose all knowledge of ——, and pass me in the streets as if he never knew me. . . . How kind and clever is the man who proposes to be Sheriff, for two months before the election; he knows everybody, smiles upon and salutes everybody, until the election is over; but then to the end of the year, he has not time to speak to you, he is so engaged in serving your property by writ of venditioni exponas, and selling your goods at vendue. . . . Thus the right of annual elections will ever oblige gentlemen to speak to you once a year, who would despise you forever were it not that you can bestow something upon them. . . . In a word, electioneering and aristocratic pride are incompatible, and if we would have gentlemen ever to come down to our level, we must guard our right of election effectually. . . . Be freemen then, and you will be companions for gentlemen annually.[9]

The writer powerfully reminds us that in a class-stratified society, to be engaged by another in "familiar" conversation (no matter how empty or insincere that conversation) is to have one's social existence validated. Because it confers social enfranchisement, face-to-face conversation, with its attendant smile and handshake, is a crucial social action. Indeed, as a marker of exclusion or inclusion, it can effect a social revolution in miniature. The social dynamic that the "mechanick" describes mixes identification with aggression. That is, the pride or self-esteem that comes from the experience of momentary social elevation is attached to the puncturing of aristocratic pride. Yet there is a pathos to the common man's pleasure, for it derives from what, in effect, is a brief stage play, a carnivalesque moment of social leveling, a marketplace drama in which a vote is exchanged for a moment of intimacy. The quality and sincerity of that moment, rather than the candidate himself or his qualifications, becomes the object of judgment. The electioneering conversation becomes a version of the oratorical moment. In the mid 1740's, the fifteen-year-old George Washington copied into an exercise book a series of maxims from Francis Hawkins's popular *Youth Behavior* entitled "Rules of Civility and Decent Behaviour in Company and Conversation." These included an injunction that typified the world the oratorical moment sought to challenge: "In speaking to men of Quality do not lean nor Look them full in the Face."[10]

As class differentiation became threatened in one sphere, markers of social difference had to be reinforced in another. Robert Blair St. George has pointed out that, at least in the Connecticut River valley, threatened elites of the 1760's and 1770's enacted "a drama of class dominance" by either building Georgian homes in the style of public buildings, thus symbolically conferring public authority on their private spaces, or, less expensively, constructing elaborate scrolled and pilastered doorway facades over rather ordinary homes as barriers against threats to the "natural" social order. However, the artisans employed to create these class markers themselves acquired so much liquid capital that by "1768 a tailor, a shoemaker, and a joiner had placed elaborate doorways on their own houses."[11] The game of class markers could not be won.

A primary instrument of the social reconfiguration suggested by the example above was the magazine. Insisting, in the introduction to its first issue in January 1778, that "a man without taste and the acquirements of genius" is an "orangutan with the human shape and the soul of a beast," *The United States Magazine*, a new Philadelphia magazine edited by Hugh Henry Brackenridge and geared to artisans, promoted itself as a vehicle of social mobility:

> The mechanic of the city or the husbandman who plows his farm by the river bank has it in his power to become, one day, the first magistrate of his respective commonwealth or to fill a seat in the Continental Congress. This happy circumstance lays an obligation upon every individual to exert a double industry to qualify himself for the great trust which may, one day, be reposed in him. It becomes him to obtain some knowledge of the history and principles of government . . . and policy and commerce of his own country. Now it may not be the lot of every individual to be able to obtain this knowledge from the first source, that is from the best writers, or the conversation of men of reading and experience. . . . The want of

these advantages must therefore be supplied by some publication that will in itself contain a library and be the literary coffee-house of public conversation. A work of this nature is *The United States Magazine.*

Because it will "supply the want of early education" and enable readers "to speak with great propriety and fluency on any subject," the new journal insists that it will qualify its readers "not only for discharging offices of honor and of profit" but for something as coveted: "the conversation of the learned and ingenious."[12]

When Jefferson became president, he issued the following "Memorandum on Rules of Etiquette" to his cabinet:

I. In order to bring the members of society together in the first instance, the custom of the country has established that residents shall pay the first visit to strangers, and, among strangers, first comers to later comers, foreign and domestic, the character of stranger ceasing after the first visits. to this rule there is a single exception. Foreign ministers, from the necessity of making themselves known, pay the first visit to the ministers of the nation, which is returned.

II. When brought together in society, all are perfectly equal, whether foreign or domestic, titled or untitled, in or out of office.

All other observances are but exemplifications of these two principles.

I. 1st The families of foreign ministers, arriving at the seat of government, receive the first visit from those of the national ministers as from all other residents.

2nd Members of the Legislature and of the Judiciary, independent of their offices, have a right as strangers to receive the first visit.

II. 1st No title being admitted here, those of foreigners give no precedence.

2nd Differences of grade among diplomatic members, gives no precedence.

3rd. At public ceremonies, to which the government invites the presence of foreign ministers and their families, a convenient seat or station will be provided for them, with any other strangers invited and the families of the national ministers, each taking place as they arrive, and without any precedence.

4th. to maintain the principle of equality, or of pele mele, and prevent the growth of precedence out of courtesy, the members of the Executive will practice at their own houses, and recommend an adherence to the ancient usage of the country, of gentlemen in mass giving precedence to the ladies in mass, in passing from one apartment where they are assembled into another.[13]

The pleasure Jefferson takes in stripping everybody of status, in creating a radical egalitarian social setting (though one that still observes gender differentiation) is made possible by the fact that participants are all members of "society" in the exclusive rather than inclusive sense. Minus even romanticized ploughmen, his pell mell (disorderly and confusedly mingled) world is safely circumscribed.

The anxiety of public speaking, whether in a socially heterogeneous or socially homogeneous environment, was further intensified by the obligation implicit in the new rhetoric to speak, as Jefferson said in *A Summary View*, in the "language of truth . . . divested of those expressions of servility," to strip away all rhetorical ornament, to remove affectation, and make one's periods conform to a natural stress pattern.[14] Yet to come from behind what the early nineteenth-century rhetorician Richard Whately would later revealingly call the "sheltering veil" of an artificial mode of delivery and adopt a natural one was to stand rhetorically naked.[15] The less well-born politicians who began to emerge in the 1770's, as Roger Atkinson described them in 1776, were "plain and of consequence less disguised . . . less intriguing, more sincere."[16]

The historian Edward Gibbon, who like most of his contemporaries saw public speaking as a moral and manly act, put it simply: "I dreaded exposing myself."[17] A physiognomically sophisticated culture intensified the anxiety of scrutiny. According to William Ellery's grandson, as the members of the Continental

Congress signed the Declaration, the signer from Rhode Island carefully examined the face of each to see the character of his "resolution," and John Adams insisted he would "give more for a perfect painting of the terror and horror upon the Faces of the Old Majority at that critical moment than for the best Piece of Raphelle."[18] For many, but especially for Jefferson, who declared that "the whole art of government consists in the art of being honest," the triple injunctions to please yet persuade, to control oneself but stimulate passions in others, to reveal oneself and yet efface oneself, combined to create an exhausting challenge.[19]

Yet that burden could not be ignored; strategies for dealing with it had to be developed. In 1785, Jefferson counseled his nephew Peter Carr: "Whenever you are to do a thing, tho' it can never be known but to yourself, ask yourself how you would act if all the world were looking at you and act accordingly."[20] Such advice was a generalized version of the advice he had given to a young friend rehearsing for the bar: "It will be of great service to pronounce your oration . . . in the presence of some person who may be considered as your judge."[21] The ambiguous phrase "your judge" suggests Jefferson's deep awareness that the judgment of a lawyer's client is always mediated by the judgment of a lawyer's performance. In his *Theory of Moral Sentiments*, Adam Smith described man as having been formed by nature with a "love not only of praise but praiseworthiness" and a dread not only of blame, but "of blameworthiness."[22] One achieved the former and escaped the latter by imagining oneself a spectator on one's own life, by endeavoring to judge one's own "sentiments and motives" the only way possible: by examining "our own conduct as we imagine any other fair and impartial spectator would examine it."[23] In the light of such a moral philosophy, an internalized version of the oratorical moment, the moment of public exposure and judgment, the moment of coming before what Jefferson called "the tribunal of the world," was the quintessential moment of one's moral existence.[24]

Behind the anxieties about self-control and self-revelation is a much larger phenomenon: the creation of new self-consciousness in an age of criticism. The centrality of private judgment to Protestant republicanism made criticism not merely an emergent professional activity but the essence and science of one's moral and social existence. "Criticism," stated Blair in his *Lectures*, "teaches us to admire and blame with judgment"; it frees us from following the "crowd blindly" by teaching a "just discernment of real merits."[25] Lord Kames, whose *Elements of Criticism* was the contemporary bible on the subject, insisted that "to censure works, not men, is the just prerogative of criticism" but at the same time made the importance and significance of being a critic in everyday life abundantly clear: "Those who live in the world and in good company, are quick-sighted with respect to every defect or irregularity in behavior: the very slightest singularity in motion, in speech, or in dress, which to a peasant would be invisible, escapes not their observation. The most minute differences in the human countenance, so minute as to be far beyond the reach of words, are distinctly perceived."[26] To be a scrutinizing critic is not only to have "taste" and "sensibility" but to reaffirm membership in a morally elite class far distant from the unperceptive peasant's. Consistently showing that disregard for justice or propriety "never fails [but] to be punished with shame and remorse," the "science of rational criticism" is a crucial "support to morality."[27] Though Kames's work, which is dedicated to George III, in effect offers a defense of the ruling class as moral arbiters, it also offers an education to middle-class readers in how to join a class of critics that, no longer exclusively defined by birth, has now opened its ranks.

The "perfect view" and "invisible omnipresence" possessed by the keeper of Jeremy Bentham's projected panopticon-shaped penitentiary, a symbol of a larger cultural preoccupation with surveillance, was but a special case of (indeed, an effort to reappropriate) a power that had already gone a long way toward being democratized. As the epigram for his "Panopticon Papers" Bentham chose a verse from Psalm 139: "Thou art about my path, and about my bed: / and spiest out all my ways."[28] That choice makes clear that the role performed by an all-seeing God (symbolized by the Masonic eye of early national iconography), the role performed by the "SEARCHER OF HEARTS for the sincerity of former declarations," as Jefferson's committee called the deity in their May 1776 instructions to the delegates of the Virginia Convention, has devolved upon society itself.[29] Because such scrutiny must also be self-scrutiny, that role has devolved anew upon one's own conscience, whose surveillance, as Roger L'Estrange put it in the period's most popular handbook of Christianized stoicism, makes a "ridiculous madness" of our desire "to creep into a corner where nobody shall see us . . . no mortal eye could find us."[30]

But the radical atomization suggested by the very concept of an existential privacy seemed to threaten the fundamental dominance (and higher claims) of society over the individual. To take the most extreme late eighteenth-century formulation, the social philosopher and novelist William Godwin insisted in his *Enquiry into Political Justice* that a redeemed society can best be brought about if every man imposes on himself a "law" of sincerity mandating that he not "conceal any part of his character and conduct." Every man must imagine himself the future "historian" of every one of his own actions in a new world where "the popish practice of auricular confession," that instrument of despotism, has been democratically appropriated so that every man now makes "the world his confessional, and the human species the keeper of his conscience." "How great would be the benefit," Godwin asks, confident of the answer, "if every man were sure of meeting in his neighbour the ingenuous censor, who would tell him in person, and publish to the world, his virtues, his good deeds, his meannesses, and his follies?"[31]

Part of the attraction of this fantasy of total divulgence—the American counterpart is Parson Weems's invention of the cherry-tree-chopping George Washington who "can't tell a lie"[32]—is that it is reciprocal: all men both give and take confession. One surrenders one's private identity in order to be able to penetrate other private identities. In addition, it permits what Godwin describes

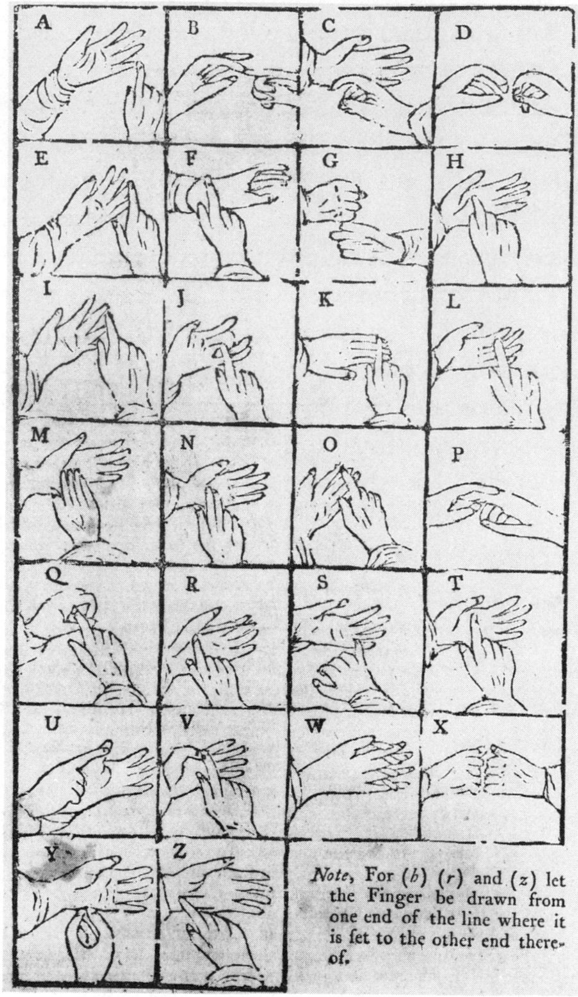

Figure 18. "Natural Alphabet . . . for a compendious, easy and secret method of *Dumb Speech*," *The Pennsylvania Magazine*, 1776. (Courtesy of the American Antiquarian Society.)

elsewhere in his text as an "unleashing of unreservedness": it inaugurates "a period of bold and unrestricted communication" that sanctions a hidden, aggressive desire to be brutally honest.[33] In this world, in which all behavior is transmuted into endless reportorial speech, it is as liberating to be able to say everything as it is inhibiting to be forced to say everything.

When John Witherspoon speaks of "the great rule of sincerity," that we should "speak nothing but what agrees with our sentiments" and "reveal the whole truth," he is referring to something greater than a cultural prescription or even a social ideal, as is Godwin in a different register.[34] "The great rule of sincerity" is an instance of the rules of behavior that lead to social happiness because they are dictated by the laws of nature. In his *Elements of Criticism*, Lord Kames inferred from his observation that men "learn to dissemble their sentiments," learn to transform their "behavior . . . into art," that "man, by his very constitution, is framed to be open and sincere." The purpose of studying natural law, as Burlamaqui, Vattel, and other eighteenth-century writers on the subject made clear, was precisely to discover the laws of that human constitution.[35] Even if, as Terry Eagleton puts it, the "discovery" of natural laws concealed society's "hegemonic" effort to inscribe its own laws "all the more effectively on the hearts and bodies of those it subjugates" by redefining the consent to those laws as consent to one's own being, natural law was simultaneously the dominant discourse of a liberal social utopianism.[36]

The alternative to Godwin's fantasy of total disclosure is that of a secret language known only to one's closest friends—the ability to undertake private communication in public, free of the threat of public criticism. The February 1776 issue of Paine's *Pennsylvania Magazine* printed in full "a compendious, easy and secret method of *Dumb Speech*" consisting of a "natural alphabet" with the thumb and four fingers of the right hand serving as the five vowels (Figure 18). The alphabet had been sent in by a correspondent not to assist the deaf but for general use, "to signify our intentions . . . in company, so as not to be perceived, and in the dark. For, whoever is master of this alphabet, need only lend his hand concealed under a hat, a table, or behind him, to one that is also versed therein, and he may soon discover this friend's mind with all the secrecy imaginable."[37] A dozen years earlier, the very young Jefferson, worrying that his confidential adolescent letters might fall into the wrong hands, wrote his friend John Page: "We must fall on some scheme of communicating our thoughts to each other, which shall be totally unintelligible to every one but to ourselves."[38]

Private Lives and Public Scrutiny

Behind the nearly two-centuries-old debate over whether Jefferson fathered children by his slave Sally Hemings is an enormous desire to ascribe to him a private (in the depreciated sense of consciously hidden) life, a life that then could be penetrated. This impulse becomes acute in the case of a public man who guarded his privacy—a man who burned virtually all his correspondence with his wife (when she died, in 1782, he inscribed his grief onto her tombstone by quoting Homer in the original); a man who, upon arriving at the Continental Congress, not only looked forward to a time when "consistently with duty, I may withdraw totally from the public stage," but who told Monroe in 1782 that he believed "public service and private misery [are] inseparably linked together"; a man who, though a lover of good conversation and dinner parties, invented a "dumb waiter" to "eliminate servants from the dining room for privacy," and who placed venetian blinds on windows at Monticello, as Jack McLaughlin puts it, "as a filter that allowed him to control light and air without being seen."[1] Even the most passionate letter in the Jefferson canon—the Head and Heart dialogue sent to Maria Cosway—was, as a result of a wrist injury, written with his left hand. Writing awkwardly and uncharacteristically "in another hand" did more than predispose the dialogic character of the letter, in which the head, the voice of stoicism, debates the heart, the voice of sensibility, over the proposition that the "most effectual means of being secure against pain is to retire within ourselves and to suffice for our own happiness."[2] By providing the equivalent of a persona, left-handedness may also have provided the self-protective masking necessary to greater emotional expression.

Jefferson's brief *Autobiography*, written when he was 77, is to the modern sensibility irritatingly unrevealing because he constructs a self that is the sum total of public actions. He locates his essential self in the arena of civic accomplishments rather than in private life and private emotions. To appropriate a useful formulation from Richard Sennett's *Fall of Public Man*, Jefferson's "expression" operates "at a distance from personal circumstances, family, and friends."[3] Indeed, in the middle of his memoir Jefferson speculates that he may not even finish recording his recollections because "I am already tired of talking about myself."[4] He resists constructing a narrative in which larger political or social principles or events are meaningful only insofar as they are visible in, and referable to, a specific individual's scrutinized actions, in which the once objective truth of a proposition becomes no more than an individual's subjective judgment as to the degree of its credibility and plausibility. Such a narrative involves a principle and a process of nearly infinite regress: an individual's actions are meaningful only insofar as they are revelatory of a specific personality or moral character; moral character is meaningful only insofar as it is vouchsafed by sincerity; sincerity is credible only insofar as it can be directly or indirectly experienced, and then preferably by an unseen witness to private behavior. In a 1775 letter to John Randolph, the Loyalist attorney general of Virginia, who was about to depart for England, Jefferson refers to the essential proposition of such a regress. Expressing his hope that their differing politics would not inhibit honest communication, he writes: "On this or any future occasion if I affirm to you any facts, your knolege of me will enable you to decide on their credibility."[5] Put thus, there is no distinction between his credibility and "their" credibility.

In his *Summary View*, which instructed the Virginia delegates to the Continental Congress to generate a resolution that a letter should be written directly to the king, Jefferson imagines addressing George himself: "This sire, is our last, our determined resolution."[6] The pun on "resolution" obscures the distinction between text and personal disposition, thus protectively concealing the latter in the former. On the dangers of excessive public exposure, Jefferson reports in his *Autobiography* on a reformist experiment to replace, for a certain class of criminals, capital punishment with hard labor conducted in public: "Exhibited as a public spectacle, with shaved heads and mean clothing, working on the high roads, produced in the criminals such a prostration of character, such an abandonment of self-respect, as, instead of reforming, plunged them into the most desperate and hardened depravity of morals and character."[7] To transform an individual into a public spectacle is itself a crime.

What most post-Freudian readers cannot accept—or should I say post-Weemsian readers (for it is Weems, in his voyeuristic fantasy of Washington's boyhood, who was the first American to insist, in the manner of Rousseau, that "Private life is always *real* life")—is that Jefferson's self-presentation is not merely a strategy of concealment.[8] Rather, it represents a particular moral and social conception of identity. Yet it must also be conceded that the Weemsians are right to the degree that Jefferson's reticence is consistent with a much more general eighteenth-century perception that, to cite Lord Chesterfield, "an unguarded frankness" makes one "the easy prey . . . of the artful and the experienced."[9] Intensified by the demand for frankness made by a critical society, that anxiety was addressed, but not resolved, by the creation of a strategic and studied naturalness.

Though Jefferson agreed with the caution in Chesterfield's *Letters to his Son* (published in Philadelphia in 1775) that "one cannot keep one's own private affairs too secret," he did so less in fear of the public gaze than for the reason Chesterfield gives his son: "your own concerns or private affairs" may be "interesting to you, [but] they are tedious and impertinent to everybody else."[10] One achieves social standing by abjuring the narcissism of constant self-revelation, by recognizing that in society, private affairs are poor "entertainment." True virtue inheres less in a transparent openness than in self-possession.

And yet this moral high ground, as the numerous contemporary critics of Chesterfield made clear, sanctions a Machiavellian concealment of real motives and real opinions by obscuring the distinction between reticence and dissimulation, between the principles of politeness (the title of Chesterfield's other popular work) and a rediscovered tyranny of artifice and artificiality. Responding in 1779 to a letter in which her son extolled the virtues and works of Chesterfield, Mercy Otis Warren wrote, "I have no quarrel with the graces; I love the *Doceurs* of civility, the placid manners, the *L'amiable* and all the innocent arts engaging the esteem, and alluring the affections of mankind."[11] She loves them, that is, as long as they are consistent with "the eternal law of rectitude," for "I love better that frankness and sincerity which bespeak a soul above dissimulation," above "the turpitude of character hid up under the flimsy Veil of deception and urged on by Mr. Stanhope as the point of perfection." Yet the problem with the insistence on frankness as an alternative to the "honey'd poison"[12] of rhetoric is that it assumes and/or reinforces a view of social relations in which the hidden is the "real" and concealment of self-interest is thought to be a universal impulse; that is, it fuels an anxious cynicism that ultimately questions the very concept of disinterestedness. As one Tory broadside put it:

> Behold yon Patriot bellowing loud
> For Liberty—that darling Theme.
> Pull off the Mask—'tis private Grudge
> Or Party Rage that forms the Scheme.[13]

If the public good is a mask for private gain, frankness must be constantly demanded.

The conflicting demands for frankness and the protection of privacy informed the dominant understanding of freedom of the press in Revolutionary America. That understanding declared that though the government could and must be criticized by a press free from prior restraint, doing injury to "the reputation of any person, as an *individual*," especially for his political views, as Virginia jurist St. George Tucker would later put it, constituted a breach of personal rights, an invasion of privacy. "The right of character is a sacred and invaluable right and is not forfeited by accepting a public employment."[14] The hard distinction between the protected private character of a public figure and his unprotected public actions, however, was an extremely difficult one to maintain in legal practice.

Such a distinction was even more difficult to maintain in a literary milieu dominated by satire and the stepchild of physiognomy, caricature. Consistent with her view of frankness, playwright Mercy Otis Warren made Thomas Hutchinson "the object of Public Derision" in her farce, *The Group*.[15] The distinction between protected character and unprotected actions was further threatened in a protected journalistic environment where nine of the eleven Revolutionary-era state constitutions explicitly insisted that liberty of the press "ought to be inviolable or ought never to be restrained,"[16] and the Bridgeton, New Jersey *Plain Dealer* could brag in February 1776 that it had a "majic spyglass" that allowed it "at any time day or night to see clearly through the brick walls of our Court House" into the secret dealings of each member of local government.[17] In 1781 Franklin complained of "malevolent Criticks and Bug-writers, who will abuse you while you are serving them, and wound your character in nameless pamphlets." In a world where appearance and public perception constitute a primary reality, character becomes synonymous with public estimation or reputation (which Franklin called "dearer to you than perhaps your life"), less a fixed, indwelling moral nature than a fluid and vulnerable social identity.[18]

In this context, one might fairly say that Jefferson's oratorical anxieties are less that his private self will be penetrated than that he will be unable and unwilling to surrender stoical self-possession for sentimental externalization, unable, that is, to deliver, in the wished-for transparencies of public behavior, the kind of private self, or endless narrative and revelation of a private self, demanded of him. Certainly Jefferson would be unable to so deliver in the manner that the obsessively self-absorbed and endlessly self-revealing John Adams could and did. Believing that the quest for attention and distinction, the desire "to be observed, considered, esteemed, praised, beloved, and admired by his fellows" ruled human life, Adams was a man who turned correspondents into confessors, audiences, and publicists.[19] He more than willingly acceded to the demand that private lives be endlessly produced so that they may be endlessly circulated and examined for authenticity.

The new admonitions to sincerity and authenticity problematized the very nature of argumentation and gave to it a new self-consciousness. Inaugurating perhaps the greatest example of a sustained argument in late eighteenth-century letters, Alexander Hamilton awkwardly tries to set forth the larger project of *The Federalist* in its first number. After announcing in the new mode that "the subject" of a new Constitution "speaks its own importance," Hamilton addresses the difficulty of evaluating the truth of arguments by the measure of the sincerity of those who make them:

> I am well aware that it would be disingenuous to resolve indiscriminately the opposition of any set of men (merely because their situations might subject them to suspicion) into interested or ambitious views: Candour will oblige us to admit, that even such men [those who oppose the Constitution] may be actuated by upright intentions; and it cannot be

doubted that much of the opposition which has made its appearance . . . will spring from sources, blameless at least, if not respectable, the honest errors of minds led astray by preconceived jealousies and fears.[20]

Hamilton's strategy is to suggest that though problematic motives operate on both sides of a dispute, his own motives, regardless of his partisan position, are congruent with and representative of those of the public at large. Thus having just conceded that "we are not always sure, that those who advocate the truth are influenced by purer principles than their antagonists," Hamilton confidently goes on to assert that "a dangerous ambition more often lurks behind the specious [that is, attractive] mask of zeal for the rights of the people than under the forbidding appearance of zeal for the firmness and efficiency of government."[21]

Throughout the Revolutionary and early national periods, opposing writers who seek to sway the same audience present them with identical ethical self-representations that point to opposite ends, with identical exhortations to distrust the (mere) rhetoric that conceals the conspiratorial aims of their opponents, and with identical tokens of their own true rhetorical sincerity. The consequence of such irreconcilable presentations, aggravated by identical claims to self-evidence, is an endless stalemating from which there are only two avenues of escape. The first is a move from "ethos" and motives to reasoned impersonal argument, a move much less frequently made in the polemical literature of the period than is imagined by those who still view this period under the misleading rubric of "the age of reason." The other (which in the context of 1775–76 might be viewed as the rhetorical origins of the American Revolution) is accepting the inevitability of physical conflict.

Hamilton concludes his introductory remarks by insisting that his readers attend to the evidence of truth alone and not to the drama of its presentation: "In the course of the preceding observations I have had an eye, my Fellow Citizens, to putting you upon your guard against all attempts, from whatever quarter, to influence your decision in a matter of the utmost moment . . . by any impressions other than those which may result from the evidence of truth." Then he turns to his own motives:

> I am convinced, that this is the safest course for your liberty, your dignity, and your happiness. I effect not reserves, which I do not feel. I will not amuse you with an appearance of deliberation, when I have decided. I frankly acknowledge to you my convictions, and I will freely lay before you the reasons on which they are founded. The consciousness of good intentions disdains ambiguity. I shall not however multiply professions of this head. My motives must remain in the depository of my own breast.[22]

Hamilton will "frankly" lay before the reader the reasons why he believes in the new Constitution, but not the dynamics that make those reasons personally compelling to him. Readers must resist the desire to seek further frankness from "Publius"—the authorial persona of *The Federalist*—whose interiority has been sealed off in "the depository of my own breast." Instead they must turn to their own interests. The position was a wise one to take for someone as conflicted as Hamilton was about the set of compromises that constituted the Constitution. On the day he signed the Constitution he declared that "No man's ideas were more remote from the plan" than his were known to be.[23]

A decade earlier, Jefferson was upset by the Continental Congress's editing out the most emotional passages of the Declaration, striking what John Adams described in his *Autobiography* as its "most oratorical Paragraphs," because in so doing they cut off the demand for independence from the deeply felt personal sentiments that testified to its emotional truthfulness.[24] In contrast, Hamilton at the end of *Federalist* 1 sought to avoid the problems of referring external representations to internal processes. That is, he sought to avoid precisely what Burke in his *Philosophical Enquiry into the Origin of our Ideas of the Sublime* urged was essential to poets and what the new elocution urged was essential to speakers: the subordination of "a clear idea of things themselves" to the more important presentation of "the effect of things on the mind of the speaker."[25] Though it sidestepped the psychological interrogation of the speaker, *The Federalist* at the same time, of course, articulated a political philosophy that was deeply psychological in its repeated consideration of the role of interest, passion, and ambition in political life. A similar desire to have it both ways characterizes *Common Sense*. Paine insists that the office of kingship be demystified and that George III be judged as a man. (In his revisionist biblical history the "high encomium" given the biblical King David takes "no notice of him *officially as a king*, but only as a *man*.") Yet he says about himself, "Who the Author of this Production is, is wholly unnecessary to the Public, as the Object for Attention is the *Doctrine itself*, not the *Man*."[26] To further complicate the matter, when the "doctrine" is laid out, it is clear that it is largely identical with the spectacle of an outraged sensibility. Thus, though the identity of "the *Man*" need not be known, it is essential that his sensibility be fully displayed.

Michael Warner has argued that print culture became identified in eighteenth-century Anglo-America with the creation of a public sphere that stood apart from, and thus was capable of being critical of, the sphere of the state. Drawing on Jürgen Habermas's account of a structural transformation of the public sphere "from a world in which power embodied in special persons is represented before the people to one in which power is constituted by a discourse in which the people are represented," Warner argues that the "civic and emancipatory" character of eighteenth-century print culture resided precisely in its impersonality. Consisting of "assertions made to be assessed by readers for just reasoning," writing is "categorically differentiated from personal modes of sociability." As he says of an early eighteenth-century pamphlet, reader and writer "encounter the exchange *not as a relation between themselves as men, but rather as their own mediation by a potentially limitless discourse*" (his emphasis).[27] Such an analysis ignores the degree to which eighteenth-century print culture, unable to stand apart from the politics of sincerity and authenticity, rejected the notion of "power embodied in special persons" only to redefine those special persons—not by office, but by sensibility. Indeed, what energizes a great deal of the polemical prose of the period is the dialectical relation between the authority of impersonality rooted in the discourse of descriptive science and the authority of sincerity rooted in the discourse of affective experience.

Insisting that no individual is free from the obligation to be "the Object for Attention," much eighteenth-century American fiction is centrally concerned with the demand for complete authenticity—a demand made within it and of it. In the introduction to her recent edition of Susanna Rowson's *Charlotte Temple* (1794), the most popular eighteenth-century American novel, Ann Douglas describes Charlotte's effort to argue her innocence before her seducer, Montraville: "She craves, as virtue in melodrama always does, absolute visibility: to be in her corporeal self coterminal with any interpretation of herself, to be believed, to be taken as testimony in the full legal and religious sense of the word," to have it known, in Rowson's words, that "the goodness of her heart is depicted in her ingenuous countenance."[28] Charlotte's desire reflects an internalization of the staple wisdom of the proliferating books of advice directed toward American youth in the period. John Bennett's much reprinted *Letters to a Young Lady*, for example, informs his readers that "An unstudied openness" is the strongest "symptom" of a "guiltless heart and a virtuous intention. Those young people are generally the most amiable, that are the most undisguised. Having nothing to *conceal* they have studied no *art*."[29]

The social demand (within the text, by the consuming reader, and by the spectator of Rowson's public readings from her novel) for Charlotte's ingenuous and artless openness, the desire to penetrate her existential interiority by insisting that it be legible in her face and thus, in a Jeffersonian mode, self-evident, is set in opposition to Montraville's desire to penetrate her sexually. But the opposition between those two penetrations only conceals the fact that the latter demand is here and elsewhere in part a literalization of the former. Yet, as someone who supported herself for several years as an actress before turning to fiction, Rowson knew that, at least sometimes, the artful impersonation of "unstudied openness" could successfully frustrate the demand for legibility.

But a larger dilemma remained inescapable. In Latin, *publicus* signifies a public man or magistrate, *publica* a public woman or prostitute.[30] Because she could never occupy the same positions in the public sphere as a man, a public woman was always an object and never a subject. The demand for a woman's public legibility thus transformed her into a version of what moral surveillance was supposedly meant to prevent her from becoming: an object for everyone's consumption. The anxiety felt by Jefferson and others about public office and office seeking was rooted, in part, in the fear that, under the demand for self-evidence, a *publicus* stood always in imminent danger of transmuting into an unmanned *publica*.

The insistence on self-evidence paradoxically demands both embodiment (the self as self) and disembodiment (the self reduced to evidence of itself). The emphasis on the expressive body identifies "the self" with the material body at the same time that the textualized body points to the primacy of the unseen interiority or character that it expresses. And if, in the affective mode, the character of a text or individual is written as much in the countenances of those responding to it as it is self-inhering, the "self" of a self-evident proposition or body becomes in part the self of the reader or consumer. In *Charlotte Temple*, the male body of the seducer contrasts with the disembodied female body, which has been reduced to expressive text. When, to take a different kind of example, Jefferson in *Notes on the State of Virginia* describes the poetry of the young black woman Phillis Wheatley as "below the dignity of criticism," he is in effect reducing the poetry from the status of independent art to the status of evidence, evidence of *his* proposition that a black had never "uttered a thought above the level of plain narration."[31]

Men were also vulnerable to violation, as Jefferson discovered, through the texts they produced and with which they identified. In an 1818 letter, he recollected that he was not "insensible to the mutilations," the "depredations on . . . parts of the instrument," wrought by the Continental Congress in 1776. In that same letter he would tell the famous story of how Franklin sought to console the author of the Declaration with the story of John Thompson, from whom "he took the lesson . . . whenever in my power to avoid becoming the draftsman of papers to be reviewed by a public body." Having submitted to his friends "for amendments" the proposed sign, "'John Thompson, Hatter, makes and sells hats for ready money' with a figure of a hat subjoined," Thompson, as Franklin tells it, found his friends eliminating one word after another. Charges of redundancy and the restatement of the obvious led ultimately to the elimination of all words but Thompson's name and the picture of the hat. At the insistence of "friendly" editors, the tautological and superfluous nature of descriptive language is replaced by the pictorialism of names as sentence gives way to the self-evidence of the sign. The "public body" once again insists on self-evidence.[32]

In a surviving presentation copy of *Notes on the State of Virginia* (Figure 19), a book Jefferson published in a limited edition for confidential distribution, Jefferson penned this third-person inscription: "Thomas Jefferson having had a few copies of these Notes printed to offer to some of his friends and to some other estimable characters beyond that line, begs the Abbé Morellet's acceptance of a copy. unwilling to expose them to the public eye he asks the favour of the Abbé Morellet to put them into the hands of no person on whose care and fidelity he cannot rely to guard them against publication."[33] Because someone on one side or the other of

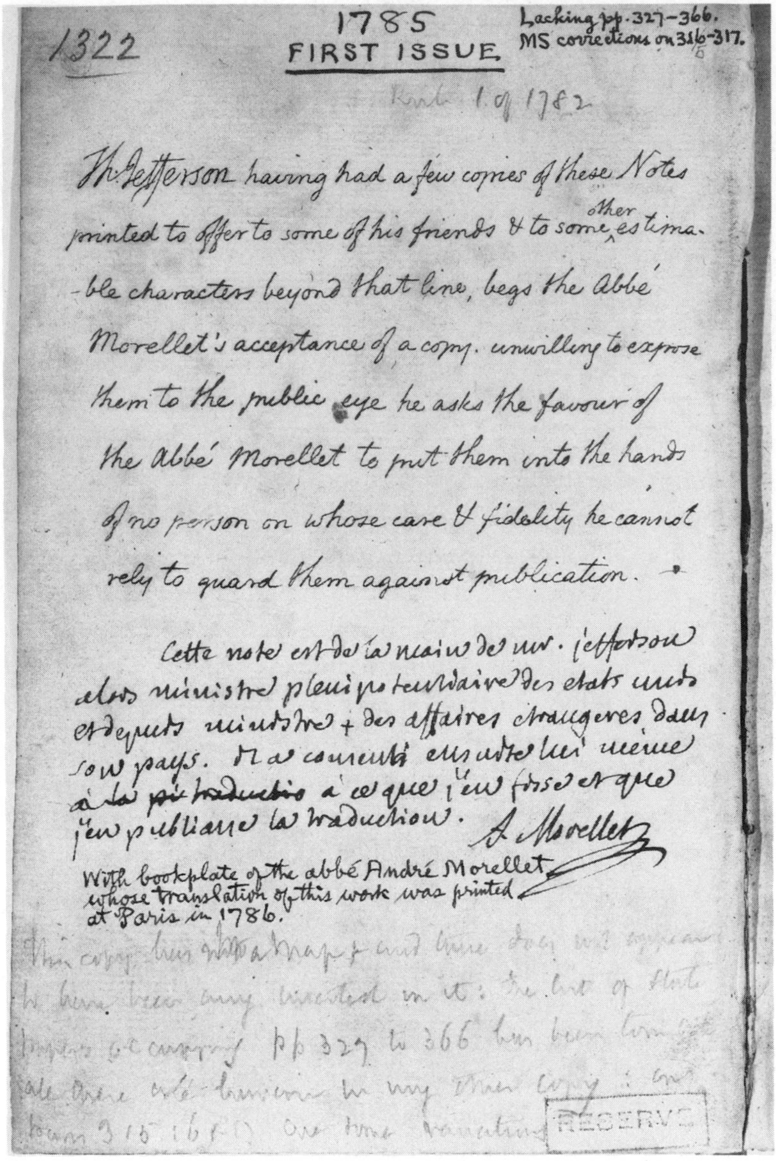
1322

1785
FIRST ISSUE

Lacking pp. 327–366.
MS corrections on 316–317.

Th: Jefferson having had a few copies of these Notes printed to offer to some of his friends & to some other estimable characters beyond that line, begs the Abbé Morellet's acceptance of a copy. unwilling to expose them to the public eye he asks the favour of the Abbé Morellet to put them into the hands of no person on whose care & fidelity he cannot rely to guard them against publication.

Cette note est de la main de mr. jefferson alors ministre plenipotentiaire des etats unis et depuis ministre des affaires etrangeres dans son pays. Il a consenti ensuite lui même à la ~~pu traductio~~ à ce que j'en fisse et que j'en publiasse la traduction. A Morellet

With bookplate of the abbé André Morellet, whose translation of this work was printed at Paris in 1786.

RESERVE

Figure 19. Inscription to Abbé André Morellet in a copy of Jefferson's privately printed 1782 edition of *Notes on the State of Virginia*. (Courtesy of the Rare Books and Manuscripts Division, The New York Public Library, Astor, Lenox and Tilden Foundations.)

Jefferson's "line" passed his text around until it seemed an unauthorized French edition might soon appear, an upset Jefferson was forced to consent to his volume being exposed to the "public eye."

When Madison later asked him to send along an English edition of Paine's *Rights of Man* to an American printer to be set for an American edition, Jefferson politely enclosed the following note: "I am extremely pleased to find it will be reprinted, and that something is at length to be publicly said about the political heresies which have sprung up among us."[34] Much to Jefferson's chagrin, the note appeared as a printed advertisement opposite the title page of the new edition. And when Ebenezer Hazard proposed to Jefferson in 1774 a multivolume collection of state papers, he cast his argument in the form of an analogy to an intensified public interest in individuals.

> When the conduct of Individuals in a Community is such as to attract public Attention, others are very naturally led to many Inquiries about them; so when civil States rise into Importance, even their earliest History becomes the object of Speculation. From a Principle of Curiosity, many who have but little, or no Connection with the British Colonies in America, are now prying into the Story of their rise and progress.[35]

If no single narrative of American history would satisfy popular prying curiosity, the naked documentary record of collected state papers might.

Hugh Henry Brackenridge's short story, "The Cave of Vanhest," serialized in *The United States Magazine* in 1779, was one of a number of popular tales about hermits, a genre that spoke directly to the larger dynamics of popular curiosity. The story opens thus:

> In my younger years I had read much of that romantic kind of writing which fills every mountain with a hermitage so that you can scarcely miss your way in any part of the country, but you stumble in upon a residence of this kind and discover some old man who, when the usual civilities are over, tells you a long story of his conflicts with the evils and accidents of

> life until, sick of the world, he has retired from it to this cell in which alone he has found happiness. I have often wished it might, one day, be my special fortune to fall in with some such individual.

The vision of a countryside populated with hermits who are only too glad to have their chosen solitude violated "in order to gratify with great pleasure," as the hermit of this tale says to the narrator, "your very natural and pardonable curiosity," links a fascination with solitude and invisibility as a form of liberty with a compensatory intolerance for leaving such liberty alone. Indeed, a fundamental principle of all forms of eighteenth-century popular culture was to simultaneously create and respond to a newly enlarged public curiosity. Perhaps the premier American example of an institution catering to that curiosity was Dr. Abraham Chovet's Anatomical Museum, one of Philadelphia's major tourist attractions for visitors during the years the Continental Congress met in that city. The museum's primary drawing card was a wax pair of male and female figures "with external parts removable for separate examination."[36]

The frontispiece of William Hill Brown's *The Power of Sympathy* illustrates an incident described in the novel as "exhibiting a picture of the wickedness and depravity of the human heart" (Figure 20). Having become pregnant in the course of an affair with the husband of her sister, the desperate Ophelia Martin confesses to her father her "incestuous" relationship. She swears that "she is penetrated with a melancholy sense of her misconduct," a penetration symbolically offered as an expiation of her sexual penetration. The outraged Mr. Martin, however, insists that though she beholds "in the most glaring colors the dangers to which she had been exposed," she must now endure another exposure. He will "publish" her disgrace to the world. Seeking desperately to hide from such exposure, to "fly from the eye of the world" and thus escape the terrible "approaching time of explanation" when she would no longer be able to conceal her pregnancy, Ophelia poisons herself. In so doing she reenacts her original sin of believing in an impenetrable private sphere safe from the public eye and of accepting her seducer's insistence that she "banish" the foolish "idea of detection" from her mind.[37]

The engraving depicts her theatrically posed parents expressing horror at seeing their dying daughter prostrate on the floor. The frontispiece that exposes her to the reader testifies to the fact that even in death Ophelia cannot escape the public gaze. There is no Horatian retirement from this public stage. Indeed, the story of Ophelia is only told because Harriot, the heroine, discovers in Mrs. Martin, Ophelia's mother, "evident traces of distress in her countenance" even though she "put on a face of vivacity."[38] The story, like the sin, cannot be hidden in a world where one's face is forever a picture of one's passions, and where pregnancy is made to symbolize the inescapable visibility and consequentiality of all sin.

A large ornate mirror hangs above Ophelia in the engraving, registering the text's insistence that the incident itself is "a mirrour by which we may regulate our conduct and amend our lives."[39] Undermining the viewer's own protected distance, the murky shield-shaped mirror inscribes the viewer (who is necessarily positioned in front of it) in the picture—both as judge (the mirror as cultural gaze) and as victim (the mirror as trope for sympathetic identification). To turn "The STORY of OPHELIA" first into a picture and then into a mirror is to transform a story from something that is reflected upon to something in which one is reflected. It is to transform the temporality of narrative into the supposed immediacy of viewing. In the same fashion that the heroine is reduced to coerced visibility, the story is reduced to the "self-evidence" of its emblematized moral. Additionally, in a genre whose power derived from its ability to encourage identification but whose danger rested in its inability to control with which character the reader identifies, the mirror symbolizes the text's own efforts to fix and control the dynamics of that identification.

The STORY of OPHELIA.
Saml. Hill, Sc.
"O Fatal! Fatal Poison!"

Figure 20. Frontispiece, William Hill Brown, *The Power of Sympathy* (Boston, 1789). (Courtesy of the American Antiquarian Society.)

If the scrutinized adolescent is the central figure in the fiction of the period, it may be argued that it is the scrutinized parent who is the crucial figure in the larger dynamics of cultural surveillance. In his *Memoirs*, Stephen Burroughs, a 1781 graduate of Dartmouth who would go on to make a career of impersonating ministers and counterfeiting money, traces the ultimate cause of his criminal preoccupation with fraudulence to parental hypocrisy in his child rearing:

> I will observe, that our actions are as strong a language, and perhaps stronger than our words; and as the observations of children are extremely keen, they discover at once, whether our words and our actions speak the same language; and when they find them interfering, they immediately conclude deception is the object of the parent, and not sincerity, that he utters words that he does not believe himself, and puts on a false appearance to answer some sinister end; a view of which insensibly leads the child to dissimulation.[40]

Because, he insisted, the mind is formed by the least impressions upon it, John Locke instructed parents in his *Thoughts on Education*: "You must do nothing before him, which you would not have him imitate."[41] Such an emphasis on example rather than precept dominated not only eighteenth-century views of child rearing, but, as I have argued elsewhere, views of political governance and social relations. It also crucially informed the period's preoccupation with performative elocution. If actions are a language more influential than words (especially in the case of parents literally creating the character of a future generation), then the performing body rather than verbal language becomes the instrument of communication, and thus the site of constant inspection. The consequence of what Hannah Foster calls in *The Coquette* "the vulgar proverb that *actions speak louder than words*" is an enormous obligation to be self-conscious about physical behavior as an almost independent and often self-betraying communicator.[42]

As a corollary to such self-consciousness, violations of privacy, the witnessing of another's unselfconscious absorption in a private behavior (including reading), often constitute, at least in the popular literature of the period, a displaced form of seduction and violation, a safely alienated version of intimacy. In support of his claim that the speech of Chief Logan was not his invention but had a wide currency long before he published it in *Notes on the State of Virginia*, Jefferson was sent in 1810 a copy of a 1780 English epistolary romance by Herbert Croft entitled *Love and Madness*. Remarkably, the heroine of the book is sent Logan's speech by her suitor, with the comment: "Would I might be in your dear, little, enchanted dressing room, while you read it!"[43] Here the Native American plaintiveness of the speech becomes a sentimental tool of seduction, one that allows the would-be lover the voyeuristic pleasure of imagining his loved one in a state of absolute receptivity.

In the post-Revolutionary period, Jefferson's friend Benjamin Rush, the physician and signer from Pennsylvania, pioneered in the medical scrutiny of the body and in a new scientific stigmatization of privacy. As a champion of penitentiaries, Rush believed solitude to be the ideal punishment. It leaves the individual alone with his conscience, hence serving the ideal of penitence, and because it was supposed to be painfully alien to the sociable instincts of man, it also constituted a psychological punishment. However, in his major work, *The Diseases of the Mind*, Rush identified privacy as the site of the "solitary vice" of masturbation, the root cause of the many physical, mental, and ultimately social problems confronting the citizens of the new nation. If self-control could not induce composure, external restriction could. Toward this end Rush devised, as a substitute for a straitjacket, the "Tranquillizer"—a chair fixed with straps for an individual's arms and legs, an architectural head brace to block out peripheral vision, and a pail to receive bodily waste. The chair permitted the physician to "open a

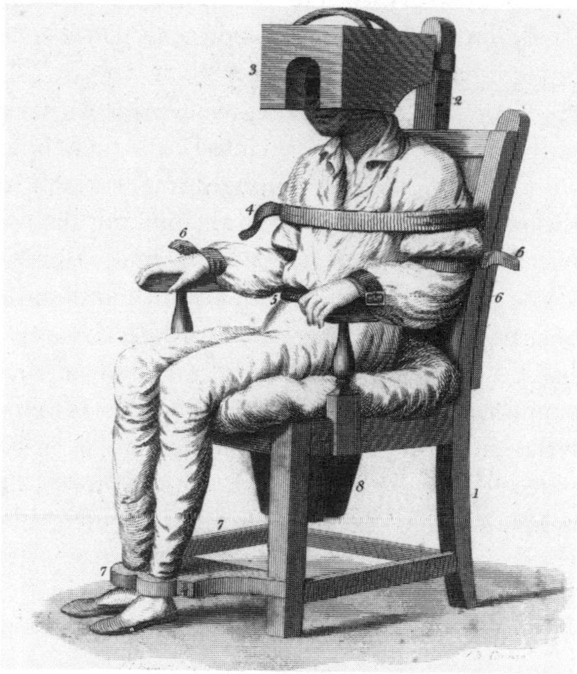

Figure 21. Benjamin Rush's "Tranquillizer," *The Philadelphia Medical Museum*, new series, 1, 1811. (Courtesy of the Library Company of Philadelphia.)

vein without relieving any other part of the body from its confinement and to administer purgative medicines without subjecting the patient to the necessity of being moved." Articulating what might be called the paradoxical ideal of the period, Rush concluded that the chair demonstrates the complementarity and mutuality of freedom and coercion: "The body of the patient in this chair, though in a state of coercion, is so perfectly free from pressure that he sometimes falls asleep in it."[44] In his essay, "Of the Mode of Education Proper in a Republic," Rush articulated a related paradox, one with which Jefferson struggled at length. He insisted that each citizen of a free country "be taught that he does not belong to himself, but that he is public property. . . . He must love his private life, but he must decline no station, however public or responsible it may be, when called to it by the suffrages of his fellow citizens."[45]

In the context of Rush's anxieties about sexuality, a contemporary engraving of a patient strapped into Rush's tranquilizing chair is highly revealing (Figure 21). Wittingly or unwittingly, the lower torso of the patient is so narrowed, so anatomically distorted, as to literally efface the area of the genitals. The image thus suggests a comforting fantasy of a desexualized body. In addition, the curved column of cushion on which the patient sits has the appearance of an externalized intestine, the ultimate extension of the logic of Rush's commitment to purging and bleeding—the forced externalization of the interior. With the patient's legs placed in such a way as to obscure and thus substitute for the front right leg of the chair, patient and chair merge into one fixed and composed object.

Agency and the Invention of Responsibility

Jefferson's anxieties about public speaking, as well as the disabling headaches lasting two to three weeks that began when he first took public office and that disappeared only when he permanently retired from it, may be seen to be rooted ultimately in a newly expanded and thus disorienting understanding of personal and historical agency. The same may be said for the debates over theatricality and the fears of excessive freedom that lay behind the ethic of surveillance and Rush's tranquilizing chair. That understanding of agency, in turn, was rooted in an insistence on defining liberty as a free, undetermined, and uncoerced will.

Gordon Wood has forcefully argued that conspiracy theories in the Revolutionary period were not instances of irrationality but represent a deep-seated desire to rationalize history, to believe events are the conscious consequence of specific intentions and efficacious wills, Newtonian causes and Newtonian effects. Much as Puritans had resisted "the seeming chaos and contingency of events" by attempting to decipher "the concealed or partially revealed will of God," individuals assuming events and actions to be like "the new genre of . . . the novel," the product of "authorial control and design," now sought to decipher "the concealed or partially exposed wills of human beings."[1] Such a rationalization of history seeks to avoid the conclusion that events are the product of either unanalyzable overdetermination or chance—of "serendipity," to use a word Horace Walpole claims to have coined in 1764 to describe the complex process whereby a result is the accidental by-product of a very different intention.[2] Enlightenment challenges to a providential model of history further underscored the wishful insistence on efficacious agency by shifting much more accountability for the process of history onto individuals, not as witting or unwitting instruments of a greater or external will but as agents of their own moral volition.

Reinforced by the emerging laissez-faire economics described by Adam Smith in *The Wealth of Nations*, which demanded that government refrain from interfering with "natural liberty," the enlarged claims for free agency both masked and responded to a fear of constraining and determinate contingencies. Similarly, the liberal idealization of a free and uncoerced will as the essence of freedom (the Declaration, it should be remembered, in part responded to the so-called *Coercion* acts of 1774) was accompanied by an acute sense of vulnerability. That vulnerability took the form of a hypersensitive and hyperbolic insistence that the operation of "any cause" that "comes in to restrain the power of self government," to cite the definition in Richard Price's influential *Observations on Civil Liberty* (1776), constitutes nothing less than "slavery."[3]

The metaphorization of slavery in Revolutionary discourse as any constraint on the private will had the rhetorical consequence of trivializing the literal reality of chattel slavery at the same time that it permitted a new kind of sympathetic identification with blacks as, ironically, another oppressed people. Thus the Declaration's account of George's "captivating & carrying . . . into slavery . . . a distant people who never offended him" seems on first reading to refer to the oppressed colonists rather than to the Crown's participation in the slave trade. Yet the fear of what Jefferson in *A Summary View* called "a deliberate, systematical plan of reducing us to slavery," a sentiment that everywhere accompanies the Revolutionary insistence on self-determination, was more than political hyperbole.[4]

The ideal of power at the heart of the new rhetoric rested on an understanding of the constitution of man as a mechanism whose springs and triggers could be controlled and manipulated. Men were conceived of, in Benjamin Rush's phrase, as "republican machines." Indeed, John Adams described the achievement of national independence as "the perfection of mechanism" no artist had ever before effected: "Thirteen clocks were made to strike together."[5] But if the discourse of mechanism suggested the fantasy of perfect control (like the elocutionists' effort to reduce natural language to a mechanical science), the other side of that fantasy was the fear of perfect enslavement, the fear of being instrument rather than musician. His "passions" under the "perfect command" of his lover's eloquence, the young minister of *The Coquette* declares: "With all the boasted fortitude and resolution of our sex, we are but mere machines."[6]

The dominant Opposition or "Country" critique of British politics and society defined their corruption less as a positive evil than as the horrifying spectacle of "a moral hollowness in men and women" who, in William Dowling's words, are "emptied of will and ethical purpose," moving "mindlessly about the social stage as mere passive creatures of a history working to its own gloomy and inexorable ends." They are "puppets of . . . underlying economic and social forces wreaking moral havoc."[7] In other words, the Whig (and in broader terms, the Enlightenment) insistence on historical agency and self-determination was not only in moral contrast to such instrumentality but in flight from a fear of such instrumentality and determinism. Yet paradoxically the discourse of mechanical determinism (recast as a determinism of psychological and natural motives) was essential to shield and exculpate individuals from the ultimate and uncomfortable responsibility of their newly heightened historical agency.

Precisely such a necessitarian context is apparent in the following phrases from Jefferson's account of the events in the Continental Congress leading up to the Declaration, an account written shortly after the event and later included in his *Autobiography*: "at all events in obedience to instructions"; "we deferred any capital step until the voice of the people drove us into it"; "not whether, by a Declaration of Independence, we should make ourselves what we are not, but whether we should declare a fact which already exists"; "we had been bound to him by allegiance, but that this bond was now dissolved by his assent to the late act of Parliament by which he declares us out of his protection."[8] Jefferson's line in the earliest draft of the Declaration, "we acquiesce in the necessity which pronounces our everlasting Adieu," literally makes necessity speak for the colonies.[9] The internal rhyme of "acquiesce" and "necessity" becomes itself a form of acquiescence. In the draft submitted to Congress, Jefferson changed the end of the line to read: "denounces our eternal separation." Jefferson's use of "denounce" in its older sense of "announce or formally proclaim" introduces an ambiguity that further clouds assertiveness and rhetorically complicates any subsequent denunciation of colonial independence by making the "denouncing" of independence identical with its declaration. If in *A Summary View* the "feelings of human nature revolt," rather than individuals, in the Declaration "revolt" is softened to "renounce." The "last stab to agonizing affection, and manly spirit bids us to renounce for ever these unfeeling brethren." Even renunciation is bidden.[10]

Indeed, the sweeping opening phrase of the preamble—"When in the course of human events"—hides the fact that the "when" is not an externally and naturally determined moment but a chosen one, no less calculated a decision than the designation of the moment when suffering is no longer "sufferable." The agent is hidden and submerged in a sea of seemingly mechanical necessity. Even the final "We . . . solemnly publish & declare that these United colonies are & of right ought to be free" is as much a description of an already achieved state as it is a performative utterance creating that independence. And the pledge of "our lives, our fortunes & our sacred honour" describes an accountability "for the support of this declaration" after the fact, rather than an accountability for the decision making itself. Finally, to put the issue of agency in yet another context, in the earliest draft version of the Declaration, George is described as committing "acts of tyranny without a mask."[11] The prepositional phrase suggests a self-evidence that calls attention away from the violence of the unmasking that constitutes a fundamental activity of the Declaration.

In contrast to the colonies, which repeatedly claim to operate in a necessitarian context, George embodies the principle of pure agency. There are no constraints on his will. His power is arbitrary, in the eighteenth-century sense: willful rather than random. Tyranny thus becomes defined not only as the abuse of power but more fundamentally as the principle of a free and independent will. "An independent ruler," declared John Adams, is "a monster in a free state."[12] By demonizing George, the Declaration stigmatizes individual willfulness at the same time that it articulates an ideology of individual liberty. Independence is thus carefully separated from, and paradoxically made antithetical to, free will. Or, put another way, George has projected onto him the uncomfortable dimension of political liberty, accountability—the very accountability from which the necessitarian language of the Declaration protected the signers and colonists. He is the responsible party, an example of the horrible cost of willful action, of designing. Although the personal pronoun is largely suppressed with reference to the colonists, each of seventeen grievances against George is prefaced with a ringing "he has." The extremity of that demonization is testimony to the deep anxiety lest the declaration be read as an act of self-interested willfulness undertaken by "lords of themselves, these kings of *Me*," as Samuel Johnson characterized the rebels in his *Taxation No Tyranny*.[13] At the same time, however, the tyranny ascribed to George embodies a fantasy of purely independent agency that lay unarticulated beneath the call for independence.

If "future ages will scarcely believe that the hardiness of one man adventured, within the short compass of twelve years only, to lay a foundation so broad & so undisguised for tyranny,"[14] Jefferson elsewhere describes another "adventurer" (his word) who makes clear the positive ideal beneath the negative characterization, a figure who laid the foundation for a future American liberty, Sir Walter Raleigh. In response to George III's speech of October 1775 in which he declared that the British nation was reluctant to give up "so many colonies that she had planted with tenderness . . . and protected and defended at much expense and treasure," Jefferson composed "A Refutation of the Argument that the Colonies Were Established at the Expense of the British Nation." Drawing principally on Hakluyt's *Voyages*, Jefferson argued that neither Raleigh nor any of the "adventurers" had "received assistance from the crown in any of these enterprizes"—though they had received a patent or a sanction.[15] Because Raleigh's corporation was independent of the Crown, Britain's claim that the colonies owed their parent nation a natural or legal debt of gratitude was a manipulative ruse at best, Jefferson claimed. Because of Raleigh's hardy adventuring, because, that is, he was his own agent and not another's instrument (only later would he be "rewarded" with the office of Governor), the American colonies had originated in a state of independence. That independence, Jefferson implied, could at any point be reclaimed.

Jefferson's attack a year later on George's arbitrary and adventuring will represents a radical departure from the dominant characterizations of him prior to 1776 as an instrument of the will of his own ministers. He is in that characterization sealed off from a true representation of the state of political affairs because there are no American ministers, a victim of partisan misinformation. His will is not his own. In *A Summary View,* for example, Jefferson warned George that "You are surrounded by British counsellers, but remember that they are parties. . . . It behooves you, therefore, to think and to act for yourself and your people." The accusation was particularly pointed because in the traditional view of monarchy the king was able to act for the good of the people, to be their protector (from Parliament or other powers), precisely because his will was free. The problem was not the extent of monarchical power or will, but the ends to which that power was put.[16]

And yet, from another perspective the essence of kingship was the king's power to delegate responsibility, to have others serve as instruments of his will, and thus to protect himself from the accountability that falls on the specific actors themselves. On New Year's Day, 1776, the Massachusetts minister John Cleaveland pondered the problem "that the king does nothing, as King, but by his ministers, and, therefore, whatever wrong is done by the Administration of the King, must be attributed to the ministers, not to him. But according to this what does the King do, as King? Why nothing, neither right nor wrong. But what is the king but an absolute nothing?"[17] The problem of delegation, like the problem of representation, complicated and aggravated the great question of accountability. Did ultimate power mean the freedom from both action and accountability, or the undertaking of their burden?

After the catalogue of George's abuses, which includes both "making the military independant of . . . civil power" and making "judges dependant on his will alone," Jefferson accuses "our British brethren" of returning to office by "their free election" the "disturbers of our harmony," and of "permitting their chief magistrate to send over not only souldiers of our common blood, but Scotch and foreign mercenaries."[18] The specific outrage at permitting the hiring of mercenaries suggests that such delegation is inherently unnatural. When one man acts coldbloodedly for another, action is severed from its ultimate rationale, its motive passion. Did accountability recognize the distinctions between final and efficient cause? And if history itself was providentially designed by God, weren't all the actors in the drama witting or unwitting hirelings of a greater will?

Periodically, throughout the war, the Continental Congress resolved that certain days be appointed as days "of Humiliation and Fasting and Prayer that we may with United Hearts confess and bewail our manifest sins, and by a sincere repentance and amendment of life, . . . humbly implore his assistance to frustrate the cruel progress of an unnatural enemy."[19] Such proclamations conveyed a mixed message. They suggested that the external political enemy was really no more than divine punishment for a sinful human nature that was the true enemy of Americans, a nature that could be changed only by surrendering to God's will. Yet the same proclamations made clear that it was England who was "deaf to the voice of reason and humanity, and inflexibly bent on war" and thus must be repelled "by open resistance."[20] A national will is asserted at the same time as that will is surrendered to God; blame is projected at the same time that it is ostensibly absorbed.

Because the American Revolution and its aftermath encouraged a radical rethinking of the relationship of individuals to the making of history, of what it means to be a historical actor, and of the concept of self-determination, it may not be surprising to learn that according to the *OED* the very noun "responsibility" makes its earliest appearance in print in *The Federalist.* In *Federalist* 70, Hamilton argues that the executive branch of government must be represented by a single individual and not by a committee because the "multiplication of the Executive" tends "to conceal faults and destroy responsibility": "It often becomes impossible, amidst mutual accusations, to determine on whom the blame or the punishment of a pernicious measure . . . ought really to fall. It is shifted from one to another with so much dexterity, and under such plausible appearances, that the public opinion is left in suspense about the real author . . . [especially] where there are a number of actors who may have had different degrees and kinds of agency."[21] In the English system, ministers "responsible to the nation for the advice they give" are an essential part of the executive because the king is "a perpetual magistrate" and the continuing loyalty of his subjects depends on his being "unaccountable for his administration." But in a free government, Hamilton continues, an executive without "responsibility" is "an idea inadmissible."[22] The dangers of concentrating power are outweighed by the necessity of concentrating "responsibility," by the crucial obligation to locate accountability definitively in an individual who takes "responsibility" for the complex process. Someone, even if it is not "the real author," must ultimately be answerable. The concept seeks to address the concealment, the dexterous shifting, of accountability, and at the same time offers up another kind of concealment.

In *Federalist* 63, Madison uses "responsibility" in a different sense. There he argues that the duration of the senatorial term must be long enough to allow senators to bring to completion those long-term measures that are as essential to the welfare of the nation as the host of short-term ones: "Responsibility, in order to be reasonable, must be limited to objects within the power of the responsible party, and in order to be effectual, must relate to operations of that power."[23] In other words, in order to be answerable to the expectations of the electorate, senators must be given the "ability to respond" to those needs, which in this case means the extended time to respond. Increased accountability must follow increased autonomous power. The word "responsibility" merges both those concepts, while at the same time carrying a decided echo of Madison's debt to Scottish Common Sense philosophy, with its insistence on the natural and involuntary ability of individuals to be responsive to the pain, pleasures, and needs of other members of their species. The ability to be responsive in feeling (response-ability) must be complemented, Madison is suggesting in *Federalist* 63, by the formal ability to respond in action.

Madison's position is consistent with the Enlightenment view that accountability is limited to actual ability. Yet at the same time Hamilton's willingness to separate actual actor from responsible party, his willingness to concentrate responsibility, constitutes his response to the new and complex understanding of accountability so much at the heart of eighteenth-century Anglo-American culture. As individual behavior came more and more to be viewed not as a function of some hypostatized individual or autonomous human will but as the complex product of parental nurture, education, social forces, and formative experiences—that is, as an individual was seen as the locus of forces rather than as a self-contained agent—twin and often conflicting needs emerged, needs that frame the still-ongoing crisis in liberalism. The first was to recognize the matrix of interdependencies that mitigate individual culpability and in consequence dramatically expand the number of "guilty" parties implicated in any one individual's actions. The second was to insist that explaining behavior by distributing guilt must not be confused with excusing it. Someone must ultimately be answerable. This indeed is the point of Hamilton's use of the newly coined term. Responsibility refers primarily to the condition of being answerable, and only secondarily, and thus not necessarily, to the condition of being personally involved or morally culpable.

In the same July 6 issue of *The Pennsylvania Evening Post* that carried the first newspaper printing of the Declaration there appeared another legal notice declaring independence—one that suggests connections between independence and responsibility. "Whereas the Wife of Joseph Cartwright having eloped from him sundry times, he requests all persons not to trust her as he will not pay any debts she may contract. Joseph Cartwright."[24] Mrs. Cartwright's elopement (no matter what its cause) has freed her husband from his financial obligations and cost her the "trust" made possible by her wifely status as a *feme covert,* to use the contemporary legal term. As this example suggests, the price of her independence is the elimination of his "responsibility" for her. And for Joseph Cartwright, that elimination, as his legal notice insists, constitutes his independence.

Dialectical Words

The ambiguities of agency were at the heart of the ordeal Governor Thomas Hutchinson endured in 1773. When his assessment of the colonial situation in a series of private letters was secretly secured and published that year, one sentence gave such offense that it ultimately led to his exile. Speculating on the character of new "measures necessary for the peace and good order of the colony," orders he expected would arrive shortly from England, he concluded "there must be an abridgement of what are called English liberties."[1] Though Hutchinson and his defenders repeatedly insisted that he had used "must" in the predictive sense—in Bernard Bailyn's words, "that it was a fact of life that could not be otherwise"—the "must" was read by his Whig opponents as expressing both his desire and his urgent recommendation. "All the art and subtlety . . . will never vindicate or excuse that expression," declared John Adams in his "Novanglus" essays.[2] In other words, the issue turned on whether "must be abridged" implied presumption of an inevitable outcome or willful self-assertion. Though Bailyn argues for the former view, the fact is that the answer does not lie in an either/or formulation or in the supposed recovery of a specific intentionality. The phrasing carries precisely the ambiguity about efficacy that characterizes the discourse of the entire period. Like Franklin's invention, the bifocals, which join two perspectives into one, the phrase blends necessity and agency, serving as a correlative to the mutuality of self-assertion and self-abnegation. It registers a desire to see it both ways, a desire intensified by the problematic character of Hutchinson's middle management position as governor.

In fact, rather than being the problem (a hiding place from accountability), the ambiguity of the word "must" stands instead as a linguistic trope for a cultural ideal: the dialectical union of liberty and constraint so intensely pursued in the period. The problem, if there was one, lay in trying to affix a determinate meaning. Like the wonderfully ambiguous "bound" of Charles Grandison Finney's nineteenth-century classic, *Sinners Bound to Change their own Hearts,* the tension in the Declaration between the description of independence as the necessary consequence of George's actions and the document's own status as a performative utterance carried precisely the same dynamic between willful determination and determinism, efficacy and necessitarianism, the same transformation of ambiguity into proto-Hegelian mediation. Indeed, in common law, as John Quincy Adams informed his students, a "declaration" was defined as "the narration" inserted into a writ or indictment to which a defendant answers.[3] Thus, in purely legalist terms a declaration was a descriptive account of grievances, not a proclamation of principles, a declaration of injuries, not of independence. As both aggrieved narration and a proclamation of rights, the Declaration of Independence wanted it both ways.

There is another crucially serviceable dialectic implicit in the title of Jefferson's only published book, *Notes on the State of Virginia.* "State" refers to both a seemingly fixed geographic entity ("A notice of the best sea-ports of the state") and a fluid condition ("the present state of manufactures") about which only provisional notes can be made.[4] In a larger sense, "state" mediates between product and process, between universal laws and the reality of contingency, and between essentialism (black "inferiority is not the effect merely of their condition of life") and developmentalism (Indian inferiority is, in contrast, largely conditional, and thus ameliorative).[5] Like Henry's oratory and Stuart's *Skater*, the word mediates between fixity and flux, order and energy, stability and instability. Indeed, even the larger book, though complete in itself, is finally judged no more than a fixed point in a fluid process. Tired from correcting the manuscript of *Notes,* Jefferson articulated the core futility of his descriptive project: "The work itself indeed is nothing more than the measure of a shadow, never stationary, but lengthening as the sun advances and to be taken anew from hour to hour. It must remain, therefore, for some other hand to sketch its appearance at another epoch."[6]

Though federalism in political theory meant that the states are primary, equal, and possessed of the lion's share of political power, the party that embraced this position and thus opposed the Constitution in 1787 was called "Anti-Federalist." In a shrewd move by the party of Madison, Jay, and Hamilton, the authors of *The Federalist,* the name rightfully belonging to their opponents had been appropriated and redefined to refer to those who supported strengthening the institutions of the federation, who placed general or "federal" authority above support for "local or particular advantages." Thus the title of our nation's greatest work of political theory may be said to contain an active dialogue between a position that asserts the primacy of the parts over the whole and one that asserts the primacy of the whole over the parts. Rather than being stigmatized as "ambiguous," the word might rather be seen once again as a verbal representative of an emerging cultural dialectic. Committed to challenging an older dichotomous thinking rooted in the essentialist assumption that every entity has a single, univocal nature, that dialectic proposes mixture rather than purity as a fundamental value in the way that the Constitution itself seeks to mix or balance federal and national models, as bicameralism seeks to mix or balance representational models, and as a government divided into executive, legislature, and judiciary seeks to combine the advantages of monarchy, aristocracy, and democracy.

When Carwin the ventriloquist, hero/villain of Brown's *Wieland,* is asked to confess to an intention to harm the heroine, Clara, he defends himself with a quintessentially dialectical remark: "Nothing less was intended than to injure you."[7] The tortured syntax here can be read to mean either: "to harm you was nothing less than what I intended," or "to harm you was what I least intended." But Carwin's statement (with its implication that the consequences of his actions should not be confused with the consequences of his intentions) is neither a poorly phrased defense nor an ironically unintended confession. Rather, it is a linguistic representation of the intractably conflicted view of accountability at the heart of a newly emerging humanitarian liberalism. That view represented the tense though dominant cultural mixture of—to invoke two influential contemporary voices—Thomas Reid's view of man as possessed of a pure agency for which he is accountable (and its liberal theological correlative that "ought" always implies "can") and Joseph Priestley's conception of man as a locus of forces that mitigate accountability. In illuminating the realm between pure freedom and compulsion, Brown is ultimately offering an analysis of what would later be called "ideology," socially determined thought that, because of the invisible dynamics of its transmission, seems to be self-determined. In the preface to his best-selling grammar book, ostentatiously called *A Grammatical Institute of the English Language, Part II* (1784), Noah Webster described at length what he saw to be the neglected topic of "auxillary verbs" like "do, be, shall, have, will, may, can, should, would, could and must." The crucial importance of verbs that precede other verbs is that they enable one to express the "mode of power, liberty, necessity, obligation, promise, determination and inclination."[8] As Thomas Hutchinson was obliged to realize with special reference to the last of Webster's verbs, they are the linguistic markers of the drama of agency.

Of all the verbs used to describe George's actions in the catalogue of grievances, only one was changed by the Continental Congress. "He has suffered the administration of Justice to cease" became "he has obstructed." Earlier in the document, *suffer*, in its sense of endure, rather than allow, is used to describe the colonists who "suffer while evils are sufferable"—biblical phrasing that acknowledges the scriptural injunction to passive obedience at the very moment it subverts it with the temporalizing "while."[9] In this instance, the ambiguity of "suffer," which mediates between activity and passivity, threatens the strategic dichotomizing of those states. In consequence, the verb must be controlled by an editorial change that limits it exclusively to its intransitive sense.

If dialectical words sought to register a more complex vision of agency, equivocal words and equivocation offered the more time-honored mode of dealing with the anxieties of agency and judgmental self-assertion. Toward the end of the rough draft of the Declaration Jefferson implicitly raises the issue of the credibility of his characterization of George when he asserts, "Future ages will scarcely believe that the hardiness of one man adventured. . . ." As if sensing a hostile audience, he shamelessly backtracks. It is not the man but his "hardiness" that adventures. George does not tyrannize but builds "a foundation . . . for tyranny." Indeed he is not even a tyrant per se, but "a prince whose character is thus marked by every act which may define a tyrant."[10] Even the "may" suggests that eighteenth-century taxonomies of character were open to question, that subjective judgment may qualify self-evidence—the compensatory adjective "undisguised" notwithstanding. The demonizing (that is, the affixing of absolute agency and efficacy) becomes mealymouthed and self-conscious, as if disrupted by a surfacing of Jefferson's awareness of the overdetermined character of history.

On the subject of such overdetermination, Jefferson's great-granddaughter retells an anecdote Jefferson reportedly told "a gentleman who had been a frequent visitor at Monticello" concerning the Declaration of Independence:

While the question of Independence was before Congress, it had its meetings near a livery-stable. The members wore short breeches and silk stockings, and, with handkerchief in hand, they were diligently employed

> in lashing the flies from their legs. So very vexatious was this annoyance, and to so great an impatience did it arouse the sufferers, that it tended, if it did not aid, in inducing them to properly affix their signatures to the great document which gave birth to an entire republic.

The correspondent adds, "This anecdote I had from Mr. Jefferson at Monticello, who seemed to enjoy it very much, as well as to give great credit to the influence of flies. He told it with much glee, and seemed to retain a vivid recollection of an attack, from which the only relief was signing the paper and flying from the scene."[11]

As an invocation of the determinate character of climate in history, as an instance of the contingent nature of historical events, as a revisionist history that replaces the power of Jefferson's prose with the annoyance of flies, the anecdote playfully redefines how Congress was "diligently employed" and recasts the freedom won by the "sufferers" as the ability to fly from the accountability of signing. Such a flight would allow them to tell their children with a becoming and self-amused modesty: the flies made me do it.

The injuries Britain inflicted on the colonists, Paine argued, "are injuries which nature can not forgive; she would cease to be nature if she did."[12] And yet for all the insistence in the 1760's and 1770's on a universal nature whose promptings—whose voice—must be attended to, there is very little agreement about what it meant to obey nature. When in March 1776 Adams was disturbed by all the anger he was feeling about the immediate political situation, he consoled himself with this sentiment confided to his diary: "Resentment is a passion, implanted by nature for the preservation of men."[13] If natural feelings must be expressed, how does one distinguish them from "unnatural" feelings which must not? The problem is illustrated by a story of "female heroism" (originally published in London in 1750) prominently featured in *Thomas's New-England Almanack . . . for 1775*. An English sailor deserts his

The Life and Adventures of a FEMALE SOLDIER.

HANNAH SNELL, was born in *Fryer-Street* in the Pariſh of St. *Hellen's*, in the city of *Worceſter*, in *England*, on the 23d day of *April*, 1723. When the Father and Mother of *Hannah* died, *Hannah* came to *London*, and contracted an acquaintance with one *James Summs*, a ſailor, who was a *Dutchman*. In a little time *Summs*, made his addreſſes to her as a lover, and gained her conſent, and was married to her at the *Fleet*, on the ſixth day of *January*, 1743-4. But all his promiſes of friendſhip, proved inſtances of the higheſt perfidy, and he turned out the worſt and moſt unnatural of huſbands. When ſhe was ſeven months gone with child, he, finding himſelf deeply involved in debt, made an elopement from her. Notwithſtanding theſe her calamities, ſhe patiently bore herſelf up under them, and two months after her huſband's departure was delivered of a daughter which lived no more than ſeven months. As ſhe was now free from all the ties ariſing from nature and conſanguinity; ſhe thought herſelf privileged to roam in queſt of the man, who, without reaſon, had injured her ſo much; for there are no bounds to be ſet either to love, jealouſy or hatred, in the female mind. That ſhe might execute her deſigns with the better grace, and the more ſucceſs, ſhe boldly com-

Figure 22. "Hannah Snell, a Female Soldier," *Thomas's New-England Almanack . . . for 1775.* (Courtesy of the American Antiquarian Society.)

new wife while she is pregnant. Though initially Hannah Snell patiently bore her calamities, after the death of her newborn the deserted woman assumes a male disguise and "boldly" joins a local regiment in an effort to locate and avenge herself against her "most unnatural" husband. "As she was now free from all the ties arising from nature and consanguinity, she thought herself privileged to roam in quest of the man, who, without reason, had injured her so much; for there are no bounds to be set either to love, jealousy or hatred, in the female mind."[14] Early in her military career Hannah receives 500 lashes because her commanding officer believes that she is a rival for the woman he is wooing, "a crime nature put it out of her power to commit." Later, in battle, she is "wounded in the groin" and sent to a hospital.[15] A sequel in which she confronts her husband is promised for the 1776 almanac, but that issue was never published or has not survived.

Is the young woman following nature, the natural passions of "the female mind," or does the ambiguous phrase "free from all ties of nature" suggest that she has betrayed nature by forswearing the "patient" acceptance of her calamities? Must she endure her groin wound and the 500 lashes as symbolically appropriate punishment for betraying her female nature through her cross-dressing? Or are her punishments for crimes that "nature put it out of her power to commit," and thus extensions of the "unnatural" tyranny she had earlier experienced at the hand of her husband? Once she has made the decision to dress as a man, is she then responsible for the consequences of that decision, or has that decision been necessitated as part of a chain of events set off by her husband's failure to respond "naturally" to parental responsibility? Though seeming to distinguish between the heroic and the unnatural, the tale repeatedly complicates their relationship.

A woodcut above the article shows Hannah Snell (now skirted) holding a musket as tall as she is (Figure 22). But it is not clear whether this illustration is intended as a heroic image, as the title suggests, or as an unnatural one. Is it consistent with the

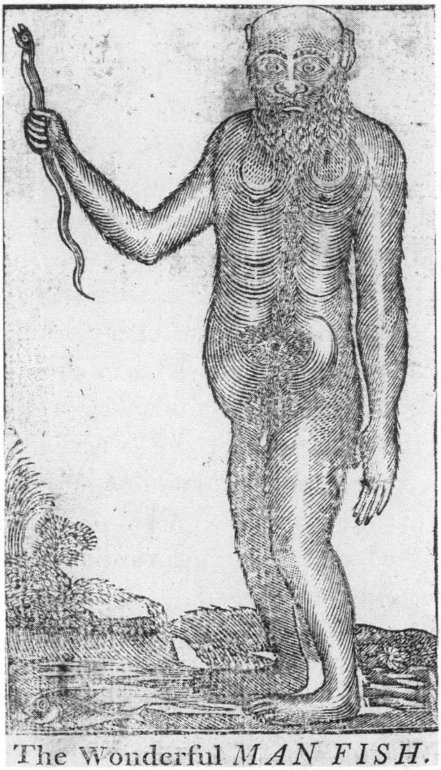

Figure 23. "The Wonderful MAN FISH," *Bickerstaff's Boston Almanack for 1772.* (Courtesy of the American Antiquarian Society.)

numerous almanac articles on anomalies of nature (or more precisely, anomalies within the taxonomies used to describe nature): dwarfs, giants, and the much-discussed "man fish" of 1772 (Figure 23), who after being presumed drowned is later discovered swimming with a shoal of fish?[16] Or is it consistent with the article that immediately follows it in Thomas's *Almanack*, on the heroic efforts of "his majesty's most loyal subjects," who have passed an embargo on the importing of British goods, no longer able to endure the "ruinous system of colonial administration evidently calculated for enslaving them"?

The Hannah Snell piece allegorizes the enormous and often unsuccessful effort to naturalize defiance in the years between 1774 and 1776, to escape the imputation that it is not only George who is the monstrous anomaly in nature, waging "cruel war against human nature itself," in the words of Jefferson's Declaration, but (as the Tories repeatedly insisted) the impatient "rebels" themselves.[17] The cross-dressed figure, like the dialectical word, yoked male agency with female victimization. The Whig position thus was obliged to concede that it may be natural, as the Declaration asserts, to suffer evils while sufferable, but then paradoxically added that beyond such a point, patience and obedience enter a realm where, in Paine's phrase, nature would "cease to be" nature. The "balloon" almanacs of the 1780's, which record the exploits of those early balloonists who literally flew in the face of nature's most fundamental law, gravity, raise an even trickier question. Is heroism a function of obeying nature, or of transcending or opposing (and thus violating) it? In support of the latter, one of the earliest balloon almanacs, *Weatherwise's Town and Countryman's Almanack for 1785*, shows a man falling from his balloon in the attitude of a punished Icarus; another depicts balloon "sailors" in triumph.[18]

The gender issues raised by the almanac story of Hannah Snell would find articulation three years later in the case of one of the women (along with Betsy Ross) most associated in the popular mind with the Revolution: Molly Hays. On the terrifically hot day of June 28, 1778 she earned the nickname Molly Pitcher by bringing water to the exhausted and wounded on the battlefield at Monmouth, and additional fame by replacing her heat-prostrated husband at a cannon that she loaded and reloaded throughout the battle. The one eyewitness account of Molly's role that has any claim to authenticity includes the following extraordinary observation:

> While in the act of reaching a cartridge and having one of her feet as far before the other as she could step, a cannon shot from the enemy passed directly between her legs without doing any other damage than carrying

away all the lower part of her petticoat. Looking at it with apparent unconcern, she observed that it was luck it did not pass a little higher, for in that case it might have carried away something else, and continued her occupation.[19]

What threatens to desex Molly is as much her behavior as the enemy's cannon shot. Her manning the cannon, her being "attached to a piece in the engagement," seems to have called forth from her chronicler, consciously or unconsciously, a scene that literalizes the gender anxiety raised by that behavior, a scene, we are told, that though indelicate it would be "unpardonable not to mention." Again, as in the story of Hannah Snell, is the threat to her sexuality a punishment for transgressions or a form of induction into the greater world of male heroism? What is most striking about the subsequent mythologizing of Molly Hays is the compensatory feminizing brought about by renaming her after the receptacle that identifies her with the nurturing role of water bringer. Consequently, it is left uncertain whether Hays's heroism, like Snell's, has to do with transcending her female nature or perfectly embodying it. Or, put differently, androgynous characterization replicates the rhetorical and oratorical ideals of the Revolution—a combination of compensating passive and aggressive postures.

The dialogue between aggressive agency and passive instrumentality, between (to turn to the central dialectical word) *revolution* as a rebellious rupture with the past and *revolution* (as with the seasons or spheres) as an ongoing natural process, is powerfully reiterated in the dialogue between the two sides of the earliest proposed national seal. On July 4, 1776, after the Declaration of Independence had been read again to the Continental Congress, it was "Resolved, That Dr. Franklin, J. Adams and Mr. Jefferson," the same committee charged with drafting the Declaration, should serve as "a committee, to prepare a device for a Seal of the United

States of America."[20] The seal would be both an iconographic declaration and an official imprimatur of independence. Because Congress rejected the design they submitted on August 10, little attention has been paid to this visual text of independence.

Drawing on a design suggested by Pierre-Eugène du Simitière, a Swiss émigré painter living in Philadelphia, the committee reported that "the arms of the United States of America" should have at its center a shield divided into six sections. "The 1st Or, a Rose enammelled gules and argent for England; the 2nd Argent, a Thistle proper for Scotland: the 3rd Vert a harp Or for Ireland: the 4th Azure a Flower de luce Or for France: the 5th Or the Imperial Eagle Sable for Germany; and the 6th Or the Belgic Lion Gules for Holland, pointing out the countries from which these States have been peopled" (Figure 24). This internal shield would be held up on one side by the "Goddess of Liberty in a corselet of Armour, alluding to the present times" and (replacing the "American soldier" who appears in the original sketch) "the Goddess Justice" on the other. Above it would be "the Eye of Providence in a radiant Triangle," below, the motto *E Pluribus Unum*. The shield would be enclosed by thirteen scutcheons, each with the initials of "the independent States of America." This, in turn, would be enclosed by a border legend reading "Seal of the United States of America MDCCLXXVI."[21]

What is fascinating about the design is that in its first official appearance, the *E Pluribus Unum* motto refers as much to the process whereby America derived from the six "countries from which these States have been peopled" as it does to America as a union of states. Such a view was consistent with Jefferson's argument in *A Summary View* that emigration itself constituted an initial act of independence, so that England had no more right over Anglo-Americans than Germany did over the descendants of the Saxon settlers of England.[22] Rather than a representation of America as a discrete, reified nation (or even a heterogeneous union of states) separate from England and Europe, the heart of the seal

Figure 24. Pierre du Simitière, pencil sketch of a design for a seal for the United States, August 1776. (Courtesy of the Library of Congress.)

figures America as a European union. The British parent has not so much been replaced as subsumed by a multiplicity of parents. Here, independence is pointedly not a self-generated new beginning but a point in a process of Northern European immigration, not a self-fashioning but a claim to wider origins.

Because America is identical with, rather than derivative from the chain of states, the shield, rather than the states, carries the representational burden of origins. And yet it competes with the chain as an image of a constituted America, a nation constituted by its peoples rather than its states. The report describes Liberty and Justice not as figures for America, but as "Supporters" of the shield. As definitional, these European origins, in pointed contrast to the rhetorical insistence of the Declaration of Independence, cannot be effaced or renounced. But as the cabinet-like shield with its six compartments also suggests, they can be contained and limited. In this protonativist and Protestant vision of past and future origins, of a limited cosmopolitanism, Southern Catholic Europe, Africa, and the Caribbean are excluded. In the design eventually approved (which followed the design of the flag adopted in June 1777), the central shield or arms is emptied of its European content and filled by thirteen stripes, alternately white, signifying "purity and innocence," and red, signifying "hardiness and Valour."[23] The new shield served as a unifying form with which to organize the now unnamed, undifferentiated, and abstracted states into a whole.

As significant as the future transformations of Jefferson's, Franklin's, and Adams's 1776 design is the dialogue between the recto of the seal's design (as described above) and its verso: "Pharaoh sitting in an open Chariot a Crown on his head . . . passing through the divided Waters of the Red Sea in pursuit of the Israelites: Rays from a [pillar] of Fire and the Cloud, expressive of the divine Presence and Command, beaming on Moses who stands on the Shore and extending his hand over the Sea causes it to overwhe[lm] Pharaoh."[24] In contrast to the heraldic formalism and implicit transatlantic genealogical narrative of the recto, the verso contains an allegory of Americans as an already separate and persecuted people. Their miraculous escape turns the Atlantic, qua Red Sea, into both a protective barrier that makes future contact and immigration impossible and an instrument of a final and violent revenge against what Paine called "The Pharaoh" of England.[25] Moses is given the decisive power of exclusion. The peopling of America is no longer an ongoing historical process, an engagement with origins that precedes, postdates, and subsumes political rupture, but a single historical moment of radical rupture (superintended by a deity immanent in fire and cloud), textually signified by the Declaration. And yet this side of the seal of America still fails to represent America as an entity unto itself. It still defines America with reference to a narrative of origins, a narrative in which once again, as was true of the reverse in a different sense, the foregrounded presence of England, typologically signified by the Pharaoh and his troops, dominates the image. The rupture is undermined by being fixed in representation, for England is never excluded. As was true of its editing of Jefferson's Declaration, the Continental Congress's rejection of his committee's design, a design that inscribed the dialogue with Europe as the essence of America, was rooted in the perception that it betrayed too much unconfident anxiety. By failing to represent a fully realized autonomy, it gave the game away.

Plagiarism, Authorship, and Improvement

In the last decade of Jefferson's life, his old Federalist adversaries as well as those simply jealous of his honored place in American history sought to undermine his popular appeal by accusing him of plagiarism in the Declaration. John Adams said that "there is not an idea in it, but what had been hackneyed in Congress for two years before, the substance of it is contained in the Declaration of rights . . . in the Journal of Congress in 1774."[1] Timothy Pickering declared "how little was his Merit" even in the humble act of "compiling." Earlier, even fellow Virginian Richard Henry Lee had said that it had been "copied from Locke's treatise on government."[2] In 1819 the Raleigh *Register and North Carolina Gazette* printed what it claimed was a declaration of independence from Great Britain, the so-called Mecklenburg Declaration, supposedly written by a group of North Carolina citizens on May 20, 1775, "fifteen Months," as a jealous John Adams took pleasure in writing Jefferson, "before your Declaration of Independence."[3] Having previously suggested that Jefferson had simply "in a day or two" patched the Declaration together from the "Minutes" of the drafting committee, on which Adams conspicuously sat, that Jefferson had done no more than "cloathe" the committee's "Articles" in "proper Dress," Adams seemed willing to entertain the credibility of a document whose obvious spuriousness enraged Jefferson.[4]

The attacks on Jefferson all explicitly, in a new mode, identified authorship with originality and the novelty of thought rather than with the act of harmonizing—identified it, that is, with the articulation of one's individual personality rather than one's social nature. No longer was the ideal of expression rooted in the authority of representativeness, the general will, and historical precedent; it appeared, rather, in the articulation of a sincere particular will, in a self-assertion that stigmatized the dissemination of traditional thought as but mechanical duplication. Jefferson's response, "that he did not consider it as any part of my charge to invent new ideas altogether," seemed part of an old aesthetic.[5]

The new aesthetic devalued the high price in self-effacement Jefferson had paid for his labor of ventriloquizing common sense and enacting so masterfully "what oft was thought, but ne'er so well express'd," as Pope recalled the central agenda of classical rhetoric.[6] "Neither aiming at originality of principle or sentiment, nor yet copied from any particular and previous writing," Jefferson insisted, the Declaration had been written as "an expression of the American mind," and its authority derived not from him but from "the harmonizing sentiments of the day, whether expressed in conversation, in letters, printed essays or in the elementary books of public right, as Aristotle, Cicero, Locke Sidney, etc."[7] The fact that Jefferson's draft of the Declaration was written on Dutch paper watermarked *Pro Patria Eiusque Libertate* (for the country and its independence) literalizes the palimpsestic character of the document. For all its specificity, it was written over, and out of, conventional nationalist and republican sentiments.[8]

But by 1800 "invention" had lost much of its old sense of a choice among set options (its technical meaning in rhetoric) and laid claim, as John Quincy Adams put it, "not merely to the praise of finding, but to the glory of creating."[9] Paraphrase, in many ways the heart of rhetoric, was deemed a poor servant to intentionality.

And originality, once understood as "that which is . . . at or near the origins, and therefore ancient or primitive"—as Homer was original—was reconceived as novel self-expression, a maximally expressive version of a unique idea. Indeed, William Godwin writing in 1793 could imagine a time when there would be no more "theatrical exhibitions" because "it may be doubted whether any men will hereafter come forward in any mode gravely to repeat words and ideas not their own."[10] Such "formal repetition" was an imprisonment of mind. In contrast, a letter writer to the Philadelphia *Weekly Magazine* in 1798 warned against confusing "original" with "never before published." Asserting that "even the great Milton's *Paradise Lost* can be traced to an Italian tragedy," and the humor of the "original Sterne" derived from Burton's *Anatomy of Melancholy,* the writer concluded, "as to real originality you must see I do not much believe in it."[11] The accused Jefferson was caught between competing aesthetics.

Gouverneur Morris, chairman of the Constitutional Convention's Committee on Style, who turned a bundle of compromise resolutions into an elegant document, is still described by historians as having "worded" rather than "written" the Constitution. Jefferson was denied the benefit of that dubious but strategic distinction.[12] His decision in 1821 to include in his *Autobiography* the then-unknown rough draft of the Declaration, to set in opposition to the final historical Declaration a document to which he was laying exclusive claim of authorship, was a move largely forced upon him by the Mecklenburg incident. Yet even at that moment in the *Autobiography,* he introduces the document with a potted history dominated by passive constructions: "The committee for drawing the Declaration of Independence, desired me to do it. It was accordingly done, and being approved by them I reported it to the House on Friday, the 28th of June, when it was read."[13] It was done and it was read. Only in the epitaph he wrote for the obelisk that was to mark his grave did he unequivocally lay prideful claim to the phrase "Author of the Declaration of American Independence." Finally, as an ironic footnote to the matter of originality, for much of his correspondence Jefferson used a pantograph or polygraph, a copying machine in which the writer's hand moved two pens simultaneously, so that, as Charles Willson Peale put it, "two originals are made with great facility at the same instant." At the level of technological agency the polygraph confounded the distinction between copy and original.[14]

Jefferson's proud but self-effacing attitude toward the authorship of texts extended to his attitude toward their ownership. Rather than placing a signature or bookplate within the books of his library, Jefferson had another procedure for indicating ownership. That procedure drew on the other definition of "signature," meaning the small letter printed in the tail margin of the first leaf of each gathering or section of a book as a guide to the binder in assembling them correctly. Jefferson would turn to the I signature (the Latin capitalized J) and complete it by penning a small T in front of it. He would then turn to the T signature and place a type-sized J after it (Figure 25).[15] Such a concealed method of signing—a double initialing, half print, half manuscript—functioned less as a public mark of ownership than as a self-effacement that distributed and gathered the owner within the order of the book, subordinating the appropriation of the book as property to a respect for it as craftsmanship and linking personal identity to the impersonality of print.

To minimize the intrusive and conspicuous presence of beds in bedrooms at Monticello, Jefferson favored alcove beds. In his own bedroom, his bed is wedged within an arch cut out of the wall that separates the bedroom from a work or cabinet room in which he did his writing. Thus, in an instance analogous to his mode of initialing books, the bed and the self in the privacy of sleep become part of the architectural structure of the room, rather than an intrusive assertion within it.

Long before the first charges of plagiarism, Jefferson acquired from Franklin a particularly revealing volume, one that addressed

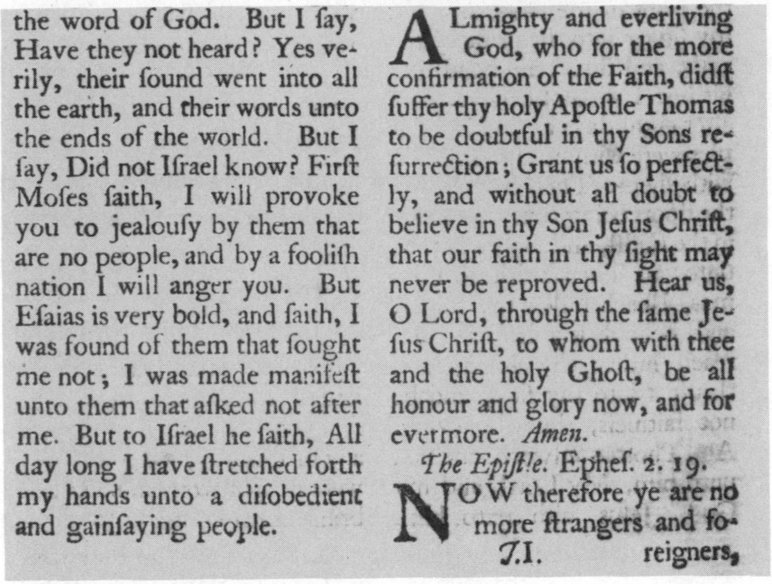

the word of God. But I ſay, Have they not heard? Yes verily, their ſound went into all the earth, and their words unto the ends of the world. But I ſay, Did not Iſrael know? Firſt Moſes ſaith, I will provoke you to jealouſy by them that are no people, and by a fooliſh nation I will anger you. But Eſaias is very bold, and ſaith, I was found of them that ſought me not; I was made manifeſt unto them that aſked not after me. But to Iſrael he ſaith, All day long I have ſtretched forth my hands unto a diſobedient and gainſaying people.

ALmighty and everliving God, who for the more confirmation of the Faith, didſt ſuffer thy holy Apoſtle Thomas to be doubtful in thy Sons reſurrection; Grant us ſo perfectly, and without all doubt to believe in thy Son Jeſus Chriſt, that our faith in thy ſight may never be reproved. Hear us, O Lord, through the ſame Jeſus Chriſt, to whom with thee and the holy Ghoſt, be all honour and glory now, and for evermore. *Amen.*

The Epiſtle. Epheſ. 2. 19.

NOW therefore ye are no more ſtrangers and fo-

T.I. reigners,

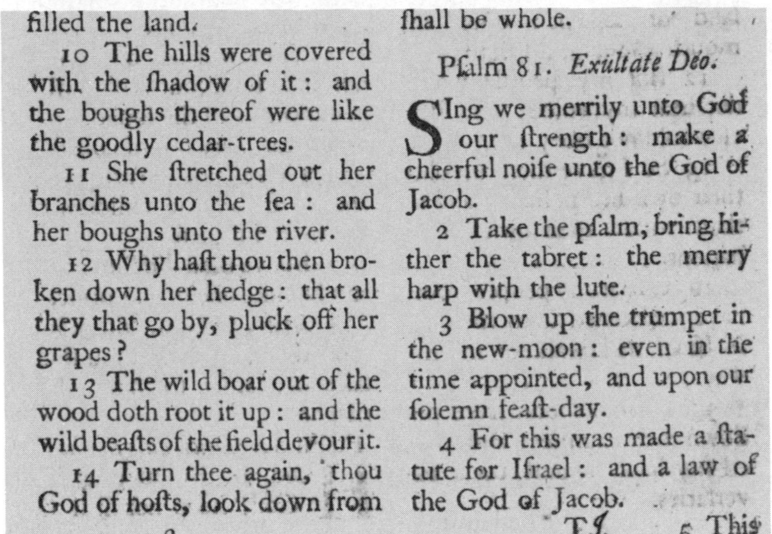

filled the land.

10 The hills were covered with the ſhadow of it: and the boughs thereof were like the goodly cedar-trees.

11 She ſtretched out her branches unto the ſea: and her boughs unto the river.

12 Why haſt thou then broken down her hedge: that all they that go by, pluck off her grapes?

13 The wild boar out of the wood doth root it up: and the wild beaſts of the field devour it.

14 Turn thee again, thou God of hoſts, look down from

3

ſhall be whole.

Pſalm 81. *Exultate Deo.*

SIng we merrily unto God our ſtrength: make a cheerful noiſe unto the God of Jacob.

2 Take the pſalm, bring hither the tabret: the merry harp with the lute.

3 Blow up the trumpet in the new-moon: even in the time appointed, and upon our ſolemn feaſt-day.

4 For this was made a ſtatute for Iſrael: and a law of the God of Jacob.

T.J. 5 This

Figure 25. Jefferson's signature marks as they appear in *The Book of Common Prayer* (Oxford, 1752), shown in two details. After 1815, Jefferson changed from cursive to block initials in imitation of printed letters. (Courtesy of the University of Virginia Library.)

the contemporary preoccupation with conflicting models of authorship. The book was a copy of John Douglas's 1771 volume, *Milton Vindicated From the Charge of Plagiarism, Brought against him by Mr. Lauder.*[16] Lauder's book, *An Essay on Milton's use and Imitation of the Moderns in his Paradise Lost*, written in 1751, accused Milton (as its ironic title suggests) of piecing together *Paradise Lost* from passages translated into English from certain minor European epics written in Latin in the sixteenth and seventeenth centuries. As an early and aggressive expression of the anxiety mid-century writers like Lauder himself felt about the enormity of Milton's cultural authority—Samuel Johnson, who wrote a preface to the book, would use more genteel means to slay the literary father—Lauder identifies the aggrieved parties as imagined surrogates for himself.

The aggrieved parties, of course, had to be moderns; imitations of the ancients, as in Watts's *Imitation of the Psalms*, would constitute not plagiarism but emulation. Charges of plagiarism, an obsessive preoccupation of literary culture in the second half of the eighteenth century and the normative practice of journalism, thus had to do not only with the emergent valorization of originality but with the struggle for cultural authority characteristic of a political and cultural milieu that defined power as the capturing of audiences. Both the common use of "Cato" or "Cicero" as pseudonyms for political writers and MacPherson's creation of Ossian suggest how the past (like the public) was constantly ventriloquized for the purposes of masquerade and legitimation, but Lauder took the process further. He invented texts that are really his plagiarisms of Milton, folded into certain seventeenth-century Latin poetry, to attack Milton's "plagiarisms," which were actually original verse.

Not only was the most famous document of the Revolutionary period the object of charges of plagiarism, but so was the most famous visual image—Paul Revere's engraving of the Boston Massacre. Three days after Revere's print, *The Bloody Massacre perpe-*

trated in King-Street, went on sale on the morning of March 26, 1770, the Boston engraver and painter Peter Pelham sent off an angry letter to Revere:

When I heard that you was cutting a plate of the late Murder, I thought it impossible as I knew you was not capable of doing it unless you coppied it from mine and as I thought I had entrusted it in the hands of a person who had more regard to the dictates of honour and Justice than to take the undue advantage you have done of the confidence and Trust I reposed in you.

Though Revere had himself made a crude sketch of the scene immediately after the March 5 event, he was, as Pelham suggests, no artist. It seems almost certain that his engraving was copied virtually line-by-line from Pelham's drawing. On April 2 Pelham issued his own engraving from that drawing entitled *The Fruits of Arbitrary Power*.[17]

Given his "Expense of making a design, paying for paper, printing, etc." as well as the loss of any "proposed advantage," Pelham told Revere, it is "as if you have plundered me on the highway." He concluded: "If you are insensible of the Dishonour you have brought on yourself by this Act, the World will not be so."[18] Pointedly described as "An Original Print . . . taken on the Spot," Pelham's engraving would thus implicitly announce to the world Revere's dishonor and betrayal—his own act of "Arbitrary Power"—as well as that of the British. If, in Pelham's view, the Revere print committed as well as depicted a crime, Pelham hoped his print would constitute a punishment by giving the lie to the former's originality. But, published belatedly, Pelham's nearly identical print appeared to be the copy, thus beginning its slide into oblivion.

The accusations of plagiarism leveled against Jefferson mark another phenomenon: the growing separation between editorial and authorial roles. The overlapping of those roles had long provided a protective context for authorial agency and articulated an older understanding of the role of the author, not as the creator of original thoughts but as a disseminator of information, as one who applied the accumulated wisdom of others to new circumstances. John Adams's *Defence of the Constitutions*, for example, is largely a pastiche of often unidentified quotations from other sources, and the crucial section on the "passion for distinction" in his *Discourses on Davila* reproduces key passages from Adam Smith's *Theory of Moral Sentiments* without ever citing him.[19]

That overlap between editorial and authorial roles is best illustrated by James Burgh's *Political Disquisitions* (1775), a three-volume work much consulted by members of the Continental Congress that Caroline Robbins calls "perhaps the most important political treatise to appear in the first half of the reign of George III." In the preface, Burgh in effect effaces his authorship: "Most writers have a set of doctrines they would lay before the public in order to strengthen their own affections by the authority of established writers. But I read in order to observe what the best historical and political writers have said and to lay *that* before the public as decisive." In other words, Burgh is saying (and his list of books cited, prominently placed before the text, bears him out) that he has put his reading into narrative form. Everywhere he seeks to quote from those writers who "inculcate with such clearness and strength as must convince every reasonable reader" except in cases "where it may be supposed a writer may be partial to a particular sentiment." Then "it is an advantage to give his reader the same sentiment in the words of another instead . . . even if not of the first rank." The ideal expression must be not only sincere and persuasive but impartial. Partisanship must be effaced. Though Burgh's *Political Disquisitions* announces itself as a narrative anthology, *e pluribus unum*, one book made out of many, its specific references to the American situation and its subtitle, *An Enquiry into public Errors, Defects, and Abuses . . . calculated to draw the timely atten-*

tion of Government . . . to Saving the State, make clear that it is a personal and passionate argument, one that invokes the author/editor distinction only to dismiss it in practice—as Jefferson's critics would not let him do—as a misleading dichotomy.[20]

In fact, in the 1775 Philadelphia edition of *Political Disquisitions,* Burgh's American editor, Robert Bell, breaks into the appended alphabetized subscribers list. Below the name of John Sullivan, one of eighteen delegates to the Continental Congress therein listed, Bell editorializes in a manner that further blurs the distinction between editor and author:

> This Gentleman hath said "It is better that 50 Thousand Men should be slain (himself among the slain) than that 50 Thousand Men should live and be made slaves." The Editor of the American Edition of the *Political Disquisitions* hath taken the liberty of eternizing this sentence, as far as this work can preserve it, because he esteems it a saying worthy of the most renowned Heroes, Legislators, and Philosophers of Antiquity.[21]

Bell, in effect, offers an updated entry for inclusion in Burgh's collection of quotations.

What Burgh's text (along with Diderot's *Encyclopédie* and a host of other examples) makes immediately clear is that, contrary to the assertions of Jefferson's "pre-Romantic" critics, editing was far more than a "humble act of compiling" that stood in opposition to the assertion, validation, and fashioning of self supposedly peculiar to authorship. In the scientific culture of the second half of the eighteenth century, which linked power with the organization of knowledge, editing, especially editing that made multiple abridged texts available in one volume, was a proprietary, interpretive, appropriative, and often imperial act. It was the textual version of Rousseau's "*la main cachée*."

Jefferson's scissor-and-paste abridgement of the Gospels, "The Life and Morals of Jesus of Nazareth Extracted textually from the Gospels in Greek, Latin, French & English," isolated Jesus' words from what he saw to be their corrupting, supernatural narrative contexts and rearranged them to shape a radically different Christ and a radically different text.[22] Out of the four gospels, Jefferson composed, in effect, one gospel, rendered in four languages running in parallel columns to facilitate philological comparisons. Writing with scissors a text that would be for private use only, he expressed his most personal and radical theological opinions. Here the sensitive author who claimed in his *Autobiography* that the deletions from his "bill for establishing religious freedom" constituted "mutilations," a word he had used earlier to describe the edits of his Declaration, could himself wield the shaping editorial blade in an act of violent revisionism, one that left no holographic trace of the editor.[23] Twenty years earlier, in order to provide a procedural text on rules and conduct for the Senate, Jefferson had "endeavoured to collect and digest as much of [the rules of Parliament]" from a variety of sources as he deemed useful "in ordinary practice."[24] The result was his *Manual of Parliamentary Practice* (1801), an American work wrought from a number of English works. Assumed to be "but" a pastiche and not an authored book, it has been largely ignored.

Indeed, the motto *E Pluribus Unum* chosen in 1776 for the seal of the United States by a committee on which Jefferson sat, though ultimately deriving from Horace, was taken most familiarly from the motto of the *Gentleman's Magazine*.[25] That journal, begun in 1732, largely reprinted the best articles from numerous newspapers and appropriated the word *magazine* (previously meaning a warehouse for military supplies) to refer to the product. Thus "one out of many" refers to the anthologizing impulse, with its implicit stigmatizing of originality and its creation of a new whole, not out of whole cloth, but out of disparate fugitive pieces originating elsewhere. Of course, such a position was also a way of obscuring the radicalness of novelty by cloaking it in the authority of the past, concealing political experimentation in the Trojan horse of classical republicanism and masking fiction in the form of "tales of truth."

Overhearing his maxims used by Father Abraham in an open-air sermon against going into debt in order to purchase fine clothes, Franklin's Poor Richard is "wonderfully delighted" with the compliment, for "nothing gives an Author so great Pleasure as to find his Works respectfully quoted by others." The fact that Franklin is "conscious that not a tenth Part of the Wisdom was my own which he ascribed to me, but rather the *Gleanings* I had made of the Sense of all Ages and nations" does not markedly reduce his authorial pleasure. Profiting from "the Echo" of his own advice, Richard, who is also waiting for the Vendue to be opened, decides against "buying stuff for a new Coat." His resolve to "wear my Old One a little longer" mirrors his endorsement of the continuing utility of traditional wisdom. Original sentiments are potentially corrupting luxuries, essential to neither life nor authorship.[26]

One of the best literary serials featured in American magazines of the 1790's was Judith Sargent Murray's *The Gleaner*. The serial's male persona introduces himself in the first number as someone who has "been seized with a violent desire to become a writer . . . the smoothness of Addison's page, the purity, strength, and correctness of Swift . . . these must all veil to me." "Veil" used as a verb suggests that Murray's character is going to not only avail himself of the examples of Addison and Swift but also take refuge from the responsibility and visibility of authorship behind their examples. The speaker in fact declares that he has taken "the name, character and advocation of a GLEANER" in order that should "an accusation of plagiarism be lodged against me, my very title will plead my apology."[27]

The emphasis on gleaning is, in part, a response to and in dialogue with the growing availability of fiction and its implicit or explicit claims for the advantages of novelty, innovation, and imagination—even when those fictions were explicitly preaching against such concepts. Indeed, the earliest American paean to the power and glory (rather than the dangers) of imagination is Philip Freneau's "The Power of Fancy," written in 1770, when he was eighteen. Rejecting a materialist metaphor of God as architect and watchmaker of the world, Freneau insists that the earth and stars, man and beast, life and death, are but "Ideas of the Almighty mind" and "Fancies of the Power of Divine!" Made in God's image, man, too, has a creative force to which Freneau declares "I owe / Half my happiness below." Annihilating time and space, fancy allows him to become a mental traveler and ubiquitous spectator. His imaginative flights take him to Arcadia, Ossian's haunts, the Hebrides, and Hector's and Virgil's tombs. In a manner consistent with the larger cultural concerns of the period, the imagination is conceived of as the ultimate instrument of penetration. That penetration permits the exercise of sympathy, but it also represents the exercise of power, a power of imagination conceived along the same metaphorical lines as the new rhetoric:

> Thine were the notes that Orpheus played;
> By thee was Pluto charmed so well
> While rapture seizd the sons of hell.[28]

In the margins of a copy of Nathaniel Evans's *Poems* (1772), a collection of Americanized but formulaic Augustan odes and elegies owned and signed by Philip Freneau's journalist brother Peter, either Peter or Philip (their handwritings are nearly identical) has added up the number of subscribers, then enviously and disdainfully written: "975 readers for this miserable trash—hardly worth reading" (Figure 26).[29] The comment makes clear that a belief in the power of fancy—that man is a creative rather than mimetic creature—sanctioned, like the war, a revolutionary challenge to certain elements of the past, including the cyclical, antiprogressive, and thus pessimistic view of history at the heart of Augustan English verse, a view that minimized the distinctive originality of the present.[30]

In the same year that saw the publication of Evans's poems, the great Orientalist, jurist, and parliamentary opponent of the American war, Sir William Jones, published his landmark essay, "The Arts called Imitative." There he influentially insisted that expression replace mimesis as the primary value in the criticism of the arts. Artistic success in all fields is achieved, he argued, "not by

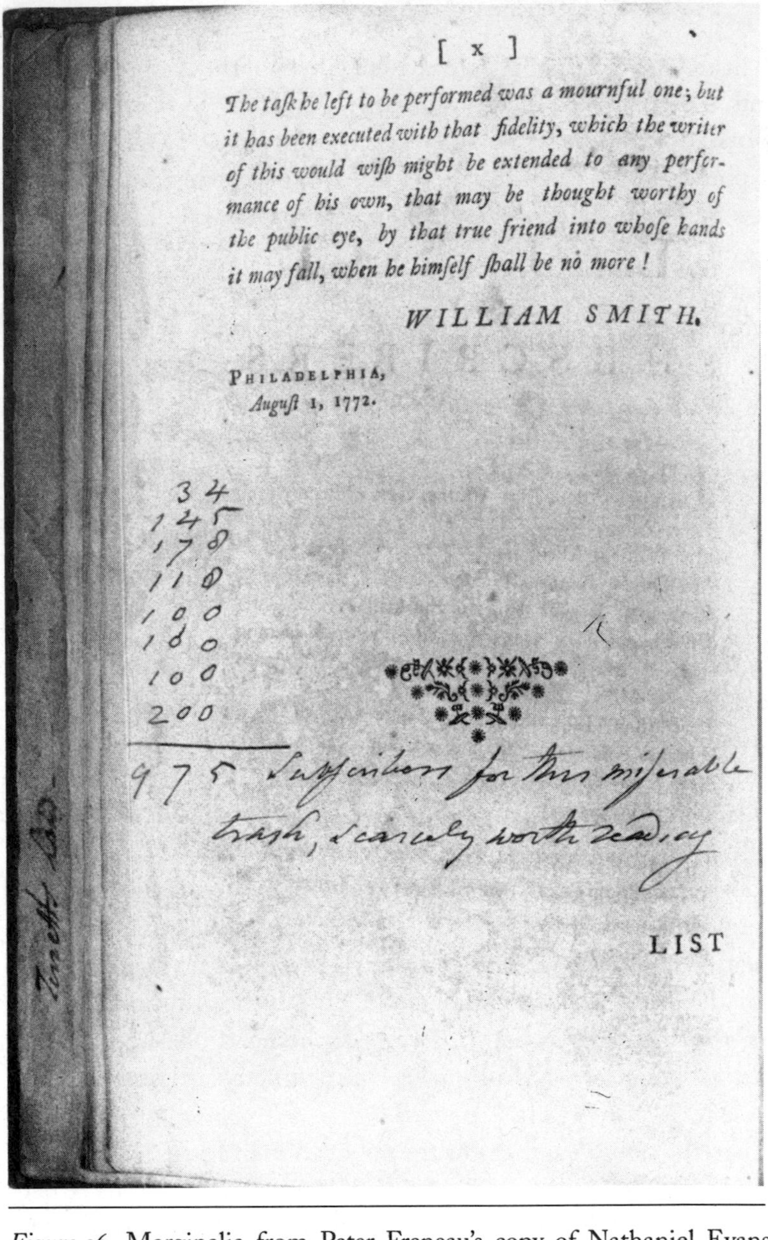

[x]

The task he left to be performed was a mournful one; but it has been executed with that fidelity, which the writer of this would wish might be extended to any performance of his own, that may be thought worthy of the public eye, by that true friend into whose hands it may fall, when he himself shall be no more!

WILLIAM SMITH.

PHILADELPHIA,
August 1, 1772.

34
145
178
110
100
100
100
200
975 Subscribers for this miserable trash, scarcely worth reading

LIST

Figure 26. Marginalia from Peter Freneau's copy of Nathaniel Evans, *The Poems on Several Occasions* (Philadelphia, 1772). (From the library of the author.)

L I S T

OF

S U B S C R I B E R S.

A

34 JOHN ALLEN, Eſq;
Andrew Allen, Eſq; Attorney Gen. of Pennſylvania
James Allen, Eſq;
Mr. William Allen, *jun.*
Mr. Dunlap Adams, Trenton
Lieutenant Stephen Adye, of the Artillery
Dr. Charles Alexander, Warfield, Frederick County, Maryland
Samuel Aliſon, Eſq; Burlington
Iſaac Allen, Eſq; Trenton, 2 Copies
Thomas Anderſon, Eſq; Suſſex County
Rev. John Andrews, A. M.
Miſs Jenny Annis
Samuel Armor, A. B.
Mr. Matthias Aſpden, 2 Copies
William Atlee, Eſq; Attorney at Law, Lancaſter
Mr. Samuel Atlee, Pequea
Mr. William Atmore, for the Library Comp. 2 Copies
William Axtell, Eſq; New-York

b 2 The

imitating the works of nature, but by assuming her power, and causing the same effect upon the imagination, which her charms produce to the senses."[31] The assumption of such power called for—as Freneau's marginalia also suggested—a new kind of author. Not surprisingly, in his essay entitled "Advice To Authors" (1786), the first American essay on that subject, Freneau defined that author by contrasting two kinds of orators. The mark of "a real author . . . an original author" is that he is no "piddling orator . . . cold and inanimate, not roused into action by the impelling flame of inspiration," but a "nervous Demosthenes who, stored with an immensity of ideas awakened within him he knows not how, has them at command upon every occasion."[32]

The early publication history of *Common Sense* makes clear that a decade before Freneau's essay, the claims and demands of a new quasi-professional class of authors (whose existence is attested to by the first national copyright act of 1790) ran a course parallel to the claims and ambitions of the new nation. That publication history sheds further light on the changing history and meaning of personal expression that frame the debate over what Jefferson's role was, or ought to have been, in the composition of the Declaration.

Having earlier, while still in England, been a victim of reprisals for his pamphlet attack on the collectors of the excise tax, Paine chose to publish *Common Sense* anonymously and to use Benjamin Rush as an intermediary to secure a publisher. He chose Robert Bell, the printer/editor of Burgh's *Political Disquisitions* and the proprietor of the Philadelphia circulating library, and the terms agreed to were half the profits for Paine, who would donate them to buy mittens for the freezing Continental soldiers, and half for Bell. Three weeks after publication, the bookseller insisted there were no profits, and an outraged Paine took an enlarged version to a new publisher, William and Thomas Bradford, announcing publicly that he had ended his agreement with Bell. Feeling betrayed, Bell printed an unauthorized second edition and lambasted Paine in *The Pennsylvania Evening Post*:

In the Evening Post of last Thursday, an author, without a name, hath asserted absolute falsehoods; he saith he gave directions and orders to the publisher of the first edition not to proceed. As soon as the printer and publisher discovered the capricious disposition of the ostensible author, he disclaimed all future connexion, and by the publication of a second edition . . . immediately declared his desirable independence from the trammels of catch-penny author-craft, whose cunning was so exceeding great as to attempt to destroy the reputation of his own first edition. . . . Said Bell farther saith, if he had either heard or received any such directions or orders, he would almost certainly have treated them immediately with that contempt which such unreasonable, illegal and tyrannic usurpations over his freedom and liberty in business deserved.[33]

Here was the American Revolution recast (and inverted) as the conflict between author and publisher. In Bell's version, the "humble Provedore to the Sentimentalists" sought to secure his freedom from the tyranny, not of state-craft or priest-craft, but "author-craft," from "a Would-be-Author" who is "whirligigged by imaginary importance," from a mere "shadow of an author with his Murdering Mask and his DARK LANTHORN, fully equipped for the ruffian business of assassination."[34] Bell's arrogant diatribe against catch-penny authors—the new populist class of professional writers supported by public patronage—suggests the then still widely held view, as Cathy Davidson has put it, that "the author was . . . a minor participant in the process of literary manufacture and one whose cash expenditures were also minor." There was "no compelling economic reason to support his or her labors."[35] Insisting on printing rights and authorial profits, if only to surrender them as he would shortly do, Paine published what he called the "declaration" of his authorial rights, setting before the audience of the *Pennsylvania Evening Post* his grievances against "this noisy man."[36]

Paine's declaration had a tradition. Eighteen years before *Common Sense*, James Ralph, a Philadelphian turned London Grub Street journalist, published the first full-length defense of the rights of that "new class" of professional authors: *The Case of Authors by Profession or Trade stated with Regard to Booksellers, the Stage and the Public.*

The larger challenge suggested by the conflict of old editorial and new authorial aesthetics, of editors and authors, of cultural preservation and innovation, was to conserve the past with its power to legitimate and authorize while at the same time embracing a certain degree of necessary novelty, thereby obeying Bacon's insistence that ancient texts no longer be blindly studied, but that nature and the world be studied directly. Thus, the cultural ideal, as the Connecticut poet David Humphreys put it, was "to aim at originality without rashness and imitation without servility." The crucial eighteenth-century concept that embodied that ideal was "emulation," a term John Adams defined in his *Discourses on Davila* as "imitation and something more, a desire not only to equal or resemble but to excel. Emulation next to self-preservation will forever be the great spring of human action."[37]

The ideal was at the heart of the apprentice/master relationship and perhaps was most famously described by Franklin in his account of using the *Spectator* as his model for good writing. After writing his own versions of the essays, comparing them, and then testing himself again, Franklin concluded in the *Autobiography*, "I sometimes had the Pleasure of Fancying that, in certain Particulars of small Import, I had been lucky enough to improve the method of the Language and this encourag'd me to think I might possibly come to be a tolerable English Writer, of which I was extremely ambitious."[38]

Emulation permitted the expression of ambition in the context of a larger reverence for the models of the past, an accommodation of authority and liberty, of ancients and moderns. It was a concept particularly suited to the agenda of neoclassicism. Art students like the American painter Benjamin West, who had gone to Rome in the 1760's to study classical sculpture, responded powerfully to the great paradox of neoclassicism set forth by Johann Winckelmann: "The only way for us to become great and, if possible, inimitable, lies in imitation of the Greeks."[39] The paradox was ironically validated by Winckelmann's repeated confusion of Roman copies with Greek originals. If properly interpreted, the past was a vehicle for liberation: imitation was a form of innovation. When Jefferson criticized England's "dread of innovation," which had "palsied the spirit of improvement" in that country, he made clear that what he meant by the absence of innovation was England's unwillingness to follow others' examples, "especially any example set by France."[40]

By 1764, Benjamin West had become so successful in London that he sent for his fiancée to join him. Accompanying her from Philadelphia were West's father and another relation, a painter by the name of Matthew Pratt. Though he was three years older than West and already had served a long apprenticeship in painting with his uncle, James Claypoole, Pratt was coming to join the West family as a student. In his journal, Pratt praised his famous teacher for rendering "me every good and kind office he could bestow on me, as if I was his father, friend and brother."[41]

In 1765, in the mode of a conversation piece, Pratt painted West's classroom studio. The painting, displayed in 1766 under the title of *The American School* (Figure 27), depicts the standing figure of West at the far left as he comments on a drawing shown to him by one of four students ranged around a small table. Two of the other students seem to have stopped their work to listen. There is some debate over which of the students is Pratt. The Metropolitan Museum of Art catalogue for the American Wing suggests that "though most of the figures are no longer identifiable . . . West is obviously the instructor and Pratt is thought to be the pupil seated next to him," the one displaying his work.[42] Robert Alberts, Ben-

Figure 27. Matthew Pratt, *The American School,* 1765. (Courtesy of the Metropolitan Museum of Art. Gift of Samuel P. Avery, 1897. (97.29.3))

jamin West's biographer, however, identifies Pratt as the balancing figure at the far right, seated in front of a canvas that is signed in the lower left corner "Matthew Pratt" (and that frames him as a painting within the painting). Like West, he also holds brushes and a palette, though his, unlike the palette of the instructor, contains the dominant colors of the painting—the green of the instructor's and youngest boy's suits, the blue of the middle student's jacket, and the red of the chairs, easel, and table.

Framing the question of Pratt's identity in terms of which figure represents him loses sight of a larger dynamic of identity in the painting. The strong horizontal that starts with the bust of a small boy, moves through three students, each older and larger than the other, and ends with the instructor himself suggests a double developmental progression, a biological one in which the child becomes a man, and an artistic one in which the student becomes the master. Indeed, a general resemblance among the students and the West figure reinforces the sense of process, the sense that the group portrait—with its echoes of family portraits—is simultaneously the portrait of a single figure at different stages of development. The cycle of emulation involves both venerating the teacher and—by submitting one's own "masterpiece," the piece by which one announces one is no longer an apprentice—supplanting or becoming him. Like a developmental theory of history that, for example, sees Native Americans as childlike versions of whites at an early stage of development, emulation involves an imperial recasting of "the other" as a version of the self at another temporal moment.

The crucial word *improve* at the heart of the concept of emulation carried less its current sense of "to make better" and more the sense of "making good use of, turning to good account," as a minister would improve a biblical passage, or "adapting to present circumstances," as Nahum Tate's *Shakespeare Improved* altered the plays to make them acceptable to the morals and taste of the day. The use of classical subject matter to address current political issues allegorically (a strategy necessitated on the English stage by the Licensing Act of 1737, which prohibited references to contemporary controversies) politicized the concept. Such improvement could also be retrospective. For example, John Adams insisted in 1805 that by changing the names in Conyers Middleton's "melancholy" life of Cicero, the "history of our own country for forty years past" could be read and "every anecdote will be applicable to us."[43] When transcribing certain passages into his commonplace book in the early 1770's, Jefferson himself often engaged in selective editing or improvement. In the case of Horace's second epode, as Gilbert Chinard has pointed out, "he did not change a word of it, but by simply omitting every detail that was purely Roman he succeeded in lifting out of time this picture of Roman farm life and in changing it into a description fitting exactly America."[44] Even the neologisms Jefferson coined either changed the form of another part of speech (*little* becomes *belittle*) or compounded two words (as with *breadstuffs*).[45] In an April 1776 letter to Samuel Cooper, Samuel Adams cautioned himself as well as his correspondent against an overeagerness to take history into one's own hands: "We cannot make Events. Our Business is wisely to improve them."[46] Improvement no less than emulation asserted the primacy of the given (be it present circumstances or past literary models) at the same time that it recognized the efficacy of human agency either to transcend its models or to redirect and transform its historical circumstances.

Franklin usually brought his political correspondence to a close with some variant of the traditional self-effacing formula, despite its antirepublican overtones: "I remain your humble and obedient servant." Though sometimes shortening it to "I have the honour to be, Sir &c." or even more casually to "I am &c.," Franklin—whether sincerely, habitually, or strategically—diligently observed the convention. Indeed, in what is a unique moment of political and personal rage in his correspondence, Franklin chose to ironize his epistolary formalism, rather than surrender it. On July 5, 1775, he wrote his longtime friend, the English printer and publisher William Strahan, what would become perhaps his most often reprinted letter:

> Mr. Strahan,
>
> You are a Member of Parliament, and one of the Majority which has doomed my Country to Destruction.—You have begun to burn our Towns and murder our People. Look upon your hands! They are stained with the Blood of your Relations!—You and I were long Friends:—You are now my enemy,—and
>
> I am
>
> Yours,
> B. Franklin[47]

But more than simple irony is at work. The line break frees Franklin from the more aggressive posture of the continuous sentence, while still linguistically enacting the break in their relations. Even more importantly, however, it introduces, by way of a control or limit, the deferential formula at precisely the moment of greatest aggression. Here, formalism becomes a strategy of conservation that implicitly denies that the assertion of one set of values necessarily must negate another. As was made clear by the inscription "Rebellion to Tyrants is Obedience to God" that Franklin claimed to have discovered on a cannon, and that Jefferson adopted as a personal motto, revolutionary separation need not mean abandoning a politics of deference. By maintaining the letter, if not the spirit, of his conventional valediction, Franklin balances his act of aggression with an act of conventional obedience. He enacts what Paine in *Common Sense* calls the "paradox" of those who "unite resistance and subjection," who will fight the British but won't yet embrace independence.[48] Furthermore, if the accountability of the "I" has been partially protected by Franklin's finesse, the accountability of "you" is progressively augmented. The first sentence is literal, descriptive, and corporate: "You are a Member of Parliament, and one of the Majority which has doomed my Country." The second and third are personalized, and insofar as they beg the question of actual agency, figurative: "You have begun to burn our Towns and murder our People. Look upon your hands!" To authorize a deed is to commit it. Add to this the fact that, as the most recent editor of the letter reads the evidence, the letter was "unquestionably" not sent.[49] In an act of self-censoring and self-control, Franklin seems to have retained the original. Writing it expressed and relieved the anger. Not sending it relieved the guilt.

In one way or another, most of the important literary texts of the postwar decade followed the double agenda of Franklin's letter and of Jefferson's Declaration. They are self-consciously written as evidence of America's literary nationalism, yet stylistically and thematically they are consciously derivative. They assert both their own and America's novelty at the same time that they insist on the necessity of preserving the authority of the European literary tradition. Barlow's *Columbiad* adopted the form of the classical epic while simultaneously rejecting the authority of Homer and Virgil, who in a postwar context were seen as militaristic and monarchical. The intertextual relations of Brackenridge's *Modern Chivalry* with *Don Quixote* or of Freneau's poem "The American Village" with Oliver Goldsmith's "The Deserted Village" suggest a mixture of aggressive revisionism with pious appreciation. Though Benjamin West violated artistic practice by painting the figures in *The Death of General Wolfe* (1770) in modern rather than classical dress, those figures strategically strike poses from antique and Christian art.

It is precisely in what might be called the subversive reverence by which an earlier work is invoked only to be taken liberties with that these works may be seen as reenactments of the late eighteenth-century debate over the proper balance or interdependence of authority and liberty, tradition and innovation. Indeed, a transmuted form of that debate defines a good deal of current scholarship on the American Revolution. For example, most notably in his magisterial *The Machiavellian Moment*, J. G. A. Pocock has argued that the American Revolution was "the last great act of the Renaissance," an extension of the tradition of civic humanism running from Machiavelli to Bolingbroke that stressed country virtue over court and commercial corruption and that insisted, in the words of Montesquieu, "a continual preference for the public interest over private ones is the source of all the individual virtues."[50] In contrast to this antimodernist view of the Revolution, Isaac Kramnick and others have championed a new version of an older understanding of the Revolution as committed to a liberal Lockean individualism, a market economy, and real principles of modernity and political novelty. For Pocock, Burgh's *Political Disquisitions* transmits an older political vision; for Kramnick, it largely articulates a new one.[51] This scholarly debate, which turns on the conjunction or disjunction of past and present, may be seen as schematizing a number of the late eighteenth-century cultural dialectics I have described in the pages above: tensions between personal expression and applied commonplace, between authorial and editorial modes, as well as the Janus-faced dynamics of emulation and improvement so central to the postcolonial project of deriving an indigenous identity from the creative appropriation of Old World materials as well as from their rejection.

If the reception of the Declaration at the end of the eighteenth century was preoccupied with the question of plagiarism, at least one immediate reaction recognized that the character of its originality lay not in its language or ideas but in its "manner," in its character as an address that one could imagine hearing "on the stage." If, as Franklin put it, "Modern Political Oratory [was] chiefly performed by the Pen and Press," Jefferson, in one particular reader's view, had succeeded in giving voice to the new oratorical ideal on paper, if not in person, in composition, if not in reading.[52] Responding on the floor of Parliament to the Marquis of Granby's attack on the Declaration of Independence, the longtime supporter of colonial rights, John Wilkes, who himself was described by a contemporary as "perhaps the best Manufacturer of paragraphs that ever lived," defended and praised the document, not on political grounds but on the grounds that it inaugurated a new theatrical era in political rhetoric, an era that correlated with a new political age. The crucial passage is worth quoting in full:

An honourable gentleman near me attacks the American Declaration of Independency in a very peculiar manner, as a wretched composition, very ill written, drawn up with the view to *captivate the people*. *That*, sir, is the very reason why I approve it most as a composition, as well as a wise political measure, for *the people* are to decide this great controversy. If they are captivated by it, the end is attained. The polished periods, the harmonious happy expressions, with all the grace, ease and elegance of a beautiful diction, which we chiefly admire, *captivate* the people of America very

> little; but manly, nervous sense, they relish even in the most awkward and uncouth language. Whatever composition produces the effect you intend in the most forcible manner is, in my opinion, the best, and that mode should always be pursued. It has the most merit, as well as succeeds, on the great theatre of the world, no less than on the stage, whether you mean to inspire *pity, terrour* or any other passion.[53]

Where sovereignty resides in the will of the people, language that "captivates" (a word that psychologizes enslavement and renders it benign) is the currency of power. Force is transformed into "forcible manner." The success of a composition rests not on the beauty of its ordered (and, as Wilkes implies, effeminate and class-specific) expression, but on the degree to which its "nervous [vigorous] manly sense" is permitted to break through the linguistic surface. It is not the admiration of the reader or auditor that one seeks to call forth, but captivated surrender to his or her passions. When Wilkes redefines compositional merit as essentially utilitarian success, stylistic perfection is denied the honor of being an end in itself. Wilkes would agree with Jefferson, who would later declare: "I have always despised the artificial canons of criticism. When I have read a work in prose or poetry . . . I have only asked myself whether it is animating, interesting and attractive? If it is, it is good for these reasons."[54]

Ironically, however, Wilkes's distinction between the rhetoric of the Declaration (and of course he is talking about the version revised by the Continental Congress) and the rhetoric of traditional parliamentary discourse might well have been invoked by Jefferson himself to distinguish the populist prose of Paine's *Common Sense* or the "uncouth," evangelically derived oratory of Patrick Henry from the dignified, albeit impassioned phrasing of his own Declaration. Though he would probably smart at parts of Wilkes's characterization, Jefferson would be obliged to acknowledge Wilkes's point: for late eighteenth-century revolutionary rhetoric to be truly revolutionary, it almost by definition was obliged to move in the direction of what Wilkes called the new theatrical and sentimental "mode."

The Oratorical Ideal, Racial Politics, and the Making of Americans

Committed to the dream of a natural language, or more precisely to the paradox of a natural theatricality, the oratorical revolution encompasses a wide range of related phenomena within the larger history of eighteenth-century expression. It may also be viewed as part of a larger history of consensus as a cultural ideal, a history lost sight of by those who would view consensus as merely the co-optation of dissent. Performative persuasion promised to generate a new and much-needed consensus by proposing sincerity as a new form of social and political legitimacy, as an antidote to various strains of epistemological skepticism, and as a control on the fact that politics was for the first time becoming a profession in ways that undermined traditional understandings of leadership. Simultaneously, by making the character of the speaker primary it introduced a crucial principle of discrimination into a rhetorical world in which more and more frequently opposing political and social groups employed the same discourse of democratic ideals.

The elocutionary texts of the period did not intend to democratize social and political leadership; they sought instead to transform the terms of its authority and accountability. Yet the larger oratorical revolution still carried considerable unintended social and personal costs, among them a tendency toward social leveling and the generation of a new and acute self-consciousness about the display (on the model of the larger market economy) of what in effect was a newly constructed model of a commodified private self. Indeed, the oratorical revolution was rife with internal conflicts—between self-control and passionate expression; between self-effacement and self-assertion; between transcendent representativeness and personal revelation; between theatrical and natural models of rhetoric; between conventional and natural signs; between spontaneity and impersonation; between an understanding of identity as the sum total of a person's different social roles and self-presentations and an essentialist understanding of identity that assumed a fixed self informed by a common humanity; between action and speech; between sincerity and hypocrisy; between self-willed agent and other-directed instrument; between rational persuasion and affective appeal; between logic and rhetoric; between stoicism and sentimentality; between argument and self-evidence; between voluntarism and involuntarism; between words and sounds; exteriority and interiority; texts and music; harmony and melody. The oratorical ideal that loomed so large in the America of 1776 presumed to contain or mediate these conflicts. To the degree that it succeeded it did so by serving as a site of those conflicts, a historically neglected but crucial battleground of American Revolutionary culture.

What ultimately made possible the Declaration's initial rhetorical act of independence—its assertion that Americans were "one people," different from "our British brethren"—was, as I have suggested at the outset, the insistence that in the aestheticized politics of pathos, those "unfeeling brethren" were "deaf to the voice of justice & of consanguinity" in a fashion that Americans were not. The dissolving of "the political bands which have connected" those two peoples followed logically from the a priori fact that Americans already occupied a separate and unequal station.[1] In an 1814 letter to Thomas Law on the subject of the moral sense, Jefferson insisted that God, intending "man for a social animal," had planted in him "social dispositions." Jefferson quickly added, however, cavalierly undermining the essentialism and universalism of the previous sentence, that "it is true they are not planted in every man, because there is no rule without exceptions." Though the moral sense was as much a part of man as "sight, hearing, and hands," some men might be born without those faculties. Others might lose them through fate or malignant folly.[2]

What was initially set forth as a universal code on which the new oratory declared itself based became in Revolutionary America a particular cultural code whose audibility signified the possession of a sensibility others lacked; in turn, possession of that sensibility was the very test definition of being an American, the principle of national differentiation. If, as Paine summarized it, the essential British argument was "that the colonies have no relation to each other but through the parent country . . . [as] sister colonies," what was needed was not a new polity but a new sociology, one that could imagine social relations on terms other than familial.[3] Though it drew much of its rhetorical power from invoking the "voice of consanguinity" (the voice of the abused child wronged by an unnatural and unfeeling parent), sensibility articulated a higher bond that transcended both the bonds of descent through the father and, by its involuntarism, the nullifiable bonds of contract and consent. At the heart of sensibility, as Paine made clear, was its insistence on the subordination of government ("a necessary evil") to the higher claims of society ("in every state a blessing")—not the Rousseauian society of common interest, but the society of common feeling.[4]

Toward the end of the draft version of the Declaration, Jefferson muses, "we might have been a free and a great people together; but a communication of grandeur & of freedom it seems is below their dignity." The larger paragraph gives no specific indication what Jefferson means by such "a communication." Garry Wills connects it with both Francis Hutcheson's view of society as founded "on the intercourse of kindness" and the French idea of "*gloire*." But this seems insufficient to explain the precise language. The "communication of grandeur & of freedom" whose expression distinguishes the American people from the British seems ultimately, if silently, to refer to the Declaration itself. In a concealed or unconscious moment of self-reference, Jefferson makes the Declaration and its writing a synecdoche for the larger capacity among members of a feeling society for free and dignified intercourse.[5]

But it was not only Tories and the British public who were excluded from that feeling society. The problem of how to speak disguised the larger social problem of who could speak. During his tenure at William and Mary, George Wythe, the first American professor of law, tutored not only the fatherless Jefferson (to whom he served as something of a surrogate parent), but Madison and John Marshall. Subsequently, he signed the Declaration as the senior member of the Virginia delegation. Several decades later he was murdered by his nephew for an inheritance. Though Wythe's slave was an eyewitness to the poisoning, Virginia law declared that a black could not testify against a white. Thus, as a vastly ironic footnote to the life of America's first law professor, the nephew went free.[6]

Indeed, the oratorical revolution had its own deeply racist dimension, especially because of its roots in physiognomy. In *Notes on the State of Virginia*, Jefferson argues for black inferiority in aesthetic terms:

> The first difference that strikes us is of color—a difference fixed in nature. . . . And is this difference of no importance? Is it not the foundation of a greater or less share of beauty in the two races? Are not the fine mixtures of red and white, the expressions of every passion by greater or less suffusions of colour in the one, preferable to that eternal monotony, which reigns in the countenances, that immovable veil of black which covers all the emotions of the other race?[7]

In contrast to the infinitely responsive interaction of white and red pigments (like the flag's alternating stripes), the "veil of black" permits no visible register of emotions, and hence no emotional communication. Without the ability to blush, that involuntary publication of private feeling, there is no register of the operations of social conscience. Though Jefferson would elsewhere draw the essentialist and racist inference that blacks feel fewer emotions (as their blackness is "immovable," so are their sensibilities), here he is stating the problem at the level of epistemology, of penetrability. In opposition to an ideal of transparency, blacks are inscrutable, thus posing the ultimate threat to a culture insisting on the legibility of its sensible citizens.

The very mask that in one context might be coveted as a protection of private feelings, a relief from social scrutiny or physiognomic scanning, becomes a literally dehumanizing prison when that mask transmutes into the countenance itself. (Even Hannah Foster's coquette, who "puts on her face," or in modern parlance "makes herself up," only blurs the distinction between face and mask, never destroying it.) At the level of argumentation, however, the fear of impenetrability becomes recast as an aesthetic distaste for monotony. Blacks, in their blackness, violate an aesthetics of variety. Significantly, that same variety is the touchstone for Jeffersonian liberalism: a state-coerced "uniformity of opinion," Jefferson insists in *Notes*, is as undesirable as a uniformity of "face and stature."[8] For Jefferson the musician, the word "monotony" was an aural term, metaphorically extended to the visual. Thus the limited textuality of blacks' countenances (for white Americans) had as analogues the fact that their speaking was limited to "the level of plain narration" and the fact that the chords of the African "banjar" were equivalent to but "the four lower chords" of the full-toned Western guitar that derived from it.[9] Their "monotony" was also a way of talking about their undevelopable and thus unchanging moral character, again in contrast to the Indians'. Indeed, in a letter written in the spring of 1776, Richard Henry Lee described the movement for independence as the logical outcome of the conviction that "a person [might as well] expect to wash an Ethiopian white, as to remove the taint of despotism from the British court."[10] Blacks were the byword for visible essentialism.

Benjamin Banneker, the son of Baltimore free blacks, put his mathematical talents to computing the "ephemeris," or positions of the sun, moon, and planets from which could be derived the solar and lunar eclipses, tide tables, and weather forecasts for a new almanac. By doing so he not only proved himself talented enough to join Andrew Ellicott in surveying the site for the new national capitol but stood, as one contemporary newspaper put it, "an Ethiopian, whose abilities . . . clearly prove that Mr. Jefferson's concluding that race of men were void of mental endowments, was without foundation."[11] To underscore the point that "the colour of the skin is in no ways connected with . . . intellectual powers," the editor of *Benjamin Banneker's Almanac* for 1793 strategically invoked the most famous use of the word *blush* in English literature, the quatrain from Thomas Gray's *Elegy in a Country Churchyard* in which the poet reflects on the great careers of which an early death has cheated those entombed before him:

> Full many a gem of purest ray serene,
> The dark unfathom'd caves of ocean bear
> Full many a flower is borne to blush unseen.
> And waste its fragrance on the desert air.[12]

The fate of talented but "untutored" blacks is to "blush unseen." Yet in so blushing they disprove the stigmatized "monotony" that, according to Jefferson, marked their race. In the same year that the Banneker almanac appeared, a yellow fever epidemic killed five thousand in Philadelphia alone. Because of their supposed racial immunity to the contagion, blacks were enjoined to care for the sick and to remove and bury the dead. When their heroism went unappreciated, Absolam Jones and Richard Allen wrote a pamphlet protesting that "our services were the production of real sensibility," not biological insensibility.[13]

But black sensibility, even if it were conceded, could not buy membership in the republic of letters, and black heroism could not technically attain the status of civic heroism. If the dominant object of both eighteenth-century oratory and fine arts was, as John Barrell puts it, "to promote the public performance of acts of public virtue," then oratory and the arts were necessarily addressed to and produced by "those who are imagined to be capable of performing such acts"—to citizens, those "capable not only of being ruled but also of ruling." Public virtue, which according to the doctrines of civic humanism was the ground and epitome of all true virtue, thus had no meaning for disenfranchised blacks, who were not part of that public, that corporate citizenry, and it had only a circumscribed meaning for women. Full membership in the republic of letters, the republic of taste, or the republic of virtue—either as producer or consumer—required prior political enfranchisement. Though Jefferson would remind the readers of *Notes* that "Epictetus, Terence, and Phaedrus were slaves" in order to make his point that color and not condition was the root cause of black inferiority, he would not dispute Hugh Blair's assertion: "Never did a slave become an orator" because "liberty . . . is the nurse of true genius."[14]

If America, like Bell's Philadelphia circulating library, was a place where "Sentimentalists, whether Ladies or Gentlemen, may become Readers," evidence of that sentimentality, of an enlarged emotional responsiveness, was essential to membership. If African-Americans and Tories failed that test (significantly, colonial grievances against the English government spoke repeatedly of its "unresponsiveness"), Jefferson achieved an equivocal and hard-won pass. For him, the lyre of Orpheus, a trope for the production of sentiment as a form of cultural power, posed enormous challenges. Those challenges inspired Jefferson to write the Declaration in what he called "the proper tone and spirit called for by the occasion."[15] But when it came to public speaking, especially in the presence of the aristocrats of the "empire of eloquence over the heart," they all too often reduced him to an anxious and self-conscious whisperer.[16] Rarely traveling without a tiny violin on which to practice quietly at night—Patrick Henry played by ear; Jefferson couldn't—and a duodecimo volume of his favorite author, Sterne, buried in his pocket, Jefferson preferred to keep his sentimental credentials to himself.[17] Yet the reading marks on the rough draft of the Declaration speak eloquently of the pervasive social drama of personal expression in which Jefferson, his document, and his culture so fully participated, a drama at the heart of Revolutionary and early national culture. In the spaces of the opening paragraphs of the official Dunlap printing of the Declaration (where, miscopied as quotation marks, those reading marks had once stood) there is a lost world of meaning. The revolution in self-expression and the American Revolution constitute crucially defining chapters in one another's history.

Epilogue

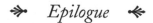

Arriving in Philadelphia in May 1776 after a ten-day trip from Williamsburg (a trip he had made several times during his fifteen-month attendance at the Continental Congress), Jefferson rented from Benjamin Graff, Jr., a room on the second floor of Graff's three-story house at Seventh and Market. In that room, on a portable desk of his own design, he drafted (or, to underscore the architectural analogy, draughted) the Declaration. A half century later that house had become a men's ready-to-wear clothing store with a large sign over its door announcing itself as the "BIRTH-PLACE OF LIBERTY." Some time in the early 1830's the proprietor, one William Brown, issued a pictorial trade card (Figure 28) advertising "The Birth-Place of Liberty" with the following copy:

> When in the course of human events it becomes necessary for Gentlemen to cast off their faded garments, and appear in such new habiliments as the laws of *Fashion and Comfort* call for, a decent respect for the *Memory of*

our Revolutionary Patriots demands that they should all call and purchase their external covering at the *Birth-Place of Liberty*, which is the identical and time-honored edifice in which the IMMORTAL PATRIOT, THOMAS JEFFERSON, *Penned the Glorious Declaration of our Unalienable Rights, Among which are Life, Liberty and Genteel Garments.*

We hold these truths to be self-evident, that all men are treated equal—that they can obtain Clothing as rich, as cheap, and as durable as at any other establishment in the nation, either by the dozen or single garment. . . . Our shelves are now filled with the choicest collection of Fashionable Ready-made Clothing consisting of . . . Cloaks, oversacks, Sack Coats, Monkey Jackets, Business Sacks, Frock Sacks, Catalonia Cloaks, Dress and Frock Coats, Pantaloons and Vests.

When Jefferson wrote that "all men are created equal," he meant they are created by "nature's God" with the same natural (that is, moral) faculties. Though nurture, environment, and experience could not efface those faculties, they would necessarily develop them differently and unequally. Thus, as a fact of natural history, Jefferson's statement of equality was far from a radical call for social equality.[1] But in the 25 years after Jefferson's death in 1826, an unfinished revolutionary agenda of social equality would be read back into the Declaration, a document endlessly appropriated and invoked. Nat Turner's slave revolt would be first planned for July 4, Thoreau would complete his cabin on July 4, the Seneca Falls Declaration of Sentiments would rewrite the Declaration to include women, and socialist John Humphrey Noyes, pushing the point as far as it could go, would set forth an instrument similar "to the Declaration of '76 renouncing my allegiance to the United States," a personal secession anticipating what someone named Jefferson Davis would later declare for the South.[2] Add to these "Wm. Brown, Proprietor," whose advertisement suggests that clothing bought at the "Birth-Place of Liberty" is capable of bringing about a symbolic effacement of class difference.

As the figures in the trade card suggest, cheap, ready-made "Genteel Garments"—and ready-made clothing was still a novelty

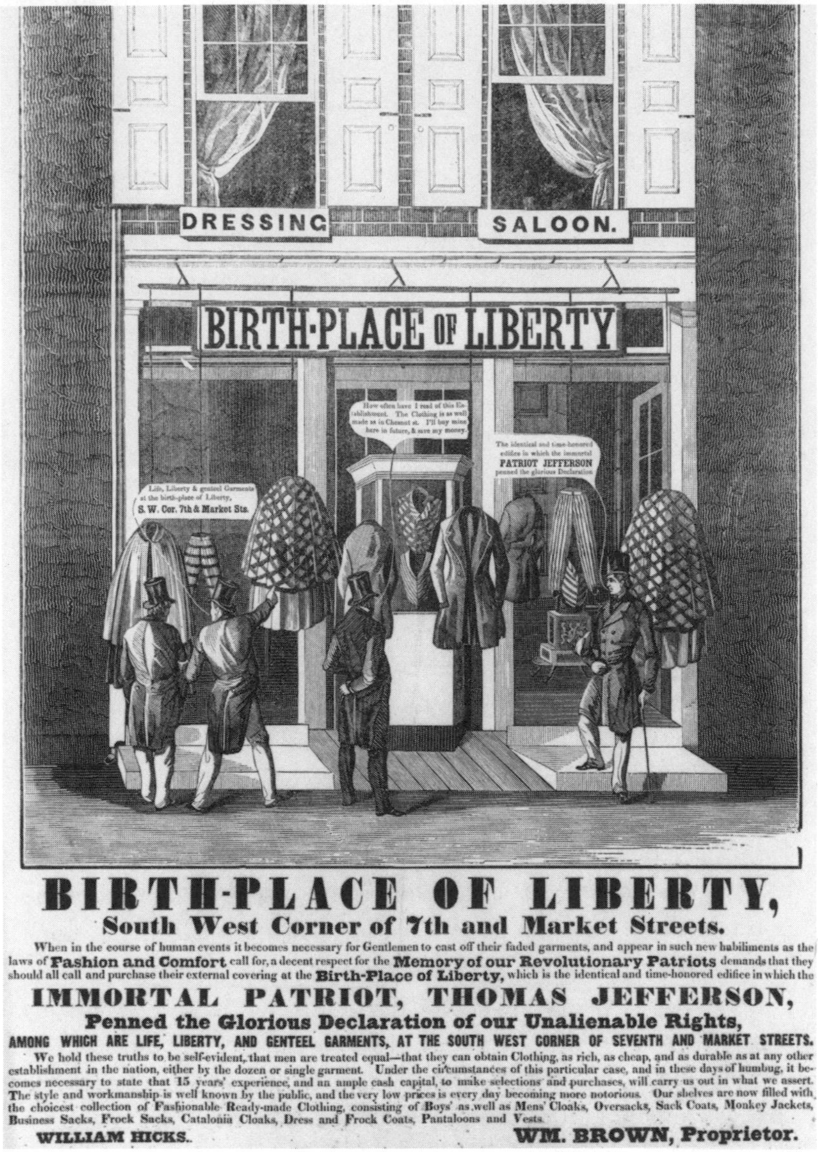

Figure 28. "The Birth-Place of Liberty," trade card, c. 1830. (Courtesy of The New-York Historical Society, New York City.)

in the 1830's—allowed everyone to look like a gentleman in lieu of ever becoming one. In a world that had witnessed the breakdown of dominance by the landed gentry (a breakdown that forced Jefferson's debt-ridden offspring to sell Monticello with an ad reading "the desire to sell is sincere"), gentility inheres in the clothes, not in the man.[3] Equality is neither natural nor social, but a function of all consumers being treated as equals by shopkeepers. If in an earlier generation clothes were precise markers of social standing, and in addition, as Carlyle put it in *Sartor Resartus*, "gave us individuality, distinction, social policy," they were now "threatening to make Clothes-screens of us."[4] No longer "incarnations of an inner substance, mastered role, or established class position," clothes had become costumes, disguises that allowed people to dress without regard to their station.[5] The quest to encounter naked nature, to encounter man as man, stripped of what Paine called the "plumage" of an artificial hierarchical society (which Burke romanticized as the "decent drapery of life"), seems a dead letter here, not just because the clothing has lost its transparency, but because the man beneath the clothing has become a mannequin. Men and mannequins stand as doubles in Brown's trade card.[6]

Once an instrument of infinite expressiveness and the repository of the mysteries of divine creation, the body itself has become denatured. It obeys the "laws of fashion" rather than those of nature, and expresses generalized consumer aspirations rather than those of an individual or national character. "As Montesquieu wrote a *Spirit of Laws*," Carlyle announced, "so could I write a *Spirit of Clothes*,"[7] for natural law (or more properly a faith in its discoverability) had been replaced by the cultural imperatives of fashion. The figures on Brown's trade card repeat in cartoon-bubble dialogue the copy of the advertisement, and vice versa. "The Birth-Place of Liberty," in contrast to its protestations, is a site not of liberation but of endless transformations masquerading as freedom. The building presents itself as a relic still possessed of the aura of living history, but it too is emptied out. The IMMORTAL

PATRIOT, THOMAS JEFFERSON becomes a sandwich sign for a commercial world of externalities that has trivialized the complex eighteenth-century drama of being a figure in public, of expressing one's self publicly. The alternately naive and cunningly strategic quest to find a voice and visual self-presentation that are true to nature, society, nation, and self has become, in this telling nineteenth-century image, little more than an existential confidence game. Yet at the same time, "The Birth-Place of Liberty" offers precious asylum from the exhausting demand that the rule of sincerity be obeyed, that private and public character cohere in a single, externalized self.

APPENDIX

The Declaration of Independence as originally reported to Congress.

(Taken from Jefferson's "Notes of Proceedings" in *Papers*, 1: 315–19. The parts struck out by Congress are in italics and brackets. Those words and phrases added are in bold type. Following Jefferson's text, the last paragraph is given in concurrent columns.)

A Declaration by the representatives of the United states of America, in [*General*] Congress Assembled

When in the course of human events it becomes necessary for one people to dissolve political bands which have connected them with another, and to assume among the powers of the earth the separate & equal station to which the laws of nature and of nature's god entitle them, a decent respect to the opinions of mankind requires that they should declare the causes which impel them to the separation.

We hold these truths to be self evident: that all men are created equal; that they are endowed by their creator with [*inherent and*] **certain** inalienable rights; that among these are life, liberty & the pursuit of happiness; that to secure these rights, governments are instituted among men, deriving their just powers from the consent of the governed; that whenever any form of government becomes destructive of these ends, it is the right of the people to alter or to abolish it, & to institute new government, laying it's foundation on such principles, & organising it's powers in such form, as to them shall seem most likely to effect their safety & happiness. prudence indeed will dictate that governments long established should not be changed for light & transient causes; and accordingly all experience hath shewn that mankind are more disposed to suffer while evils are sufferable than to right themselves by abolishing the forms to which they are accustomed. but when a long train of abuses & usurpations, [*begun at a distinguished period and*] pursuing invariably the same object, evinces a design to reduce them under absolute despotism it is their right, it is their duty to throw off such government, & to provide new guards for their future security. such has been the patient sufferance of these colonies; & such is now the necessity which constrains them to [*expunge*] **alter** their former systems of government. the history of the present king of Great Britain is a history of [*unremitting*] **repeated** injuries & usurpations, [*among which appears no solitary fact to contradict the uniform tenor of the rest but all have*] **all having** in direct object the establishment of an absolute tyranny over these states. to prove this let facts be submitted to a candid world [*for the truth of which we pledge a faith yet unsullied by falsehood*].

he has refused his assent to laws the most wholsome & necessary for the public good.

he has forbidden his governors to pass laws of immediate & pressing importance, unless suspended in their operation till his assent should be obtained; & when so suspended, he has utterly neglected to attend to them.

he has refused to pass other laws for the accomodation of large districts of people, unless those people would relinquish the right of representation in the legislature, a right inestimable to them, & formidable to tyrants only.

he has called together legislative bodies at places unusual, uncomfortable, and distant from the depository of their public records, for the sole purpose of fatiguing them into compliance with his measures.

he has dissolved representative houses repeatedly [*& continually*] for opposing with manly firmness his invasions on the rights of the people.

he has refused for a long time after such dissolutions to cause others to be elected, whereby the legislative powers, incapable of annihiliation, have returned to the people at large for their exercise, the state remaining in the mean time exposed to all the dangers of invasion from without & convulsions within.

he has endeavored to prevent the population of these states; for that purpose obstructing the laws for naturalization of foreigners, refusing to pass others to encourage their migrations hither, & raising the conditions of new appropriations of lands.

he has [*suffered*] **obstructed** the administration of justice [*totally to cease in some of these states*] **by** refusing his assent to laws for establishing judiciary powers.

he has made [*our*] judges dependant on his will alone, for the tenure of their offices, & the amount & paiment of their salaries.

he has erected a multitude of new offices, [*by a self assumed power*] and sent hither swarms of new officers to harass our people and eat out their substance.

he has kept among us in times of peace standing armies [*and ships of war*] without the consent of our legislatures.

he has affected to render the military independant of, and superior to the civil power.

he has combined with others to subject us to a jurisdiction foreign to our constitutions & unacknoleged by our laws, giving his assent to their act of pretended legislation for quartering large bodies of armed troops among us; for protecting them by a mock trial from punishment for any murders which they should commit on the inhabitants of these states; for cutting off our trade with all parts of the world; for imposing taxes on us without our consent; for depriving us **in many cases** of the benefits of trial by jury; for transporting us beyond seas to be tried for pretended offences; for abolishing the free system of English laws in a neighboring province, establishing therein an arbitrary government, and enlarging it's boundaries, so as to render it at once an example and fit instrument for introducing the same absolute rule into these [*states*] **colonies**; for taking away our charters, abolishing our most valuable laws, and altering fundamentally the forms of our governments; for suspending our own legislatures, & declaring themselves invested with power to legislate for us in all cases whatsoever.

he has abdicated government here [*withdrawing his governors, and declaring us out of his allegiance & protection*] **by declaring us out of his protection & waging war against us**.

he has plundered our seas, ravaged our coasts, burnt our towns, & destroyed the lives of our people.

he is at this time transporting large armies of foreign mercenaries to compleat the works of death, desolation & tyranny already begun with circumstances of cruelty and perfidy **scarcely paralleled in the most barbarous ages, & totally** unworthy the head of a civilized nation.

he has constrained our fellow citizens taken captive on the high seas to bear arms against their country, to become the executioners of their friends & brethren, or to fall themselves by their hands.

he has **excited domestic insurrections amongst us, & has** endeavored to bring on the inhabitants of our frontiers the merciless Indian savages, whose known rule of warfare is an undistinguished destruction of all ages, sexes, & conditions [*of existence*].

[*he has incited treasonable insurrection of our fellow-citizens, with the allurements of forfeiture & confiscation of our property.*

he has waged cruel war against human nature itself, violating it's most sacred rights of life and liberty in the persons of a distant people who never offended him, captivating & carrying them into slavery in another hemisphere or to incur miserable death in their transportation thither. this piratical warfare, the opprobrium of infidel *powers, is the warfare of the* Christian *king of Great Britain. determined to keep open a market where* Men *should be bought & sold, he has prostituted his negative for suppressing every legislative attempt to prohibit or to restrain this execrable commerce. and that this assemblage of horrors might want no fact of distinguished die, he is now exciting those very people to rise in arms among us, and to purchase that liberty of which he has deprived them, by murdering the people on whom he also obtruded them: thus paying off former crimes committed against the* Liberties *of one people, with crimes which he urges them to commit against the* lives *of another.*]

In every stage of these oppressions we have petitioned for redress in the most humble terms: our repeated petitions have been answered only by repeated injuries. a prince whose character is thus marked by every act which may define a tyrant is unfit to be the ruler of a **free** people [*who mean to be free. future ages will scarcely believe that the hardiness of one man adventured, within the short compass of twelve years only, to lay a foundation so broad & so undisguised for tyranny over a people fostered & fixed in principles of freedom*].

Nor have we been wanting in attentions to our British brethren. We have warned them from time to time of attempts by their legislature to extend [*a*] **an unwarrantable** jurisdiction over **us** [*these our states*]. we have reminded them of the circumstances of our emigration & settlement here, [*no one of which could warrant so strange a pretension: that these were* *effected at the expence of our own blood & treasure, unassisted by the wealth or the strength of Great Britain: that in constituting indeed our several forms of government, we had adopted one common king, thereby laying a foundation for perpetual league and amity with them: but that submission to their parliament was no part of our constitution, nor ever in idea, if history may be credited: and,*] we **have** appealed to their native justice and magnanimity [*as well as to*] **and we have conjured them by** the ties of our common kindred to disavow these usurpations which [*were likely to*] **would inevitably** interrupt our connection and correspondence. they too have been deaf to the voice of justice & of consanguinity, [*and when occasions have been given them, by the regular course of their laws, of removing from their councils the disturbers of our harmony, they have, by their free election, re-established them in power. at this very time too they are permitting their chief magistrate to send over not only souldiers of our common blood, but Scotch & foreign mercenaries to invade & destroy us. these facts have given the last stab to agonizing affection, and manly spirit bids us to renounce for ever these unfeeling brethren. we must endeavor to forget our former love for them, and hold them as we hold the rest of mankind enemies in war, in peace friends. we might have been a free and a great people together; but a communication of grandeur & of freedom it seems is below their dignity. be it so, since they will have it. the road to happiness & to glory is open to us too. we will tread it apart from them, and*] **we must therefore** acquiesce in the necessity which denounces our [*eternal*] separation [*!*] **and hold them as we hold the rest of mankind, enemies in war, in peace friends**.

We therefore the representatives of the United states of America in General Congress assembled do in the name, & by the authority of the good people of these [*states reject & renounce all allegiance & subjection to the kings of Great Britain & all others who may hereafter claim by, through or under them: we utterly dissolve all political connection which may heretofore have sub-*

We therefore the representatives of the United states of America in General Congress assembled, appealing to the supreme judge of the world for the rectitude of our intentions, do in the name, & by the authority of the good people of these colonies, solemnly publish & declare that these United colonies are & of right ought to be free & independant

sisted between us & the people or parliament of Great Britain: & finally we do assert & declare these colonies to be free & independant states,] & that as free & independant states, they have full power to levy war, conclude peace, contract alliances, establish commerce, & to do all other acts & things which independant states may of right do. and for the support of this declaration we mutually pledge to each other our lives, our fortunes & our sacred honour.

states; that they are absolved from all allegiance to the British crown, and that all political connection between them & the state of Great Britain is, & ought to be, totally dissolved; & that as free & independant states they have full power to levy war, conclude peace, contract alliances, establish commerce & to do all other acts & things which independant states may of right do.

and for the support of this declaration, with a firm reliance on the protection of divine providence we mutually pledge to each other our lives, our fortunes & our sacred honour.

REFERENCE MATTER

Notes

INTRODUCTION

1. On the elocutionary revolution, see Wilbur Samuel Howell, *Eighteenth-Century British Logic and Rhetoric*, chapter 4; Clarence W. Edney, "English Sources of Rhetorical Theory in Nineteenth-Century America"; Peter de Bolla, *The Discourse of the Sublime: Readings in History, Aesthetics and the Subject*, chapter six; Murray Cohen, *Sensible Words: Linguistic Practice in England, 1640–1785*. The opening chapter of Kenneth Cmiel's *Democratic Eloquence: The Fight over Popular Speech in Nineteenth-Century America* offers an excellent account of rhetoric and the social order in late eighteenth-century America. Chapter three of Howell provides a full account of the older Ciceronian tradition, which, though challenged, remained influential.

2. John Adams to Jedidiah Morse, March 10, 1815, in *Works*, 10: 182.

JEFFERSON'S PAUSES

1. William Wirt, *Sketches of the Life and Character of Patrick Henry*, p. 23.

2. John Adams, *Diary and Autobiography*, 3: 335. Adams speculates that Jefferson was put on the Committee on Style charged with drafting the Declaration in part because the famed orator "Mr Richard Henry Lee was not beloved by the most of his Colleagues from Virginia and Mr. Jefferson was sett up to rival and supplant him. This could be done only by the Pen, for Mr. Jefferson could stand no competition with him or any one else in Elocution and public debate." (*Diary and Autobiography*, 3: 336.)

3. Garry Wills, *Inventing America: Jefferson's Declaration of Independence*, p. 16.

4. Frank L. Dewey, *Thomas Jefferson, Lawyer*, p. 98.

5. Alf J. Mapp, *Thomas Jefferson*, p. 397.

6. Jeffrey K. Tulis, *The Rhetorical Presidency*, pp. 70–71.

7. John H. Hazelton, *The Declaration of Independence and Its History*, p. 178.

8. Julian Boyd, "The Declaration of Independence: The Mystery of the Lost Original," p. 458. On Jefferson's early ownership of Rice's *Art of Reading*, see Millicent Sowerby, *Catalogue of the Library of Thomas Jefferson*, 1: 51. Jefferson assembled several libraries during his lifetime. Using the physical evidence of the surviving books from those libraries, as well as Jefferson's manuscript catalogues, invoices, and references in his letters. Sowerby's heavily annotated work tries to establish when Jefferson was in possession of a particular book and what edition he possessed.

9. Boyd, "Declaration," p. 458.

10. Thomas Jefferson, "Thoughts on Prosody," in *The Complete Jefferson*, p. 846.

11. Thomas Sheridan, *The Art of Reading; First Part: Containing The Art of Reading Prose*, pp. 181, 210.

12. Thomas Sheridan, *A Course of Lectures on Elocution*, p. 79. On Jefferson's purchase of Sheridan, see Marie Kimball, *Jefferson: The Road to Glory, 1743–1776*, p. 83.

13. Sheridan, *Lectures on Elocution*, pp. 79–80.

14. Ibid., p. 77.

15. Randolph is quoted in Wills, *Inventing America*, p. 9.

16. Sheridan, *Lectures on Elocution*, p. 77.

17. The letter recommending Mason's volume is reproduced in Morris L. Cohen, "Thomas Jefferson Recommends a Course of Law Study." John Mason, *Essay on the Power and Harmony of Prosaic Numbers*, p. 2. Jefferson is quoted in Henry S. Randall, *The Life of Thomas Jefferson*, 1: 131. The works on musical theory that appear in Jefferson's 1783 book catalogue are conveniently listed in Helen Cripe, *Thomas Jefferson and Music*, p. 97. She describes his traveling violin on pp. 14–15. Several months before his 1761 legal arguments against the Writs of Assistance set the stage for future challenges to British authority, the incendiary lawyer James Otis published *The Rudiments of Latin Prosody with . . . the Principles of Harmony in Poetic and Prosaic Composition.* Drawing heavily on "Mason on Pronunciation," Otis's first published work used the subject of prosody—pronunciation informed by a knowledge of the "spirit, accent, and qualities of words"—to address what was a social and political question as much as a literary one: how best to "convey the passions of the speaker into the breasts of the audience" (pp. 2, 66).

18. Francesco Geminiani, *The Art of Playing the Violin*, p. v. Published in 1769 in Boston, Geminiani's volume was the first book on the subject printed in America; John Holden, *Essay Towards a Rational System of Music*, p. 35.

19. John Bender and David E. Wellbery, "Rhetoricality," p. 21.

20. Jefferson to Henry Lee, May 8, 1825, in *Writings*, 16: 118.

21. John Rice, *An Introduction to the Art of Reading*, pp. 236–37.

22. Lord Kames, *Elements of Criticism*, p. 404; Jefferson to Skipwith, in *Papers*, 1: 79; Thomas Paine, *The Thomas Paine Reader*, p. 123.

23. Jefferson to (name missing in original letter), June 28, 1778, in Eleanor D. Berman, *Thomas Jefferson Among the Arts*, p. 172.

24. Morris L. Cohen, "Thomas Jefferson Recommends," p. 824.

25. Cripe, *Jefferson and Music*, p. 69.

26. *The Complete Jefferson*, p. 846.

27. Jefferson, *Commonplace Book*, p. 351.

28. For an intellectual and cultural history of sincerity with particular reference to changing notions of personal identity, see Lionel Trilling, *Sincerity and Authenticity*. On sincerity in eighteenth-century English letters, see Leon Guilhamet, *The Sincere Ideal: Studies on Sincerity in Eighteenth-Century English Literature*.

29. Worthington Chauncey Ford, ed., *Journals of the Continental Congress*, 5: 516.

30. Mason Lowance and Georgia B. Bumgardner, eds., *Massachusetts Broadsides of the American Revolution*, p. 47.

31. John Adams, *Papers*, 4: 372–73.

32. The first two phrases are from Jefferson's 1776 "Notes of Proceedings in the Continental Congress," in *Papers*, 1: 309, 314. The third is from the draft of the Declaration as originally reported to Congress. Drawing on his 1776 "Notes of Proceedings," Jefferson reproduced that draft with the changes made by the Continental Congress in his *Autobiography*. For convenience, I have reprinted that draft as an appendix to this volume. Though I have used a slightly different mode of display, I have followed the text as given in Jefferson, *Papers*, 1: 315–19. Unless otherwise indicated, all citations to the Declaration are to this appendix. In this case see Appendix, pp. 207, 206.

33. Kames, *Elements of Criticism*, p. 470. On Kames's popularity in American colleges, see George V. Bohman, "Rhetorical Practice in Colonial America," p. 55.

34. Sheridan, *Lectures on Elocution*, p. xii.

35. Thomas Jefferson, *Autobiography*, p. 70.

36. Madison is quoted in Jeffrey Smith, *Printers and Press Freedom: The Ideology of Early American Journalism*, p. 164.

37. Hugh Blair, *Lectures on Rhetoric and Belles Lettres*, p. 312.

38. Morris L. Cohen, "Thomas Jefferson Recommends," p. 843.

39. William Wordsworth, "Preface" to *Lyrical Ballads*, p. 437.

40. Gordon Wood, "Democratization of Mind in the American Revolution," p. 74. Congressional public galleries were opened in 1794.

41. Bohman, "Rhetorical Practice," p. 66.

THE ELOCUTIONARY REVOLUTION

1. Stevenson's translation of Fénelon is quoted in Howell, *Logic and Rhetoric*, p. 440.

2. Ibid., p. 442.

3. Adam Smith, *Lectures on Rhetoric and Belles Lettres*, p. 182.

4. See note 1 in the Introduction.

5. Warren Guthrie, "Rhetorical Theory in Colonial America," p. 59; Sowerby, *Catalogue*, 1: 511.

6. James Burgh, *The Art of Speaking*, p. 4.

7. Sheridan, *Lectures on Elocution*, p. x.

8. Burgh, *The Art of Speaking*, p. 3; John Moore, *The Young Gentleman and Lady's Monitor and English Teacher's Assistant*, p. 369.

9. Burgh is quoted in Frederick W. Haberman, "English Sources of American Elocution," in Karl Wallace, ed., *A History of Speech Education in America*, p. 115. In an article entitled "Observations on Faces" appearing in the July 1775 issue of the *Pennsylvania Magazine*, the anonymous author enumerates the variety of things that can be inferred from "the fashion of wearing our faces, or rather the features of the face." These include nationality, the state of national manners, occupation, and the character of present feeling. Because "there is a certain kind of countenance or fashion of the features, which a man insensibly puts on in the way of his business," the author can tell the trades of all those who assemble outside the Philadelphia coffeehouses. Because "men who have things at heart, cannot expunge them from their faces," he can also infer the "general tenor" of any "fresh intelligence" by marking the differing countenances of Whigs and Tories. He needn't read the latest newspaper if he can read the face of its reader (p. 304).

10. Burgh, *The Art of Speaking*, pp. 28–29.

11. Ibid., p. 7.

12. Ibid., p. 38.

13. Immanuel Kant, *Critique of Judgment*, p. 398.

14. L. H. Butterfield, ed., *Adams Family Correspondence*, 1: 97. In their classic study *Dialectic of Enlightenment* (1944), Max Horkheimer and Theodor Adorno argue that the central agenda of the Enlightenment was

the disenchantment of the world by a dominating rational inquiry. At the heart of the Enlightenment's banishment of superstition, irrationality, and mystery was a "dread of losing the self and of abrogating together with the self the barrier between oneself and other life" (p. 33). Horkheimer and Adorno offer as the situation of the individual bound by Enlightenment rationality the figure of Odysseus lashed to the mast in an effort to avoid surrendering to the seductive beauty of the Sirens' song. With its abjuring of rational argumentation in favor of a form of affective seduction, however, the new oratory appropriated the Sirens' song itself, with its promise of a transcendent surrender. Yet Horkheimer's and Adorno's emphasis on the Enlightenment dread of losing the self to passion (a loss moralized against in the sentimental novel) remained an important and pervasive concern of eighteenth-century American culture. Feeling guilty about leaving his country in March 1776 for the island of Santa Cruz, the poet Philip Freneau compares himself to Ulysses tempted by "delicious nectar" to quit "his friends, his country, and his all." *Poems of Philip Freneau*, 1: 260.

15. Paine, in *Reader*, p. 213.

16. Thomas Paine, *Common Sense*, p. 65; Paine, *Reader*, 283; Ramsay is quoted in Gordon S. Wood, *The Radicalism of the American Revolution*, p. 235.

17. Revere's dentistry advertisement is in Esther Forbes, *Paul Revere and the World He Lived In*, p. 130.

18. Edmund Morgan is quoted in Thomas Miller's introduction to his edition of John Witherspoon, *Selected Writings*, p. 26.

19. Witherspoon, *Selected Writings*, p. 233.

20. Blair, quoted in P. W. K. Stone, *The Art of Poetry, 1750–1820: Theories of Poetic Composition and Style*, p. 52. Stone offers a brief history of the "language as the dress of thought" trope.

21. For perhaps the best example of Copley's lace work, see *Mrs. Daniel Sargent* (1763). A color reproduction is included in Marc Simpson et al., *The American Canvas*, p. 31.

SOFT COMPULSION

1. Jefferson to Henry Lee, May 8, 1825, in *Writings*, 16: 118.

2. Benjamin Franklin, *Autobiography*, p. 88.

3. Jefferson, *Papers*, 10: 451.

4. Adams is quoted in Lewis P. Simpson, *The Brazen Face of History: Studies in the Literary Consciousness in America*, p. 54.

5. Hume is quoted in Terry Eagleton, *The Ideology of the Aesthetic*, p. 45.

6. Johann Caspar Lavater, *Essays on Physiognomy*, p. 7.

7. Stephen Burroughs, *Memoirs*, p. 224.

8. Franklin, *Autobiography*, pp. 180, 178. Responses to Whitefield are cited in Alan Heimert, *Religion and the American Mind: From the Great Awakening to the Revolution*, p. 228.

9. Jefferson to Page, in *Papers*, 1: 11.

10. John Quincy Adams, *Memoirs*, 3: 441–42.

11. Ibid., 442. "Soft compulsion" is Adams's translation of a phrase from Manilius; Jefferson, *Papers*, 1: 12; Charles Brockden Brown, *Wieland, or The Transformation*, p. 5.

12. Adam Smith, *The Theory of Moral Sentiments*, p. 3.

13. Eagleton, *Ideology of the Aesthetic*, pp. 25, 24.

14. John Quincy Adams, *Lectures*, 1: 17.

15. John Adams, *Earliest Diary*, p. 74.

16. Murray Cohen, *Sensible Words*, p. 109; John Adams, *Papers*, 4: 87; George Mason is quoted in Edmund Morgan, *Inventing the People: The Rise of Popular Sovereignty in England and America*, p. 272.

17. Sheridan, *Lectures on Elocution*, pp. 2–3.

18. Thomas Reid, *An Inquiry into the Human Mind on the Principles of Common Sense*, p. 32.

19. Barlow is quoted in William C. Dowling, *Poetry and Ideology in Revolutionary Connecticut*, p. 119.

20. Paine, *Common Sense*, p. 68.

21. Isaiah Thomas, *History of American Printing*, 2: 250–51.

22. John Barrell, *English Literature in History, 1730–1780*, p. 34; Noah Webster, *Dissertations on the English Language*, p. 20. On the subject of "local standards," regional idioms, and accents, Alexander Cowie has concluded: "Speech varied so sharply in different parts of the country that at the time of the First Continental Congress members from different localities had difficulty understanding each other." *The Rise of the American Novel*, p. 1.

23. John Herries, *Elements of Speech*, pp. 24–25.

24. Bentham is quoted in Steintrager, *Bentham*, p. 26; Paine, *Common Sense*, p. 92; Paine, *Rights of Man*, in *Reader*, p. 227. For an intellectual history of the relationship between political corruption and linguistic corruption, see Thomas Gustafson, "Representative Words: Politics, Literature, and the American Language, 1776–1865."

25. Rice, *The Art of Reading*, p. 5.

26. Franklin, *Autobiography*, p. 88.

27. Reid, *Inquiry*, pp. 38, 34.

28. Hans Aarsleff, *The Study of Language in England, 1780–1860*, p. 22; Blair, *Lectures*, p. 47; Tooke is quoted in Aarsleff, *The Study of Language*, p. 23.

29. Murray Cohen, *Sensible Words*, p. 109.

30. William Hill Brown, *The Power of Sympathy*, p. 6.

31. Ibid., p. 7.

32. John Perkins, *Theory of Agency or, An Essay on the Nature, Source and Extent of Moral Freedom*, 1: 147. On the rattlesnake, see Benjamin Smith Barton, *A Memoir Concerning the Fascinating Faculty which has been ascribed to the Rattle-Snake, and other American Serpents* (1796).

33. Brown, *The Power of Sympathy*, p. 83.

34. John Ward is quoted in Howell, *Logic and Rhetoric*, p. 74.

35. Lord Kames, *Sketches of the History of Man*, 2: 183, 2: 257.

36. Campbell is quoted in Howell, *Logic and Rhetoric*, p. 405.

37. Wilbur Samuel Howell, "The Declaration of Independence and Eighteenth-Century Logic," p. 471.

38. Geoffrey Seed, *James Wilson: Scottish Intellectual and American Statesman*, p. 127.

39. Howell, "Declaration," p. 480. In the course of his detailed and instructive reading of the political content, structure, and style of the Declaration, "Justifying America: The Declaration of Independence as a Rhetorical Document," Stephen E. Lucas challenges Howell's argument. See footnote 64, p. 126. Its title apart, Lucas's essay largely ignores the rhetorical theories and issues with which I am concerned.

40. Aristotle is quoted in John Richetti, *Philosophical Writing: Locke, Berkeley, Hume*, p. 6. Richetti offers a very useful account of the nonrhetorical pose of eighteenth-century philosophy and its stylistic consequences. Jefferson to Henry Lee, May 8, 1825, in *Writings*, 16: 118.

41. Thomas Jefferson, *A Summary View of the Rights of British America*, in *Papers*, 1: 134.

42. Thomas Jefferson, *Notes on the State of Virginia*, p. 275 n. 98. See Appendix, p. 204.

43. Jefferson, *Summary View*, in *Papers*, 1: 134. See Appendix, p. 205.

44. On Jefferson and Bacon, see Albert Furtwangler, *American Silhouettes: The Rhetorical Identities of the Founders*, p. 124. A problem that Jefferson, scientific positivism, and the new oratory did not address would later be suggested by a comment made by the detective in Edgar Allan Poe's "The Purloined Letter." On the whereabouts of the letter, Dupin comments that its hiding place may be "a little *too* self-evident" (*Collected Works: Tales and Sketches*, 2: 975). Poe's larger point is that the most

pervasive aspects of reality—psychological, social, and environmental—are the most difficult to see.

45. John Adams is quoted in Barnet Baskerville, *The People's Voice: The Orator in American Society*, p. 17.

46. Thomas Paine, *The Age of Reason*, in *Reader*, pp. 420, 404.

47. Alexander Hamilton, *Papers*, 1: 121–22.

48. Franklin's nostalgia for printing "between the restoration and the accession of George 2d" is quoted in Rollo G. Silver, *The American Printer, 1787–1825*, p. 146.

49. Joseph Priestley is quoted in Brian Vickers, *In Defense of Rhetoric*, p. 304.

50. For a sophisticated account of the character of print culture in eighteenth-century America, an account that rightly warns against the sentimental assumption that print is elitist and speech egalitarian, see Michael Warner, *Letters of the Republic: Publication and the Public Sphere in Eighteenth-Century America*, chapter 1. For the dynamics of oral culture in Revolutionary America, see Rhys Issac, *The Transformation of Virginia, 1740–1790*; Donald Weber, *Rhetoric and History in Revolutionary New England*; Richard D. Brown, *Knowledge is Power: The Diffusion of Information in Early America, 1700–1865*, chapters 4 and 5; and Harry S. Stout, "Religion, Communication, and the Ideological Origins of the American Revolution." On the interaction of orality and print, see Walter Ong, *Orality and Literacy: The Technologizing of the Word*. However, it is crucial to recognize that rather than merely standing in opposition to print, orality can also be, and in the eighteenth century often was, a defining characteristic of print, a set of cues within a text that signal it is to be heard by the ear (as performance) as much as it is to be read by the eye.

51. Francis Hopkinson's 1786 article, which first appeared in the *Pennsylvania Packet*, is collected in *Miscellaneous Essays*, 2: 179–93; William Thornton, *Cadmus*, p. 90. Bemoaning the fact that written English has so little attachment to spoken English that "to read and write and speak the same things" requires learning "two different languages," Thornton, a friend of Jefferson, proposed an American language with a number of new letters to make written speech phonetically capable of accommodating the full range of spoken sounds. He addressed his readers: "Mai diir kuntrimen" (p. iv). Franklin is quoted in Silver, *The American Printer*, pp. 146–47. In the same 1789 letter to Noah Webster, Franklin discusses the "physiognomies" of typefaces.

52. Boswell is quoted in Fredrick Bogel, *Literature and Insubstantiality in Later Eighteenth-Century England*, p. 184.

53. Walker is quoted in Murray Cohen, *Sensible Words*, p. 116.

54. Robert Darnton, *The Great Cat Massacre and Other Episodes in French Cultural History*, pp. 234–35.

55. Charles Brockden Brown, *Arthur Mervyn: Or, Memoirs of the Year 1793*, p. 427.

56. *The Adventures of Jonathan Corncob*, p. 3.

57. Olaudah Equiano, *The Interesting Narrative of the Life of Olaudah Equiano or Gustavus Vassa, the African*, p. 44. The review is quoted on p. 8.

58. J. Hector St. John de Crèvecoeur, *Letters from an American Farmer*, pp. 41, 48, 35. On Bell's library, see Edwin Wolfe II, *The Book Culture of a Colonial American City: Philadelphia Books, Bookmen, and Booksellers*, p. 197.

59. Jefferson, *Papers*, 1: 77.

60. Leon Howard, *The Connecticut Wits*, p. 46.

61. Ibid., p. 47.

62. See Appendix, pp. 203, 206, 207; *The Complete Jefferson*, p. 849.

HARMONIES: HOMER, FUGUES, AND CHAIRS

1. Steven Shankman, *Pope's "Illiad"*, pp. 74, 78; Jefferson to John Waldo, August 16, 1813, in *The Complete Jefferson*, p. 884.

2. Franklin is quoted in Mitchell Breitwieser, *Mather and Franklin: The Price of Representative Personality*, p. 299; Franklin on Scottish ballads is quoted in Carl Van Doren, *Benjamin Franklin*, p. 325.

3. James H. Stam, *Inquiries into the Origin of Language*, p. 72. For representative extracts from Blackwell and Wood, see Burton Feldman and Robert D. Richardson, *The Rise of Modern Mythology, 1680–1860*.

4. On silhouettes in general, see E. Nevill Jackson, *Silhouettes: A History and Dictionary of Artists*. For another metaphorical use of silhouettes, see Furtwangler, *American Silhouettes*, p. 13.

5. Lord Kames, *Introduction to the Art of Thinking*, 62.

6. Jefferson to Thomas Jefferson Randolph, November 24, 1808, in *The Portable Jefferson*, p. 513.

7. Thomas Jefferson, *Manual of Parliamentary Practice*, p. 40.

8. The distinction between the two documents is made by Jürgen Habermas in his *Theory and Practice*, p. 89.

9. Quoted in David McKay and Richard Crawford, *William Billings of Boston*, pp. 14, 15. I am indebted to the McKay and Crawford biography for my account of the state of church singing in the period.

10. John Adams, *Papers*, 2: 104.

11. Peter Oliver, *Peter Oliver's Origin and Progress of the American Revolution, A Tory View*, 41. Another instance of the normalizing power of

print was the regularizing of Jefferson's inconsistent spelling (e.g., dependant/independent) in the printed Declaration. Because spelling in this period was usually phonetic and thus a clue to pronunciation, editorial decisions to normalize spelling silence the contemporary voice.

12. For words and music, see Vera Brodsky Lawrence, *Music for Patriots, Politicians, and Presidents*, p. 62.

13. Oliver Strunk, ed., *Source Readings in Music History: The Classic Era*, p. 27.

14. See Breitwieser, *Mather and Franklin*, chapter 6; John Holden, *Rational System of Music*, p. 8.

15. On Jefferson and Burney, see Cripe, *Jefferson and Music*, p. 10. Charles Burney, *The Present State of Music in France and Italy*, p. 19. On Jefferson and opera, see Berman, *Jefferson Among the Arts*, p. 19.

16. William Billings, *New England Psalm Singer*, p. 3.

17. Billings's essay on the fugue, which first appeared as the introduction to his *Continental Harmony* (1794), is quoted in McKay and Crawford, *William Billings*, pp. 176–77.

18. Ibid., p. 177.

19. *The Portable Jefferson*, p. 301.

20. Charles F. Montgomery and Patricia Kane, eds., *American Art, 1750–1800: Towards Independence*, p. 166. See also Charles Santore, *The Windsor Style in America*.

21. On the politicizing of consumer behavior, see Timothy Breen, "'Baubles of Britain': The American and Consumer Revolutions of the Eighteenth Century."

22. The phrase is Breen's, ibid., p. 75.

23. Chastellux is quoted in Mitchell Breitwieser, "Jefferson's Prospect," p. 315. On Jefferson's chair, which probably was built by Francis Trumbull, who also supplied the chairs for Carpenters Hall, in which the Continental Congress met, see Silvio Bedini, *Declaration of Independence Desk*, p. 7. The definition is to be found in Noah Webster, *A Dictionary of the English Language* (1828).

24. Kames, *Elements of Criticism*, pp. 466, 467, 468, 466.

25. Warren is quoted in Wood, "Democratization," p. 71. Quincy is quoted in Bertram Wyatt-Brown, *Southern Honor: Ethics and Behavior in the Old South*, p. 40. Declaration, see Appendix, p. 207.

26. Thomas Bolton, *An Oration*, is reprinted in David Potter and Gordon L. Thomas, eds., *The Colonial Idiom*, pp. 301–3.

27. The musical attack on "Whorators" is in Lawrence, *Music for Patriots*, p. 41.

28. Boucher's history (which was not published until 1797) is quoted in

Stout, "Religion," p. 539. By way of Whig counterpoint, see Benjamin West's politically charged painting *Daniel Interpreting to Belshazzar the Handwriting on the Wall* (1775), in which the king only understands the prophecy of doom once the mysterious text on the wall is translated into the oratorical gestures of Daniel that dominate the image. West at the time was court painter to George III.

29. The Tory broadside, which has no other title, is item 14518 in Charles Evans, *American Bibliography*, vol. 5.

30. Allen is quoted in Stout, "Religion," p. 537.

31. Though Preston did not say the word "fire" (Private Hugh Montgomery seems to have shouted the word when knocked to the ground), one irony of the event was that even before shots were fired, in what seems to have been a calculated effort to draw an anti-British crowd into the fray, church bells rang the alarm for "fire." In consequence, "fire"—the noun rather than the verb—was shouted by numerous frightened citizens, thus providing, with the sound of the bells, a strange choral backdrop to the voices of those who actually taunted the Redcoats by daring them to fire. Beyond any particular agency, the sound of "fire" took on a life of its own on the night of March 5. See Hiller B. Zobel, *The Boston Massacre*, pp. 196–97. It did so again five years later. After Dr. Joseph Warren, dressed in a "Ciceronian Toga," delivered his 1775 oration on the anniversary of the Boston Massacre, several British officers cried out "O fie, O fie." Misheard as "fire," this created a panic and a mad exodus from the Old South Meetinghouse. Those fleeing ran into a British regiment on maneuvers outside and "assumed they were about to be slaughtered." John C. Miller, *Sam Adams: Pioneer in Propaganda*, p. 330.

32. Paine, *Reader*, pp. 211, 123.

NATURAL THEATRICALITY

1. Quintilian is quoted in John Quincy Adams, *Lectures*, 1: 138.

2. See Appendix, p. 206.

3. Blair, *Lectures*, pp. 312, 314.

4. Herries is quoted in Murray Cohen, *Sensible Words*, pp. 108, 112. A facsimile of one of Herries' charts appears on p. 113.

5. Burgh, *The Art of Speaking*, p. 5.

6. Adams, *Earliest Diary*, p. 74. Charles Willson Peale, *An Essay to Promote Domestic Happiness*, p. 17. Current scientific thinking seems to confirm Peale's view that a constructed facial expression can often stimulate the same autonomic activity that is stimulated by the "real" experiencing of the emotion that the expression "naturally" represents. See Paul

Ekman et al., "Autonomic Nervous System Activity Distinguishes Among Emotions."

7. Burgh, *The Art of Speaking*, p. 12; William Cockin, *The Art of Delivering Written Language*, p. 9.

8. Burgh, *The Art of Speaking*, p. 9.

9. Jean-Jacques Rousseau, *Emilius and Sophia, or a New System of Education*, 2: 183.

10. Charles Brockden Brown, *Ormond: or, The Secret Witness*, p. 116.

11. Rousseau is quoted in Jean-Christophe Agnew, *Worlds Apart: The Market and the Theater in Anglo-American Thought, 1550–1750*, p. 190. For good accounts of the antitheatrical tradition, see *Worlds Apart* and Jonas Barish, *The Antitheatrical Prejudice*.

12. Charles Stearns, *Dramatic Dialogues for the Use of Schools*, p. 12.

13. Dorinda Evans, *Mather Brown: An Early American Artist in England*, p. 51.

14. All quotations in this paragraph are culled from Charles Coleman Sellers, *Patience Wright: American Artist and Spy*, pp. 94, 49, 4, 204.

15. Kalman A. Burnim, *David Garrick, Director*, p. 58.

16. Sellers, *Patience Wright*, pp. 169–70.

17. Ibid., p. 145.

18. Kenneth Silverman, *A Cultural History of the American Revolution*, p. 383.

19. John Woolman, *Journal*, p. 131.

20. Jefferson, *Papers*, 1: 456.

21. Ibid., 471.

22. Broadside is quoted in Silverman, *Cultural History*, p. 249.

23. M. Guralnick, "The All-Seeing Eye," p. 66. See Steven C. Bullock, "The Revolutionary Transformation of American Freemasonry, 1752–1792."

24. Newspapers are quoted in Silverman, *Cultural History*, pp. 241, 211.

25. Adams and the congressional resolution are quoted ibid., pp. 365, 271. The word "discountenance" figures disapproval as a facial sign and stricture. Versions of the word "countenance" as a verb and noun are omnipresent in the period. In a letter printed in Franklin's *Autobiography*, Benjamin Vaughn urges Franklin to publish his "Biography and Art of Virtue" to assist those "who try to keep themselves in countenance [free from shame or discouragement] by examples of other truly great men." Fully aware of the irony, Franklin later describes giving up his project for "moral Perfection" lest his surely inimitable example put out of countenance friends he wishes to keep "in Countenance." *Autobiography*, pp. 138, 156.

26. Witherspoon is quoted in Agnew, *Worlds Apart*, p. 191.

27. On this trope, see David Marshall, *The Figure of the Theater*. Indeed, David Hume describes the mind itself as "a kind of theatre, where several perceptions successively make their appearance; pass, re-pass, glide away, and mingle in an infinite variety of postures and situations," *Enquiries Concerning Human Understanding and the Principles of Morals*, p. 253. The couplet from "The Universal Prayer" is "Teach me to feel another's Woe / To hide the Fault I see," in Alexander Pope, *Pope: Poetical Works*, p. 626.

28. Adams, *Diary and Autobiography*, 1: 282.

29. Hopkinson, *Miscellaneous Essays*, 1: 103.

30. Bishop Berkeley, "On the Prospect of Planting Arts and Learning in America," quoted in Silverman, *Cultural History*, p. 232.

31. William Dunlap, *A History of the American Theater*, 1: 123. Philip Freneau, *Poems*, 2: 108. Jeffrey H. Richards, *Theater Enough: American Culture and the Metaphor of the World Stage, 1607–1789*, which draws on some of the same passages I do, came to my attention after my manuscript was complete. Richards's concern, however, is with tracing the *theatrum mundi* trope in American letters, rather than with exploring tensions between the natural and the theatrical.

32. Adams, *Diary and Autobiography*, 3: 397.

33. See Franklin, *Autobiography*, p. 180.

34. Adams, *Diary and Autobiography*, 3: 263.

35. Butterfield, ed., *Adams Family Correspondence*, 3: 93–94.

36. John Quincy Adams, *Lectures*, 2: 375–76. One salient fact Adams omits is that it is from the Greek word for actor, *hupokrites*, that "hypocrite" emerges.

37. John Adams to Benjamin Rush, June 21, 1811, in John A. Schutz and Douglass Adair, eds., *The Spur of Fame: Dialogues of John Adams and Benjamin Rush*, p. 182.

38. Ibid., pp. 42–43. For another reading of this passage and of Adams's competitive feelings, see Larzer Ziff's new book, *Writing in the New Nation*, pp. 108–12.

39. John Adams to Jefferson, July 30, 1815, and Jefferson to John Adams, August 10, 1815, in Lester J. Cappon, ed., *The Adams-Jefferson Letters*, pp. 451–52.

40. John Adams to Benjamin Rush, December 25, 1811, in Schutz and Adair, eds., *The Spur of Fame*, pp. 201–2.

41. Adams on Hutchinson is quoted in Peter Shaw, *The Character of*

John Adams, p. 228. On Adams and titles, see James H. Hutson, "John Adams' Titles Campaign."

THE FIGURE OF PATRICK HENRY

1. Daniel Webster, *Papers*, 1: 372.
2. Jefferson, *Autobiography*, p. 26.
3. Ibid., p. 22.
4. Edmund Randolph, *History of Virginia*, p. 179.
5. Ibid., p. 180.
6. Quoted in Merritt Ierley, *The Year that Tried Men's Souls*, p. 328.
7. Jefferson, *Papers*, 1: 96.
8. Ibid., 97.
9. Ibid., 495.
10. Jefferson, *Notes*, p. 227.
11. Ibid., p. 63.
12. Ibid., pp. 62, 58.
13. Jefferson, *Notes*, p. 240.
14. In Lester J. Cappon, ed., *The Adams-Jefferson Letters*, p. 307.
15. Jefferson is quoted in Noble E. Cunningham, *The Life of Thomas Jefferson*, p. 3.
16. Roane is quoted in George Morgan, *Patrick Henry*, p. 443.
17. Jefferson, *Notes*, p. 54.
18. Dickinson is quoted in Robert A. Ferguson, "'We Hold these Truths': Strategies of Control in the Literature of the Founders," p. 16.
19. Adams is quoted in Shaw, *The Character of John Adams*, p. 87.
20. See Friedrich Schiller, *On the Naive and Sentimental in Literature*.
21. Deane is quoted in Baskerville, *The People's Voice*, p. 12.
22. Jefferson's comments are transcribed in Daniel Webster, *Papers*, 1: 372.
23. Mason is quoted in Haberman, "English Sources," p. 114.
24. William Wirt, *The Life of Patrick Henry*, p. 65.
25. Robert Wiebe, *The Opening of American Society: From the Adoption of the Constitution to the Eve of Disunion*, p. 15.
26. Douglass Adair, *Fame and the Founding Fathers*, p. 11.
27. "Epaminondas," untitled essay, *Pennsylvania Magazine* (June 1775), pp. 262, 263.
28. William Scott, *Lessons in Elocution and Elements of Gesture*, p. 360.
29. For example, Sam Adams asked Benjamin Kent in a letter of July 27, 1776, "Was there ever a Revolution brot about, especially as important as this, without great internal Tumults & violent Convulsions!" Quoted in Jack N. Rakove, *The Beginnings of National Politics: An Interpretive History of the Continental Congress*, p. 109.

30. Stuart is quoted by the nineteenth-century artist James Ross Snowden in Q. David Bowers, *The History of United States Coinage*, p. 270.

31. Douglas L. Wilson's editorial comment is in Thomas Jefferson, *Jefferson's Literary Commonplace Book*, p. 193.

32. See Appendix, p. 206. See Figure 1.

SOCIAL LEVELING AND STAGE FRIGHT

1. George Fisher, *The American Instructor, or The Young Man's Best Companion*, p. 3. On Jefferson's ownership of the book, see Sowerby, *Catalogue*, 1: 508.

2. See Appendix and Figure 1.

3. Daniel J. Boorstin, *The Americans: The Colonial Experience*, p. 115.

4. Jack P. Greene, *Landon Carter: An Inquiry into the Personal Values and Social Imperatives of the Eighteenth Century*, p. 47.

5. Blair, *Lectures*, p. 299.

6. Jefferson, *Notes*, p. 165. Jefferson is using "casualities" in the sense of chance that produces accidental death.

7. Jefferson, *Summary View*, in *Papers*, 1: 134.

8. Jefferson to Edmund Pendleton, August 26, 1776, in *Papers*, 1: 503.

9. Quoted in Philip S. Foner, *Labor and the American Revolution*, pp. 164–65.

10. Washington is quoted in Wood, *Radicalism*, p. 198.

11. Robert Blair St. George, "Artifacts of Regional Consciousness in the Connecticut River Valley, 1700–1780," p. 349.

12. Hugh Henry Brackenridge, *A Hugh Henry Brackenridge Reader*, pp. 70, 71–72.

13. Judith Martin, *Common Courtesy in which Miss Manners Solves the Problem that Baffled Mr. Jefferson*, p. 6.

14. Jefferson, *Papers*, 1: 121.

15. Whately is quoted in Edney, "Rhetorical Theory," p. 100.

16. Roger Atkinson is quoted in Wood, "Democratization," p. 76.

17. W. B. Carnochan, "Gibbon's Silences," p. 377.

18. See Clifford C. Hubbard, "William Ellery," in *Dictionary of American Biography*, 6: 86; John Adams to William Plumer, March 28, 1813, in Edmund C. Burnett, ed., *Letters of Members of the Continental Congress*, 1: 537.

19. Jefferson, *Summary View*, in *Papers*, 1: 134.

20. Jefferson to Peter Carr, August 19, 1785, in *The Portable Jefferson*, pp. 380–81.

21. Morris L. Cohen, "Thomas Jefferson Recommends," p. 844.
22. Smith, *Theory of Moral Sentiments*, p. 113.
23. Ibid., p. 110.
24. The phrase is from Jefferson's letter to Henry Lee, May 8, 1825, in *Writings*, 16: 118, in which he discusses the audience for the Declaration.
25. Blair, *Lectures*, p. 4.
26. Kames, *Elements of Criticism*, pp. 17, 472.
27. Ibid., pp. 6–7.
28. Jeremy Bentham, *A Bentham Reader*, p. 194. On Bentham and the ethic of surveillance, see Michel Foucault, *Discipline and Punish*.
29. Jefferson, *Papers*, 1: 291.
30. Sir Roger L'Estrange, *Seneca's Morals by Way of Abstract*, p. ix.
31. William Godwin, *Enquiry into Political Justice*, 1: 262–63. In this context suicide is the heinous reassertion of self-ownership.
32. Mason Locke Weems, *The Life of Washington*, p. 12.
33. Godwin, *Enquiry*, 1: 265.
34. Witherspoon is quoted in Michael Kramer, *Imagining Language in America: From the Revolution to the Civil War*, p. 129.
35. Kames, *Elements of Criticism*, p. 433.
36. Eagleton, *Ideology of the Aesthetic*, p. 43.
37. *Pennsylvania Magazine*, February 1776, p. 75.
38. Jefferson, *Papers*, 1: 15.

PRIVATE LIVES AND PUBLIC SCRUTINY

1. Jefferson, *Papers*, 1: 24; Jefferson to James Monroe, May 20, 1782, in *The Portable Jefferson*, p. 365; McLaughlin, *Jefferson and Monticello*, pp. 365, 327. The draperies in the Assembly Room of the State House where the Continental Congress met had been replaced shortly before their arrival with venetian blinds. They are visible in Figure 11 above. Because Venice was associated with political conspiracy in the popular imagination of the late eighteenth century, in part as a result of plays like Thomas Otway's *Venice Preserved*, venetian blinds had political and epistemological resonances beyond their practicality.
2. Jefferson, *Papers*, 10: 449.
3. Richard Sennett, *The Fall of Public Man*, p. 89.
4. Jefferson, *Autobiography*, p. 62.
5. Jefferson, *Papers*, 1: 242. Jefferson acquired Randolph's violin before the latter left.
6. Jefferson, *Summary View*, in *Papers*, 1: 135. William L. Hedges com-

ments on the pun in "Telling Off the King: Jefferson's *Summary View* as American Fantasy."

7. Jefferson, *Autobiography*, p. 59. On the *Autobiography*, see James M. Cox, "Recovering Literature's Lost Ground Through Autobiography."

8. Weems, *Life of Washington*, p. 2.

9. Chesterfield is quoted in Sennett, *Public Man*, p. 62.

10. Ibid., p. 63.

11. Edmund M. Hayes, "Mercy Otis Warren versus Lord Chesterfield," pp. 618–19.

12. Ibid., p. 618.

13. Arthur M. Schlesinger, *Prelude to Independence: The Newspaper War on Britain, 1764–1776*, p. 142.

14. Jeffrey Smith, *Printers and Press Freedom*, p. 88. See also Richard Buel, Jr., "Freedom of the Press in Revolutionary America: The Evolution of Libertarianism, 1760–1820." In addition to libel, the press could be used to perpetuate another kind of misrepresentation. In a 1778 letter, the New York polemicist William Livingston described a series of letters he had sent to the *New Jersey Gazette* "written as if by different hands, not even excluding the tribe of petticoats, all calculated to caution America against the insidious arts of enemies. This method of rendering a measure unpopular, I have frequently experienced in my political days to be of surprising efficacy, as the common people collect from it that everybody is against it." Quoted in Paul Langford, "British Correspondence in the Colonial Press," p. 300.

15. Frank Shuffleton, "In Different Voices: Gender in the American Republic of Letters," p. 293.

16. Smith, *Printers and Press Freedom*, p. 11.

17. Ierley, *The Year*, p. 58.

18. Franklin is quoted in Smith, *Printers and Press Freedom*, pp. 151, 152.

19. Adams, *Works*, 6: 233.

20. Isaac Kramnick, ed., *The Federalist Papers*, pp. 87, 88. I am indebted to Bud Bynack for his useful comments on rhetorical strategies in *The Federalist*.

21. Ibid., pp. 88, 89.

22. Ibid., p. 89. In *The Rights of Man* Paine applies the substance of Hamilton's argument against a corporate Executive to a critique of mixed government itself. A government that incorporates elements of democracy, aristocracy, and monarchy does so "by cementing and soldering the discordant parts together by corruption, to act as a whole." In "Mixed Governments there is no responsibility: the parts cover each other till

responsibility is lost; and the Corruption which moves the machine, contrives at the same time its own escape." A checks and balances system in reality means that "the advisers, the actors, the approvers, the justifiers, the persons responsible, and the persons not responsible, are the same persons." There is no responsibility in a heterogeneous government, only endless blaming. Paine, *Reader*, p. 258.

23. Hamilton, *Papers*, 4: 253.

24. Adams is quoted in Hazelton, *The Declaration*, p. 142.

25. Burke is quoted in James Engell, *The Creative Imagination: Enlightenment to Romanticism*, p. 148.

26. Paine, *Common Sense*, pp. 75, 64.

27. Warner, *The Letters of the Republic*, pp. 39, 9, 40.

28. Ann Douglas, "Introduction" to *Charlotte Temple*, p. xxxi.

29. John Bennett, *Letters to a Young Lady, on a Variety of Useful and Interesting Subjects*, p. 49. Using "character" in the dominant eighteenth-century sense that collapses external "characterization" and internal nature, the hero of Samuel Richardson's *Sir Charles Grandison* (1753–54) introduces Harriet Byron, the woman to whom he will later propose, to a Dr. Bartlett: "Were there fifty Ladies here, my good Dr. Bartlett, whom you had never seen before, you would, I am sure, from the character you have had of Miss Byron, be under no difficulty of reading that character in her face." Harriet returns the compliment with reference to the good doctor: "The character he has given you, Sir, is stamped in your countenance. I should have venerated you wherever I had seen you." Quoted in Guilhamet, *The Sincere Ideal*, p. 295. The insistence that inward intentions should be legible in outward actions and appearances (the essence of sincerity) speaks, in a wholly different context, to an ongoing problematic in eighteenth-century Protestantism: the evidentiary relationship between good works and faith. For an even earlier account of the defining importance of sincerity to professions of faith, see Thomas Shepherd, *The Sincere Convert* (1641).

30. I am indebted to John Barrell, *The Political Theory of Painting from Reynolds to Hazlitt: 'The Body of the Public'*, p. 64, for the Latin distinction.

31. Jefferson, *Notes*, p. 140. The anonymous English sex manual *Aristotle's Master-Piece*, which according to Shipton and Mooney's *National Index of American Imprints* went through numerous American editions in the second half of the eighteenth century, offers an interesting contemporary counterpoint to the sentimental novel's preoccupation with the expressive female body. Beginning with a description of "the Pudenda (from the shame-facedness that is in women to have them seen)," *Aris-*

totle's Master-Piece not only proceeds to "lay open" the "secret parts in Women," but offers detailed keys to reading the faces, gaits, statures, and palms of both men and women. *Aristotle's Complete Master-Piece . . . Displaying the Secrets of Nature in the Generation of Man*, p. 7.

32. Jefferson to Robert Walsh, December 14, 1818, in Hazelton, *The Declaration*, pp. 178–79. The rough draft of Jefferson's Declaration, to which Franklin, Adams, and Jefferson made small changes before a fair copy was presented to the Congress, includes one change of real substance: the phrase "sacred and undeniable" is replaced with "self-evident." Protecting "these truths" from the realm of opinion suggested by "undeniable" and from the requirement of divine origin, the word "self-evident" is believed by virtually all modern authorities to be in Jefferson's hand. A minority view, however, is that it is in Franklin's. Were that true, Franklin's anecdote would be an ironic gloss on his editorial contribution. See Jefferson, *Papers*, 1: 427, and Boyd, "Declaration," p. 22.

33. See Richard B. Bernstein, *Are We to be a Nation? The Making of the Constitution*, p. 241.

34. Jefferson, *Papers*, 20: 290.

35. Ibid., 1: 144.

36. Brackenridge, *Reader*, pp. 78, 88; Chovet is discussed in Sellers, *Patience Wright*, p. 35.

37. Brown, *The Power of Sympathy*, pp. 35, 36, 38, 41, 37.

38. Ibid., p. 35.

39. Ibid., p. 41. Composing the right countenance was a national problem as well. In *Federalist* 39 Madison describes the debate over the Constitution as centering on the problem of balancing federal and national "features" so as to prevent "the national countenance of the Government" from being "disfigured" (p. 258).

40. Burroughs, *Memoirs*, p. 6. On the politics of eighteenth-century child rearing, see Jay Fliegelman, *Prodigals and Pilgrims: The American Revolution Against Patriarchal Authority, 1750–1800*.

41. John Locke, *Educational Writings*, p. 172.

42. Hannah Foster, *The Coquette*, p. 79.

43. Sowerby, in *Catalogue*, 4: 449, records Jefferson's receipt of the letter and quotes the relevant passage. See Gilbert Burgess's introduction to his edition of *The Love Letters of Mr. H and Miss R.*

44. Benjamin Rush to John Redman Coxe, September 5, 1810, in *Letters*, 2: 1059. On solitary confinement, see *Letters*, 1: 511–12.

45. Benjamin Rush, "Of the Mode of Education Proper in a Republic," p. 7. Having served a stormy term as governor, Jefferson defensively confessed to Monroe in a May 20, 1782, letter that he was enjoying

retirement from public life. "If we are made in some degree for others, yet in a greater are we made for ourselves." Virginia's "*perpetual* right" to his services would constitute a form of "slavery." *Papers*, 6: 185–86.

AGENCY AND THE INVENTION OF RESPONSIBILITY

1. See Gordon Wood, "Conspiracy and the Paranoid Style: Causality and Deceit in the Eighteenth Century."

2. The *OED* quotes Walpole's claim.

3. Bernard Peach, ed., *Richard Price and the Ethical Foundations of the American Revolution: Selections from His Pamphlets*, pp. 68–69.

4. Jefferson, *Papers*, 1: 125. On the fear of enslavement, see Bailyn, *Ideological Origins*, chapter 3.

5. Rush, "Education Proper in a Republic," p. 9; John Adams, *Works*, 10: 283.

6. Foster, *The Coquette*, p. 11.

7. Dowling, *Poetry and Ideology*, p. 20.

8. Jefferson, *Autobiography*, pp. 29, 31.

9. Jefferson, *Papers*, 1: 427.

10. See Appendix, p. 207; Jefferson, *Summary View*, in *Papers*, 1: 132. The *OED* indicates that by the time Jefferson uses "denounce" in its formal sense, that meaning was usually associated with a warning about a calamity or portent—thus pushing the word in the direction of its other sense, "inveighing against or condemning."

11. Julian P. Boyd, *The Declaration of Independence: The Evolution of the Text as Shown in Facsimiles of Various Drafts*, p. 21. The phrase "on so many acts of tyranny without a mask" is replaced in the version Jefferson brought to Congress with "to build a foundation so broad & undisguised for tyranny." See Figure 1. See also Appendix, pp. 203, 207, 208.

12. Adams is quoted in Richard L. Bushman, *King and People in Provincial Massachusetts*, p. 173.

13. Johnson is quoted in David Simpson, *The Politics of American English, 1776–1850*, p. 20.

14. Appendix, p. 206.

15. Jefferson, *Papers*, 1: 281.

16. Jefferson, *Summary View*, in *Papers*, 1: 134.

17. Quoted in Bushman, *King and People*, p. 221. Bushman describes at length the changing perceptions of the king's power. On the significance of the simultaneity of present and future in the phrase "are & of right ought to be," see Jacques Derrida, "Declarations of Independence," p. 12.

18. See Appendix, pp. 205, 206, 207.
19. Resolution of March 16, 1776, in Ford, *Journals*, 4: 208–9.
20. Ibid., 209.
21. Isaac Kramnick, ed., *The Federalist Papers*, p. 406.
22. Ibid., p. 407.
23. Ibid., p. 370. According to *The Federalist Concordance*, Thomas Engeman, ed., the word appears in 15 of the Federalist papers, though most frequently in numbers 63 and 70.
24. *The Pennsylvania Evening Post*, July 6, 1776, p. 338. Issues were paginated consecutively. Advertisements for runaway slaves also appeared in the *Post*, though not in this particular issue.

DIALECTICAL WORDS

1. Thomas Hutchinson, *Copy of Letters Sent to Great Britain*, p. 15.
2. Bernard Bailyn, *The Ordeal of Thomas Hutchinson*, p. 251; Bernard Mason, ed., *The American Colonial Crisis: The Daniel Leonard–John Adams Letters to the Press, 1774–1775*, p. 213.
3. John Quincy Adams, *Lectures*, 2: 4.
4. Jefferson, *Notes*, pp. 17, 164.
5. Ibid., p. 141.
6. Jefferson to John Melish, December 10, 1814, quoted in William Peden's "Introduction" to Jefferson, *Notes*, p. xxi.
7. Brown, *Wieland*, p. 233. For a more extensive account of the relationship of Brown's novel to the discourse of accountability (and to the elocutionary revolution), see my introduction to the Penguin edition of this novel.
8. Noah Webster, *A Grammatical Institute of the English Language, Part II*, p. 5.
9. See Appendix, pp. 205, 203. Linking anxieties of agency to a heightened preoccupation with human misery, "suffer" is a crucial verb in Enlightenment discourse. In *Notes*, Jefferson declares "it is to be lamented then . . . that we have suffered so many of the Indian tribes already to extinguish, without our having previously collected . . . the general rudiments at least of the languages they spoke," p. 101. At the level of diction, the suffering is taken from the suffering group. Here "suffered" suggests that white Americans have both endured and permitted the spectacle of an ongoing Indian extinction rather than actively participated in it. Indians are left "to extinguish" rather than to be extinguished. Furthermore the tragedy is that the extinguishing precedes the completion of the scientific record. The thwarted proto-ethnologist is the real sufferer.

10. Appendix, p. 206.

11. Quoted in Sarah N. Randolph, *The Domestic Life of Thomas Jefferson*, p. 49.

12. Paine, *Common Sense*, p. 99.

13. John Adams, *Diary and Autobiography*, 2: 336.

14. Ezra Gleason, *Thomas's New-England Almanack: or The Massachusetts Calendar, for the Year of Our Lord Christ, 1775*, p. 13. The full title of the almanac gives a good indication of the mix of universal Christian and secular history in which American history was in this period largely seen to operate. Following on the above: *Being the Third after Bissextile or Leap-Year. From the Creation of the World, According to the best of Prophane History, 5742; . . . From Noah's Flood, 4069; From the Destruction of Sodom, 3677; . . . Building of Boston, the Capital of N.E., 145; . . . Of King George the III's Reign, 15; Containing Every Thing Necessary and Useful in an Almanack. To Which is Added, The Life and Adventures of a Female Soldier.*

15. Ibid., p. 14.

16. See Marion Barber Stowell, *Early American Almanacs*, p. 216. For another politically interesting image of cross-dressing, see Charles Wilson Peale's 1771 painting of the actress Nancy Hallam in the role of Imogen in Shakespeare's *Cymbeline.* Peale depicts her at the moment in the play when, to ensure her safety, the English princess is dressed as the boy Fidele.

17. See Appendix, p. 206.

18. Reproduced in Stowell, *Almanacs*, p. 115.

19. Joseph P. Martin, *A Narrative of Some of the Adventures, Dangers and Sufferings of A Revolutionary Soldier* (1830), quoted in Henry Steele Commager and Richard B. Morris, eds., *The Spirit of Seventy-Six: The Story of the American Revolution as Told by Participants*, pp. 714–15.

20. Ford, *Journals*, 5: 517–18.

21. Proposal in Jefferson, *Papers*, 1: 496.

22. For Jefferson on emigration, see *Summary View*, in *Papers*, 1: 121–25. In *Common Sense*, Paine uses the argument that "Europe and not England is the parent country of America" to expose how England has "jesuitically adopted" the "phrase of parent or mother country" in order to create a false sense of natural obligation (pp. 84–85).

23. Ford, *Journals*, 4: 39.

24. Proposal in Jefferson, *Papers*, 1: 497.

25. Paine, *Common Sense*, p. 92.

PLAGIARISM, AUTHORSHIP, AND IMPROVEMENT

1. John Adams to Timothy Pickering, August 22, 1822, in Burnett, ed., *Letters*, 1: 516.

2. Lee is cited in a letter from Jefferson to James Madison, August 30, 1823, quoted in Hazelton, *The Declaration*, p. 144.

3. John Adams to Jefferson, June 22, 1819, in Cappon, ed., *Adams-Jefferson Letters*, p. 542.

4. John Adams, *Diary and Autobiography*, 3: 336. For a similar set of charges leveled against Noah Webster for "compiling" his grammar and speller out of previous works, notably Thomas Dilworth's immensely popular *New Guide to the English Tongue*, see E. Jennifer Monaghan, *A Common Heritage: Noah Webster's Blue-Back Speller*, pp. 46–50. On Adams's attitude toward Jefferson's authorship of the Declaration, see Elizabeth M. Renker, "'Declaration-men' and the Rhetoric of Self-Presentation." On eighteenth-century views of plagiarism, see Thomas McFarland, *Originality and Imagination*, pp. 22–30.

5. Jefferson to James Madison, August 30, 1823, in *Writings*, 15: 462.

6. Alexander Pope, *Essay on Criticism*, line 298, in *Poetical Works*, p. 72.

7. Jefferson to Henry Lee, May 8, 1825, in *Writings*, 16: 118. On the subject of agency, note that Jefferson does not say he "harmonized" the sentiments of the day, but that the sentiments themselves harmonized. Though Jefferson says no previous writing was consulted, the fact is that the Declaration's list of charges against the king draws heavily on a comparable list that occupies the first page of Jefferson's rough draft for the Virginia Constitution written the month before. See *Papers*, 1: 332.

8. On the paper and watermark, see Boyd, *Declaration*, p. 41.

9. John Quincy Adams, *Lectures*, 1: 165.

10. Godwin, *Enquiry*, p. 378. In *Federalist* 47, Madison defines the originality of Homer by an analogy between government and an epic: "The British constitution was to Montesquieu, what Homer has been to the didactic writers on epic poetry. As the latter have considered the work of the immortal Bard, as the perfect model from which the principles and rules of the epic art were to be drawn, and by which all similar works were to be judged; so this great political critic appears to have viewed the constitution of England, as the standard, or to use his own expression, as the mirrour of political liberty" (p. 303).

11. Philadelphia *Weekly Magazine*, February 1798, p. 106.

12. "Worded" is, for example, used by Albert Furtwangler in *The Authority of Publius: A Reading of the Federalist Papers*, p. 55.

13. Jefferson, *Autobiography*, p. 34.

14. Peale is quoted in Silvio A. Bedini, *Thomas Jefferson and his Copying Machines*, p. 85.

15. On the few books that survive from Jefferson's earliest library, volumes inherited from his father, Jefferson wrote "ex libris Thomae Jefferson." After shifting in the late 1760's or early 1770's to the internal initialing, Jefferson actually erased his name from several of these volumes (leaving another kind of mark) in order to initial them. See James A. Bear, Jr., *Thomas Jefferson's Book-Marks*.

16. Sowerby, *Catalogue*, 5: 55. The date of acquisition is uncertain.

17. The Pelham letter as well as the Pelham print are reproduced in Clarence S. Brigham, *Paul Revere's Engravings*, pp. 52–54.

18. Ibid., p. 53.

19. George Peek, ed., *The Political Writings of John Adams*, p. 175.

20. Caroline Robbins, *The Eighteenth-Century Commonwealthman*, p. 365; James Burgh, *Political Disquisitions*, 1: viii.

21. Burgh, *Political Disquisitions*, 2: unpaginated.

22. See Susan Bryan, "Reauthorizing the Text: Jefferson's Scissor-Edit of The Gospels."

23. Jefferson, *Autobiography*, p. 58.

24. Jefferson, *Manual of Parliamentary Practice*, p. v.

25. On this source, see Malone, *Jefferson The Virginian*, p. 243.

26. Franklin, *The Way to Wealth* (1758), in *A Benjamin Franklin Reader*, p. 301. The tension between an editorial and an authorial model of writing played out in another context as well: the contemporary debate about the active versus passive role of the mind in thought. Thomas Reid dismissed Hume's argument that mediating ideas are the only objects of thought because it leads to the corollary "absurdity" that "thought and ideas may be without any thinking being." Reid then introduces a withering analogy between Hume's view and the process of writing. "It seemed," he observes, "very natural to think, that the 'Treatise of Human Nature' required an author, and a very ingenious one too; but now we learn that it is only a set of ideas which came together and arranged themselves by certain associations and attractions." *Inquiry*, p. 21.

27. Judith Sargent Murray, *The Gleaner: A Miscellaneous Production*, 1: 15. When Murray revealed her true identity at the end of her series, she gave a different reason for adopting the mask of the Gleaner: the "contempt, with which female productions are regarded," and the fact that "I was ambitious of being considered independent as a writer" (3: 314).

28. Philip Freneau, *Poems*, 1: 208, 211. Phillis Wheatley's "On Imagina-

tion" (1773) reverses the power dynamic. Fancy flies only "Till some loved object strikes her wand'ring eyes, / Whose silken fetters all the senses bind." *Poems on Various Subjects, Religious and Moral*, p. 65.

29. An excised strip of the title page above Peter's signature, apparently the work of an autograph collector, may once have contained Philip's signature.

30. On the pervasiveness of this cyclical view in American poetry of the last quarter of the eighteenth century, see Dowling, *Poetry and Ideology*.

31. Quoted in Stam, *Inquiries*, p. 74.

32. Philip Freneau, *Miscellaneous Works*, pp. 42–43.

33. Quoted in Richard Gimbel, *Thomas Paine: A Bibliographical Check List of "Common Sense" with an Account of its Publication*, p. 34.

34. Ibid., pp. 28–29.

35. Cathy Davidson, *Revolution and the Word: The Rise of the American Novel*, p. 30.

36. Paine is quoted in Gimbel, *Thomas Paine*, p. 27.

37. David Humphreys, *The Miscellaneous Works*, p. 123. Adams is quoted in Brooke Hindle, *Emulation and Invention*, p. 167.

38. Franklin, *Autobiography*, p. 62.

39. Winckelmann is quoted in Robert Alberts, *Benjamin West*, p. 44.

40. Jefferson to John Waldo, August 16, 1813, in *The Complete Jefferson*, p. 888.

41. Pratt is quoted in Alberts, *Benjamin West*, p. 67.

42. Marshall Davidson and Elizabeth Stillinger, *The American Wing at the Metropolitan Museum of Art*, p. 280.

43. Adams is quoted in Shaw, *The Character of John Adams*, p. 271.

44. Gilbert Chinard, "Introduction," *The Literary Bible of Thomas Jefferson*, p. 32.

45. H. L. Mencken, *The American Language*, pp. 5, 130.

46. Adams is quoted in Pauline Maier, *The Old Revolutionaries: Political Lives in the Age of Samuel Adams*, p. 20.

47. Franklin, *Papers*, 22: 85.

48. For the story of the inscription, see Jefferson, *Papers*, 1: 679. Paine, *Common Sense*, p. 111.

49. Franklin, *Papers*, 22: 85. A facsimile of the original letter appears in Richard E. Amacher, "Benjamin Franklin," in *Dictionary of Literary Biography*, 24: 140.

50. Pocock is quoted in Isaac Kramnick, *Republicanism and Bourgeois Radicalism: Political Ideology in Late Eighteenth-Century England and America*, p. 167. Kramnick's chapter "Republican Revisionism Revisited"

sets forth the debate. Montesquieu is quoted in Howard Mumford Jones, *Revolution and Romanticism*, p. 157.

51. See Kramnick's chapter, "James Burgh and Opposition Ideology," in *Republicanism*.

52. Franklin, *Papers*, 3: 413.

53. John Wilkes, *The Speeches of Mr. Wilkes in the House of Commons*, p. 89. The description of Wilkes as the "best Manufacturer of paragraphs" is William Strahan's, cited in Jeffrey Smith, *Printer and Press Freedom*, p. 24.

54. Jefferson is quoted in Max I. Baym, *A History of Literary Aesthetics in America*, p. 8.

THE ORATORICAL IDEAL, RACIAL POLITICS, AND THE MAKING OF AMERICANS

1. Appendix, pp. 203, 206, 207.

2. *The Portable Jefferson*, p. 542.

3. Paine, *Common Sense*, p. 84.

4. Ibid., p. 65.

5. Appendix, p. 207; Wills, *Inventing America*, p. 316.

6. See Bernard Schwartz, *The American Heritage History of Law in America*, p. 37. On the relationship between Wythe and Jefferson, see Harold Hellenbrand, *The Unfinished Revolution: Education and Politics in the Thought of Thomas Jefferson*, chapter 1.

7. Jefferson, *Notes*, p. 138.

8. Ibid., p. 160.

9. Ibid., p. 288.

10. Lee is quoted in Kimball, *Jefferson*, p. 281.

11. Sidney Kaplan and Emma Nogrady Kaplan, *The Black Presence in the Era of the American Revolution*, p. 137.

12. Quoted ibid., p. 148.

13. The Jones and Allen pamphlet, *A Narrative of the Proceedings of the Black People during the late Awful Calamity in Philadelphia*, is quoted ibid., p. 102.

14. John Barrell, "'The Dangerous Goddess': Masculinity, Prestige, and the Aesthetic in Early Eighteenth-Century Britain," p. 102; Jefferson, *Notes*, p. 142; Blair is quoted in Barrell, *The Political Theory of Painting*, p. 23.

15. Jefferson to Henry Lee, May 8, 1825, in *Writings*, 16: 118.

16. John Quincy Adams, *Lectures*, 1: 370.

17. On his traveling violin and Jefferson as a reader of music, see Cripe,

Jefferson and Music, pp. 14, 12. On Henry playing by ear, see Malone, *Jefferson*, p. 90. On Jefferson and Sterne, see Mapp, *Thomas Jefferson*, p. 97.

EPILOGUE

1. See Boorstin, *The Lost World of Thomas Jefferson*, p. 60. In *The Radicalism of the American Revolution*, Gordon Wood glosses the phrase as meaning that "no one of them should be dependent on the will of another" (p. 234).

2. Noyes is quoted in David Brion Davis, ed., *Antebellum American Culture*, p. 449. In contrast to those who sought to appropriate and extend it, Frederick Douglass powerfully rejected the Declaration in his *Address Delivered in Rochester, New York, on July 5, 1852*, as belonging only to white American citizens.

3. The advertisement, appearing in the Richmond *Enquirer* for July 22, 1828, is reproduced in William Howard Adams, *Jefferson's Monticello*, p. 237.

4. Thomas Carlyle, *Sartor Resartus*, p. 41.

5. Michael Paul Rogin, *Subversive Genealogy: The Politics and Art of Herman Melville*, p. 25. Melville's father was an importer and dealer in fine fabrics until the ready-to-wear clothing industry, among other factors, destroyed his business.

6. Paine, *Rights of Man*, in *Reader*, p. 213; Burke, *Reflections on the Revolution in France*, p. 61; on "Men and Mannequins" see Sennett, *Public Man*, pp. 65–73.

7. Carlyle, *Sartor Resartus*, p. 35.

Works Cited

Aarsleff, Hans. *The Study of Language in England, 1780–1860*. Princeton, N.J.: Princeton University Press, 1967.

Adair, Douglass. *Fame and the Founding Fathers*. New York: Norton, 1974.

Adams, John. *Diary and Autobiography of John Adams*. 4 vols. Ed. L. H. Butterfield. New York: Atheneum, 1964.

———. *John Adams's Earliest Diary*. Ed. L. H. Butterfield. Cambridge, Mass.: Harvard University Press, 1966.

———. *Papers of John Adams*. 8 vols. Ed. Robert J. Taylor. Cambridge, Mass.: Harvard University Press, 1977.

———. *The Works of John Adams*. 10 vols. Ed. Charles Francis Adams. Boston, 1851.

Adams, John Quincy. *Lectures on Rhetoric and Oratory*. 2 vols. Cambridge, 1810.

———. *The Memoirs of John Quincy Adams*. 12 vols. Ed. Charles Francis Adams. Boston, 1874.

Adams, William Howard. *Jefferson's Monticello*. New York: Abbeville, 1983.

The Adventures of Jonathan Corncob, Loyal American Refugee. Boston: D. R. Godine, 1976.

Agnew, Jean-Christophe. *Worlds Apart: The Market and the Theater in Anglo-American Thought, 1550–1750*. Cambridge: Cambridge University Press, 1986.

Alberts, Robert C. *Benjamin West*. Boston: Houghton Mifflin, 1978.

Amacher, Richard E. "Benjamin Franklin." In *Dictionary of Literary Biography*, vol. 24. Ed. Emory Elliott. Detroit: Gale Research Company, 1984.

Aristotle's Complete Master-Piece . . . Displaying the Secrets of Nature in the Generation of Man. Philadelphia, 1798.

Bailyn, Bernard. *Ideological Origins of the American Revolution*. Cambridge, Mass.: Harvard University Press, 1967.

———. *The Ordeal of Thomas Hutchinson*. Cambridge, Mass.: Harvard University Press, 1974.

Barish, Jonas. *The Antitheatrical Prejudice*. Berkeley: University of California Press, 1981.

Barrell, John. "'The Dangerous Goddess': Masculinity, Prestige, and the Aesthetic in Early Eighteenth-Century Britain." *Cultural Critique* (Spring 1989): 101–31.

——. *English Literature in History, 1730–80: An Equal, Wide Survey*. London: Hutchinson, 1983.

——. *The Political Theory of Painting from Reynolds to Hazlitt: 'The Body of the Public'*. New Haven: Yale University Press, 1986.

Barton, Benjamin Smith. *A Memoir Concerning the Fascinating Faculty which has been ascribed to the Rattle-Snake, and other American Serpents*. Philadelphia, 1796.

Baskerville, Barnet. *The People's Voice: The Orator in American Society*. Lexington: University of Kentucky Press, 1979.

Baym, Max I. *A History of Literary Aesthetics in America*. New York: Frederick Ungar, 1973.

Bear, James A., Jr. *Thomas Jefferson's Book-Marks*. Charlottesville: University Press of Virginia, 1958.

Bedini, Silvio A. *Declaration of Independence Desk: Relic of Revolution*. Washington, D.C.: Smithsonian Institution Press, 1981.

——. *Thomas Jefferson and his Copying Machines*. Charlottesville: University Press of Virginia, 1984.

Bender, John, and David E. Wellbery. "Rhetoricality." In John Bender and David Wellbery, eds., *The Ends of Rhetoric: History, Theory, Practice*. Stanford: Stanford University Press, 1990.

Bennett, Rev. John. *Letters to a Young Lady, on a Variety of Useful and Interesting Subjects*. Hartford, 1792.

Bentham, Jeremy. *A Bentham Reader*. Ed. Mary Peter Mack. New York: Pegasus, 1969.

Berman, Eleanor D. *Thomas Jefferson Among the Arts*. New York: Philosophical Library, 1947.

Bernstein, Richard B. *Are We to be a Nation? The Making of the Constitution*. Cambridge, Mass.: Harvard University Press, 1987.

Billings, William. *The New-England Psalm Singer*. Boston, 1770.

Blair, Hugh. *Lectures on Rhetoric and Belles Lettres*. Philadelphia, 1784.

Bogel, Fredrick. *Literature and Insubstantiality in Later Eighteenth-Century England*. Princeton, N.J.: Princeton University Press, 1984.

Bohman, George V. "Rhetorical Practice in Colonial America." In Karl Wallace, ed., *A History of Speech Education in America*. New York: Appleton-Century-Crofts, 1954.

Bolton, Thomas. *An Oration Delivered March 15th, 1775*. Boston, 1775. In David Potter and Gordon L. Thomas, eds., *The Colonial Idiom*. Carbondale: Southern Illinois University Press, 1970.

Boorstin, Daniel J. *The Americans: The Colonial Experience*. New York: Random House, 1958.

——. *The Lost World of Thomas Jefferson*. Boston: Beacon Press, 1960.

Bowers, Q. David. *The History of United States Coinage*. Wolfeboro, N.H.: Bowers and Merena Galleries, 1983.

Boyd, Julian P. *The Declaration of Independence: The Evolution of the Text as Shown in Facsimiles of Various Drafts*. Princeton, N.J.: Princeton University Press, 1945.

——. "The Declaration of Independence: The Mystery of the Lost Original." *The Pennsylvania Magazine of History and Biography* (1976): 438–67.

Brackenridge, Hugh Henry. *A Hugh Henry Brackenridge Reader, 1770–1815*. Ed. Daniel Marder. Pittsburgh: University of Pittsburgh Press, 1970.

Breen, Timothy. "'Baubles of Britain': The American and Consumer Revolutions of the Eighteenth Century." *Past and Present* 119 (1988): 73–104.

Breitwieser, Mitchell. *Cotton Mather and Benjamin Franklin: The Price of Representative Personality*. Cambridge: Cambridge University Press, 1984.

——. "Jefferson's Prospect." *Prospects* 10 (1985): 315–53.

Brigham, Clarence S. *Paul Revere's Engravings*. New York: Atheneum, 1969.

Brown, Charles Brockden. *Arthur Mervyn: Or, Memoirs of the Year 1793*. Ed. Sydney J. Krause. Kent, Ohio: Kent State University Press, 1980.

——. *Ormond: or, The Secret Witness*. Ed. Sydney J. Krause and S. W. Reid. Kent, Ohio: Kent State University Press, 1982.

——. *Wieland, or The Transformation*. Ed. Jay Fliegelman. New York: Penguin, 1991.

Brown, Richard D. *Knowledge is Power: The Diffusion of Information in Early America, 1700–1865*. New York: Oxford University Press, 1989.

Brown, William Hill. *The Power of Sympathy*. Boston: New Frontiers, 1961.

Bryan, Susan. "Reauthorizing the Text: Jefferson's Scissor-Edit of The Gospels." *Early American Literature* 22, no. 1 (1987): 19–42.

Buel, Richard, Jr. "Freedom of the Press in Revolutionary America: The Evolution of Libertarianism, 1760–1820." In Bernard Bailyn and

John B. Hench, eds., *The Press and the American Revolution*, pp. 59–99. Boston: Northeastern University Press, 1981.

Bullock, Steven C. "The Revolutionary Transformation of American Freemasonry, 1752–1792." *William and Mary Quarterly* 47 (1990): 347–69.

Burgess, Gilbert, ed. *The Love Letters of Mr. H and Miss R, 1775–1779*. Chicago, 1895.

Burgh, James. *The Art of Speaking*. Danbury, 1795.

——. *Political Disquisitions*. 3 vols. Philadelphia, 1775.

Burke, Edmund. *Reflections on the Revolution in France*. New York, 1791.

Burnett, Edmund C., ed. *Letters of Members of the Continental Congress*. 8 vols. Gloucester, Mass.: Peter Smith, 1963.

Burney, Charles. *The Present State of Music in France and Italy* (1771). New York: Boude, 1969.

Burnim, Kalman A. *David Garrick, Director*. Carbondale: Southern Illinois University Press, 1961.

Burroughs, Stephen. *The Memoirs of Stephen Burroughs*. Ed. Philip Gura. Boston: Northeastern University Press, 1988.

Bushman, Richard L. *King and People in Provincial Massachusetts*. Chapel Hill: University of North Carolina Press, 1985.

Butterfield, L. H., ed. *Adams Family Correspondence*. 4 vols. Cambridge, Mass.: Harvard University Press, 1963.

Cappon, Lester J., ed. *The Adams-Jefferson Letters*. New York: Simon and Schuster, 1971.

Carlyle, Thomas. *Sartor Resartus*. Ed. Charles Frederick Harold. New York: Odyssey, 1937.

Carnochan, W. B. "Gibbon's Silences." In James Engell, ed., *Johnson and his Age*. Harvard English Studies, 12. Cambridge, Mass.: Harvard University Press, 1984.

Chinard, Gilbert. "Introduction." *The Literary Bible of Thomas Jefferson*. Baltimore: Johns Hopkins University Press, 1928.

Cmiel, Kenneth. *Democratic Eloquence: The Fight over Popular Speech in Nineteenth-Century America*. Berkeley: University of California Press, 1989.

Cockin, William. *The Art of Delivering Written Language* (1775). Menston, Eng.: Scolar Press, 1969.

Cohen, Morris L. "Thomas Jefferson Recommends a Course of Law Study." *University of Pennsylvania Law Review* 119 (1971): 823–44.

Cohen, Murray. *Sensible Words: Linguistic Practice in England, 1640–1785*. Baltimore: Johns Hopkins University Press, 1977.

Commager, Henry Steele, and Richard B. Morris, eds. *The Spirit of Seventy-Six: The Story of the American Revolution as Told by Participants*. New York: Bonanza Books, 1983.

Cowie, Alexander. *The Rise of the American Novel*. New York: American Book Company, 1931.

Cox, James M. "Recovering Literature's Lost Ground Through Autobiography." In James Olney, ed., *Autobiography: Essays Theoretical and Critical*, pp. 123–45. Princeton, N.J.: Princeton University Press, 1980.

Crèvecoeur, J. Hector St. John de. *Letters from an American Farmer*. Ed. Albert E. Stone. New York: Penguin, 1981.

Cripe, Helen. *Thomas Jefferson and Music*. Charlottesville: University Press of Virginia, 1974.

Cunningham, Noble E. *The Life of Thomas Jefferson*. New York: Ballantine, 1987.

Darnton, Robert. *The Great Cat Massacre and Other Episodes in French Cultural History*. New York: Vintage, 1984.

Davidson, Cathy. *Revolution and the Word: The Rise of the American Novel*. New York: Oxford University Press, 1986.

Davidson, Marshall, and Elizabeth Stillinger. *The American Wing at the Metropolitan Museum of Art*. New York: Knopf, 1985.

Davis, David Brion, ed. *Antebellum American Culture*. Boston: D. C. Heath, 1979.

De Bolla, Peter. *The Discourse of the Sublime: Readings in History, Aesthetics and the Subject*. Oxford: Basil Blackwell, 1989.

Derrida, Jacques. "Declarations of Independence." *New Political Science* 15 (1986): 7–17.

Dewey, Frank L. *Thomas Jefferson, Lawyer*. Charlottesville: University Press of Virginia, 1986.

Dictionary of American Biography. Ed. Allen Johnson and Dumas Malone. 20 vols. New York: Charles Scribner, 1931.

Douglas, Ann. "Introduction." *Charlotte Temple*, by Susanna Rowson. New York: Penguin, 1991.

Douglass, Frederick. *An Address Delivered in Rochester, New York, on July 5, 1852*. Rochester, 1852.

Dowling, William C. *Poetry and Ideology in Revolutionary Connecticut*. Athens: University of Georgia Press, 1990.

Dunlap, William. *A History of the American Theater*. New York, 1832.

Eagleton, Terry. *The Ideology of the Aesthetic*. Oxford: Basil Blackwell, 1990.

Edney, Clarence W. "English Sources of Rhetorical Theory in Nineteenth-Century America." In Karl Wallace, ed., *A History of Speech Education in America*. New York: Appleton-Century-Crofts, 1954.

Ekman, Paul, Robert W. Levenson, and Wallace V. Friesen. "Autonomic Nervous System Activity Distinguishes Among Emotions." *Science* 221 (1983): 1208–10.

Engell, James. *The Creative Imagination: Enlightenment to Romanticism*. Cambridge, Mass.: Harvard University Press, 1981.

Engeman, Thomas S., ed. *The Federalist Concordance*. Chicago: University of Chicago Press, 1980.

"Epaminondas." Untitled essay. *Pennsylvania Magazine*, June 1775.

Equiano, Olaudah. *The Interesting Narrative of the Life of Olaudah Equiano or Gustavus Vassa, the African*. In Henry Louis Gates, ed., *The Classic Slave Narratives*. New York: Mentor, 1987.

Evans, Charles. *American Bibliography*. 13 vols. New York: Peter Smith, 1941.

Evans, Dorinda. *Mather Brown: An Early American Artist in England*. Middletown, Conn.: Wesleyan University Press, 1982.

Feldman, Burton, and Robert D. Richardson. *The Rise of Modern Mythology, 1680–1860*. Bloomington: Indiana University Press, 1972.

Ferguson, Robert A. "'We Hold these Truths': Strategies of Control in the Literature of the Founders." In Sacvan Bercovitch, ed., *Reconstructing American Literary History*, pp. 1–29. Cambridge, Mass.: Harvard University Press, 1986.

Fisher, George. *The American Instructor, or The Young Man's Best Companion*. Burlington, 1775.

Fliegelman, Jay. *Prodigals and Pilgrims: The American Revolution Against Patriarchal Authority, 1750–1800*. Cambridge: Cambridge University Press, 1982.

Foner, Philip S. *Labor and the American Revolution*. Westport, Conn.: Greenwood Press, 1976.

Forbes, Esther. *Paul Revere and the World He Lived In*. Boston: Houghton Mifflin, 1969.

Ford, Worthington Chauncey, ed. *Journals of the Continental Congress, 1774–1789*. 12 vols. Washington: Government Printing Office, 1906.

Foster, Hannah. *The Coquette, or the History of Eliza Wharton*. Boston, 1802.

Foucault, Michel. *Discipline and Punish: The Birth of the Prison*. Trans. Alan Sheridan. New York: Vintage, 1979.

Franklin, Benjamin. *The Autobiography*. Ed. Leonard W. Labaree,

Ralph L. Ketcham, Helen C. Boatfield, and Helene H. Fineman. New Haven: Yale University Press, 1964.
——. *A Benjamin Franklin Reader*. Ed. Nathan G. Goodman. New York: Crowell, 1971.
——. *The Papers of Benjamin Franklin*. 24 vols. Ed. Leonard W. Labaree, Whitfield J. Bell, Jr., Helen C. Boatfield, and Helene H. Fineman. New Haven: Yale University Press, 1959.
Freneau, Philip. *The Miscellaneous Works of Philip Freneau*. Philadelphia, 1788.
——. *The Poems of Philip Freneau*. 3 vols. Ed. Fred Lewis Pattee. Princeton, N.J.: The University Library, 1903.
Fried, Michael. *Absorption and Theatricality*. Berkeley: University of California Press, 1980.
Furtwangler, Albert. *American Silhouettes: The Rhetorical Identities of the Founders*. New Haven: Yale University Press, 1987.
——. *The Authority of Publius: A Reading of the Federalist Papers*. Ithaca: Cornell University Press, 1984.
Geminiani, Francesco. *The Art of Playing the Violin* (1751). Ed. David Boyden. London: Oxford University Press, n.d.
Gimbel, Richard. *Thomas Paine: A Bibliographical Check List of "Common Sense" with an Account of its Publication*. Port Washington, N.Y.: Kennikat Press, 1973.
Gleason, Ezra. *Thomas's New-England Almanack . . . for 1775*. Boston, 1774.
Godwin, William. *Enquiry into Political Justice*. 2 vols. Philadelphia, 1796.
Greene, Jack P. *Landon Carter: An Inquiry into the Personal Values and Social Imperatives of the Eighteenth-Century Virginia Gentry*. Charlottesville: University Press of Virginia, 1965.
Guilhamet, Leon. *The Sincere Ideal: Studies on Sincerity in Eighteenth-Century English Literature*. Montreal: McGill-Queen's University Press, 1974.
Guralnick, M. "The All-Seeing Eye." *Art and Antiques* (Jan. 1988): 62–67, 102.
Gustafson, Thomas B. "Representative Words: Politics, Literature, and the American Language, 1776–1865." Stanford University Diss., 1986.
Guthrie, Warren. "Rhetorical Theory in Colonial America." In Karl Wallace, ed., *A History of Speech Education in America*. New York: Appleton-Century-Crofts, 1954.
Haberman, Frederick W. "English Sources of American Elocution." In Karl Wallace, ed., *A History of Speech Education in America*. New York: Appleton-Century-Crofts, 1954.

Habermas, Jürgen. *Theory and Practice.* Boston: Beacon Press, 1973.
Hamilton, Alexander. *The Papers of Alexander Hamilton.* 20 vols. Ed. Harold C. Syrett. New York, 1961–72.
Hayes, Edmund M. "Mercy Otis Warren versus Lord Chesterfield." *William and Mary Quarterly* 40 (1983): 617–21.
Hazelton, John H. *The Declaration of Independence and Its History.* New York: Dodd, Mead, 1906.
Hedges, William L. "Telling Off the King: Jefferson's *Summary View* as American Fantasy." *Early American Literature* 22, no. 2 (1987): 166–75.
Heimert, Alan. *Religion and the American Mind: From the Great Awakening to the Revolution.* Cambridge, Mass.: Harvard University Press, 1966.
Hellenbrand, Harold. *The Unfinished Revolution: Education and Politics in the Thought of Thomas Jefferson.* Newark: University of Delaware Press, 1990.
Herries, John. *Elements of Speech and Vocal Music on a New Plan* (1773). Menston, Eng.: Scolar Press, 1968.
Hindle, Brooke. *Emulation and Invention.* New York: Norton, 1981.
Holden, John. *Essay Towards a Rational System of Music.* London, 1770.
Hopkinson, Francis. *The Miscellaneous Essays.* 3 vols. Philadelphia, 1792.
Howard, Leon. *The Connecticut Wits.* Chicago: University of Chicago Press, 1943.
Howell, Wilbur Samuel. "The Declaration of Independence and Eighteenth-Century Logic." *William and Mary Quarterly* 18 (1961): 463–84.
——. *Eighteenth-Century British Logic and Rhetoric.* Princeton, N.J.: Princeton University Press, 1971.
Hume, David. *Enquiries Concerning Human Understanding and the Principles of Morals.* Ed. L. A. Selby-Bigge. Oxford: Oxford University Press, 1978.
Humphreys, David. *The Miscellaneous Works.* New York, 1804.
Hutchinson, Thomas. *Copy of Letters Sent to Great Britain.* Boston, 1773.
Hutson, James H. "John Adams' Titles Campaign." *New England Quarterly* 41 (1968): 22–42.
Ierley, Merritt. *The Year that Tried Men's Souls: The World of 1776.* South Brunswick: A. S. Barnes, 1977.
Issac, Rhys. *The Transformation of Virginia, 1740–1790.* Chapel Hill: University of North Carolina Press, 1982.
Jackson, E. Nevill. *Silhouettes: A History and Dictionary of Artists.* New York: Dover, 1981.

Jefferson, Thomas. *Autobiography*. Ed. Dumas Malone. New York: Capricorn, 1959.
——. *The Commonplace Book of Thomas Jefferson: A Repertory of His Ideas on Government*. Ed. Gilbert Chinard. Baltimore: Johns Hopkins University Press, 1926.
——. *The Complete Jefferson*. Ed. Saul Padover. New York: Tudor, 1943.
——. *Jefferson's Literary Commonplace Book*. Ed. Douglas L. Wilson. Princeton, N.J.: Princeton University Press, 1989.
——. *Manual of Parliamentary Practice*. New York, 1867.
——. *Notes on the State of Virginia*. Ed. William Peden. New York: Norton, 1972.
——. *The Papers of Thomas Jefferson*. Ed. Julian Boyd et al. 25 vols. Princeton, N.J.: Princeton University Press, 1959–.
——. *The Portable Thomas Jefferson*. Ed. Merrill D. Peterson. New York: Penguin, 1977.
——. *The Writings of Thomas Jefferson*. Ed. Andrew Lipscomb and Albert Ellery Bergh. 20 vols. Washington, D.C.: Thomas Jefferson Memorial Association, 1903.
Johnson, Samuel. *The Yale Edition of the Works of Samuel Johnson*, vol. 12. New Haven: Yale University Press, 1977.
Jones, Howard Mumford. *Revolution and Romanticism*. Cambridge, Mass.: Harvard University Press, 1974.
Kames, Lord (Henry Home). *Elements of Criticism* (1762). New York, 1854.
——. *Introduction to the Art of Thinking*. Edinburgh, 1761.
——. *Sketches of the History of Man*. 2 vols. Dublin, 1779.
Kant, Immanuel. *Critique of Judgment*. In Hazard Adams, ed., *Critical Theory Since Plato*. New York: Harcourt Brace Jovanovich, 1971.
Kaplan, Sidney, and Emma Nogrady Kaplan. *The Black Presence in the Era of the American Revolution*. Amherst: University of Massachusetts Press, 1989.
Kimball, Marie. *Jefferson: The Road to Glory, 1743–1776*. New York: Coward-McCann, 1943.
Kramer, Michael P. *Imagining Language in America: From the Revolution to the Civil War*. Princeton, N.J.: Princeton University Press, 1992.
Kramnick, Isaac. *Republicanism and Bourgeois Radicalism: Political Ideology in Late Eighteenth-Century England and America*. Ithaca: Cornell University Press, 1990.
——, ed. *The Federalist Papers*. New York: Penguin, 1987.
Langford, Paul. "British Correspondence in the Colonial Press, 1763–

1775." In Bernard Bailyn and John B. Hench, eds., *The Press and the American Revolution*, pp. 273–315. Boston: Northeastern University Press, 1981.

Lavater, Johann Caspar. *Essays on Physiognomy*. Boston, 1794.

Lawrence, Vera Brodsky. *Music for Patriots, Politicians, and Presidents*. New York: Macmillan, 1975.

L'Estrange, Sir Roger. *Seneca's Morals by Way of Abstract*. Boston, 1794.

Locke, John. *Educational Writings*. Ed. James Axtell. Cambridge: Cambridge University Press, 1968.

Lowance, Mason, and Georgia B. Bumgardner, eds. *Massachusetts Broadsides of the American Revolution*. Amherst: University of Massachusetts Press, 1976.

Lucas, Stephen E. "Justifying America: The Declaration of Independence as a Rhetorical Document." In Thomas W. Benson, ed., *American Rhetoric: Context and Criticism*. Carbondale: Southern Illinois University Press, 1989.

McFarland, Thomas. *Originality and Imagination*. Baltimore: Johns Hopkins University Press, 1985.

McKay, David, and Richard Crawford. *William Billings of Boston: Eighteenth-Century Composer*. Princeton, N.J.: Princeton University Press, 1975.

McLaughlin, Jack. *Jefferson and Monticello: The Biography of a Builder*. New York: Henry Holt, 1988.

Maier, Pauline. *The Old Revolutionaries: Political Lives in the Age of Samuel Adams*. New York: Knopf, 1980.

Malone, Dumas. *Jefferson The Virginian*. New York: Little, Brown, 1948.

Mapp, Alf J. *Thomas Jefferson: A Strange Case of Mistaken Identity*. New York: Madison, 1987.

Marshall, David. *The Figure of the Theater: Shaftesbury, Defoe, Adam Smith, and George Eliot*. New York: Columbia University Press, 1986.

Martin, Judith. *Common Courtesy in which Miss Manners Solves the Problem that Baffled Mr. Jefferson*. New York: Atheneum, 1985.

Mason, Bernard, ed. *The American Colonial Crisis: The Daniel Leonard–John Adams Letters to the Press, 1774–1775*. New York: Harper and Row, 1972.

Mason, John. *An Essay on the Power and Harmony of Prosaic Numbers* (1749). Menston, Eng.: Scolar Press, 1967.

Mencken, H. L. *The American Language*. New York: Knopf, 1977.

Miller, John C. *Sam Adams: Pioneer in Propaganda*. Stanford: Stanford University Press, 1964.

Monaghan, E. Jennifer. *A Common Heritage: Noah Webster's Blue-Back Speller*. Hamden: Archon Books, 1983.

Montgomery, Charles F., and Patricia Kane, eds. *American Art, 1750–1800: Towards Independence*. New Haven: Yale University Art Gallery, 1976.

Moore, John. *The Young Gentleman and Lady's Monitor and English Teacher's Assistant*. New York, 1791.

Morgan, Edmund S. *Inventing the People: The Rise of Popular Sovereignty in England and America*. New York: Norton, 1989.

Morgan, George. *Patrick Henry*. Philadelphia: Lippincott, 1929.

Murray, Judith Sargent. *The Gleaner: A Miscellaneous Production*. 3 vols. Boston, 1798.

"Observations on Faces." *Pennsylvania Magazine*, July 1775.

Oliver, Peter. *Peter Oliver's Origin and Progress of the American Revolution, A Tory View*. San Marino, Calif.: Huntington Library, 1961.

Ong, Walter. *Orality and Literacy: The Technologizing of the Word*. London: Methuen, 1982.

Otis, James. *The Rudiments of Latin Prosody with . . . the Principles of Harmony in Poetic and Prosaic Composition*. Boston, 1760.

The Oxford English Dictionary. Ed. James A. H. Murray. 13 vols. Oxford: Oxford University Press, 1933.

Paine, Thomas. *Common Sense*. Ed. Isaac Kramnick. New York: Penguin, 1989.

——. *The Thomas Paine Reader*. Ed. Michael Foot and Isaac Kramnick. New York: Penguin, 1987.

Peach, Bernard, ed. *Richard Price and the Ethical Foundations of the American Revolution: Selections from His Pamphlets*. Durham: Duke University Press, 1979.

Peale, Charles Willson. *An Essay to Promote Domestic Happiness*. Philadelphia, 1812.

Peek, George A., ed. *The Political Writings of John Adams: Representative Selections*. Indianapolis: Bobbs-Merrill, 1954.

Perkins, John. *Theory of Agency or, An Essay on the Nature, Source and Extent of Moral Freedom* (1771). In Charles S. Hyneman and Donald S. Lutz, eds., *American Political Writing during the Founding Era*, 1: 137–57. 2 vols. Indianapolis: Liberty Press, 1983.

Pocock, J. G. A. *The Machiavellian Moment*. Princeton, N.J.: Princeton University Press, 1975.

Poe, Edgar Allan. *The Collected Works: Tales and Sketches*. 3 vols. Ed.

Thomas Ollive Mabbott. Cambridge, Mass.: Harvard University Press, 1977.

Pope, Alexander. *Pope: Poetical Works*. Ed. Herbert Davis. Oxford: Oxford University Press, 1978.

Rakove, Jack N. *The Beginnings of National Politics: An Interpretive History of the Continental Congress*. New York: Knopf, 1979.

Ralph, James. *The Case of Authors by Profession or Trade Stated*. London, 1758.

Randall, Henry S. *The Life of Thomas Jefferson*. 3 vols. Philadelphia, 1865.

Randolph, Edmund. *History of Virginia*. Ed. Arthur Shaffer. Charlottesville: University Press of Virginia, 1970.

Randolph, Sarah N. *The Domestic Life of Thomas Jefferson* (1871). New York: Frederick Ungar, 1958.

Reid, Thomas. *Inquiry and Essays*. Ed. Ronald E. Beanblossom. Indianapolis: Hackett, 1983.

Renker, Elizabeth M. "'Declaration-men' and the Rhetoric of Self-Presentation." *Early American Literature* 24, no. 2 (1989): 120–34.

Rice, John. *An Introduction to the Art of Reading with Energy and Propriety* (1765). Menston, Eng.: Scolar Press, 1969.

Richards, Jeffrey H. *Theater Enough: American Culture and the Metaphor of the World Stage, 1607–1789*. Durham: Duke University Press, 1991.

Richetti, John J. *Philosophical Writing: Locke, Berkeley, Hume*. Cambridge, Mass.: Harvard University Press, 1983.

Robbins, Caroline. *The Eighteenth-Century Commonwealthman*. Cambridge, Mass.: Harvard University Press, 1959.

Rogin, Michael Paul. *Subversive Genealogy: The Politics and Art of Herman Melville*. New York: Knopf, 1983.

Rousseau, Jean-Jacques. *Emilius and Sophia, or a New System of Education*. 4 vols. London, 1762–63.

Rush, Benjamin. *The Letters of Benjamin Rush*. 2 vols. Ed. L. H. Butterfield. Princeton, N.J.: Princeton University Press, 1951.

——. "Of the Mode of Education Proper in a Republic." In Michael Meranze, ed., *Benjamin Rush: Essays Literary, Moral and Philosophical*. Schenectady: Union College Press, 1988.

St. George, Robert Blair. "Artifacts of Regional Consciousness in the Connecticut River Valley, 1700–1780." In Robert Blair St. George, ed., *Material Life in America, 1600–1860*. Boston: Northeastern University Press, 1988.

Santore, Charles. *The Windsor Style in America*. Philadelphia: Running Press, 1981.

Schiller, Friedrich. *On the Naive and Sentimental in Literature*. Trans. and ed. Helen Watanabe-O'Kelly. Manchester, Eng.: Carcanet New Press, 1981.

Schlesinger, Arthur M. *Prelude to Independence: The Newspaper War on Britain, 1764–1776*. Boston: Northeastern University Press, 1980.

Schutz, John A., and Douglass Adair, eds. *The Spur of Fame: Dialogues of John Adams and Benjamin Rush, 1805–1813*. San Marino, Calif.: Huntington Library, 1966.

Schwartz, Bernard. *The American Heritage History of the Law in America*. New York: American Heritage, 1975.

Scott, William. *Lessons in Elocution . . . and Elements of Gesture*. New York, 1799.

Seed, Geoffrey. *James Wilson: Scottish Intellectual and American Statesman*. Boston: KTO Press, 1978.

Sellers, Charles Coleman. *Patience Wright: American Artist and Spy in George III's London*. Middletown, Conn.: Wesleyan University Press, 1976.

Sennett, Richard. *The Fall of Public Man*. New York: Knopf, 1977.

Shankman, Steven. *Pope's "Illiad"*. Princeton, N.J.: Princeton University Press, 1983.

Shaw, Peter. *The Character of John Adams*. Chapel Hill: University of North Carolina Press, 1976.

Shepherd, Thomas. *The Sincere Convert*. London, 1641.

Sheridan, Thomas. *A Course of Lectures on Elocution* (1762). Menston, Eng.: Scolar Press, 1968.

———. *Lectures on the Art of Reading*. London, 1775.

Shipton, Clifford K., and James E. Mooney. *National Index of American Imprints Through 1800: The Short Title Evans*. 2 vols. Worcester, Mass.: American Antiquarian Society, 1969.

Shuffleton, Frank. "In Different Voices: Gender in the American Republic of Letters." *Early American Literature* 25, no. 3 (1990): 289–304.

Silver, Rollo G. *The American Printer, 1787–1825*. Charlottesville: University Press of Virginia, 1967.

Silverman, Kenneth. *A Cultural History of the American Revolution*. New York: Crowell, 1976.

Simpson, David. *The Politics of American English, 1776–1850*. New York: Oxford University Press, 1986.

Simpson, Lewis P. *The Brazen Face of History: Studies in the Literary Consciousness in America*. Baton Rouge: Louisiana State University Press, 1980.

Simpson, Marc, Sally Mills, and Jennifer Saville. *The American Canvas: Paintings from the Collection of the Fine Arts Museums of San Francisco.* New York: Hudson Hills, 1989.

Smith, Adam. *Lectures on Rhetoric and Belles Lettres.* Ed. J. C. Bryce. Oxford: Clarendon Press, 1983.

——. *The Theory of Moral Sentiments.* Ed. D. D. Raphael and A. L. Macfie. Oxford: Clarendon Press, 1976.

Smith, Jeffrey. *Printers and Press Freedom: The Ideology of Early American Journalism.* Oxford: Oxford University Press, 1988.

Sowerby, E. Millicent. *Catalogue of the Library of Thomas Jefferson.* 5 vols. Charlottesville: University Press of Virginia, 1983.

Stam, James H. *Inquiries into the Origin of Language.* New York: Harper and Row, 1976.

Stearns, Charles. *Dramatic Dialogues for the Use of Schools.* Leominster, Mass., 1978.

Steele, Joshua. *An Essay toward Establishing the Melody and Measure of Speech.* London, 1775.

Steintrager, James. *Bentham.* Ithaca: Cornell University Press, 1977.

Stone, P. W. K. *The Art of Poetry, 1750–1820: Theories of Poetic Composition and Style in the Late Neo-Classic and Early Romantic Periods.* New York: Barnes and Noble, 1967.

Stout, Harry S. "Religion, Communication, and the Ideological Origins of the American Revolution." *William and Mary Quarterly* 34 (1977): 519–41.

Stowell, Marion Barber. *Early American Almanacs.* New York: Burt Franklin, 1977.

Strunk, Oliver, ed. *Source Readings in Music History: The Classic Era.* New York: Norton, 1965.

Thomas, Isaiah. *History of American Printing.* 2 vols. Worcester, 1810.

Thornton, William. *Cadmus: Or, a Treatise on the Elements of Written Language.* Philadelphia, 1793.

To the Very Learned, Loquacious . . . Chairman. New York, 1775.

Trilling, Lionel. *Sincerity and Authenticity.* Cambridge, Mass.: Harvard University Press, 1970.

Tucker, Abraham. *Vocal Sounds.* London, 1773.

Tulis, Jeffrey K. *The Rhetorical Presidency.* Princeton, N.J.: Princeton University Press, 1987.

Van Doren, Carl. *Benjamin Franklin.* New York: Viking, 1938.

Vickers, Brian. *In Defense of Rhetoric.* Oxford: Clarendon Press, 1988.

Walker, John. *The Melody of Speaking Delineated: or, Elocution Taught like Music, by Visible Signs*. London, 1787.
Warner, Michael. *The Letters of the Republic: Publication and the Public Sphere in Eighteenth-Century America*. Cambridge, Mass.: Harvard University Press, 1990.
Weber, Donald. *Rhetoric and History in Revolutionary New England*. New York: Oxford University Press, 1988.
Webster, Daniel. *The Papers of Daniel Webster*. 5 vols. Hanover: Dartmouth University Press, 1974.
Webster, Noah. *An American Selection of Lessons in Reading and Speaking . . . and Directions for Expressing the Principal Passions of the Mind*. Hartford, 1785.
——. *A Dictionary of the English Language*. 2 vols. New York, 1828.
——. *Dissertations on the English Language, with Notes Historical and Critical*. Boston, 1789.
——. *A Grammatical Institute of the English Language, Part II*. Hartford, 1784.
Weems, Mason Locke. *The Life of Washington*. Ed. Marcus Cunliffe. Cambridge, Mass.: Harvard University Press, 1962.
Wheatley, Phillis. *Poems on Various Subjects, Religious and Moral*. London, 1773.
Wiebe, Robert H. *The Opening of American Society: From the Adoption of the Constitution to the Eve of Disunion*. New York: Knopf, 1984.
Wilkes, John. *The Speeches of Mr. Wilkes in the House of Commons*. London, 1786.
Wills, Garry. *Inventing America: Jefferson's Declaration of Independence*. New York: Doubleday, 1978.
Wirt, William. *Sketches of the Life and Character of Patrick Henry*. Richmond, 1817.
Witherspoon, John. *The Selected Writings of John Witherspoon*. Ed. Thomas Miller. Carbondale: Southern Illinois University Press, 1990.
Wolfe, Edwin, II. *The Book Culture of a Colonial American City: Philadelphia Books, Bookmen, and Booksellers*. Oxford: Clarendon Press, 1988.
Wood, Gordon S. "Conspiracy and the Paranoid Style: Causality and Deceit in the Eighteenth Century." *William and Mary Quarterly* 39 (1982): 401–41.
——. "The Democratization of Mind in the American Revolution." In *Leadership in the American Revolution*, pp. 64–68. Washington, D.C.: Library of Congress, 1974.
——. *The Radicalism of the American Revolution*. New York: Knopf, 1992.

Woolman, John. *The Journal of John Woolman*. Gloucester, Mass.: Peter Smith, 1971.
Wordsworth, William. "Preface" to *Lyrical Ballads*. In Hazard Adams, ed., *Critical Theory Since Plato*. New York: Harcourt Brace Jovanovich, 1971.
Wyatt-Brown, Bertram. *Southern Honor: Ethics and Behavior in the Old South*. New York: Oxford University Press, 1982.
Ziff, Larzer. *Writing in the New Nation: Prose, Print, and Politics in the Early United States*. New Haven: Yale University Press, 1991.
Zobel, Hiller B. *The Boston Massacre*. New York: Norton, 1970.

Index

In this index an "f" after a number indicates a separate reference on the next page, and an "ff" indicates separate references on the next two pages. A continuous discussion over two or more pages is indicated by a span of page numbers, e.g., "57–59." *Passim* is used for a cluster of references in close but not consecutive sequence.

Index

Library of Congress Cataloging-in-Publication Data

Fliegelman, Jay.
Declaring independence : Jefferson, natural language, and the culture of performance / Jay Fliegelman.
p. cm.
Includes bibliographical references and index.
ISBN 0-8047-2075-4 (cl.) — ISBN 0-8047-2076-2 (pbk.)
1. Jefferson, Thomas, 1743–1826—Language. 2. Rhetoric—Political aspects—History—18th century. 3. United States. Declaration of Independence. I. Title.
E332.2.F55 1993
973.4′6′092—dc20
92-17928 CIP

∞ This book is printed on acid-free paper. It was designed by Copenhaver Cumpston and typeset by Keystone Typesetting, Inc. in 11/14 Adobe Caslon.

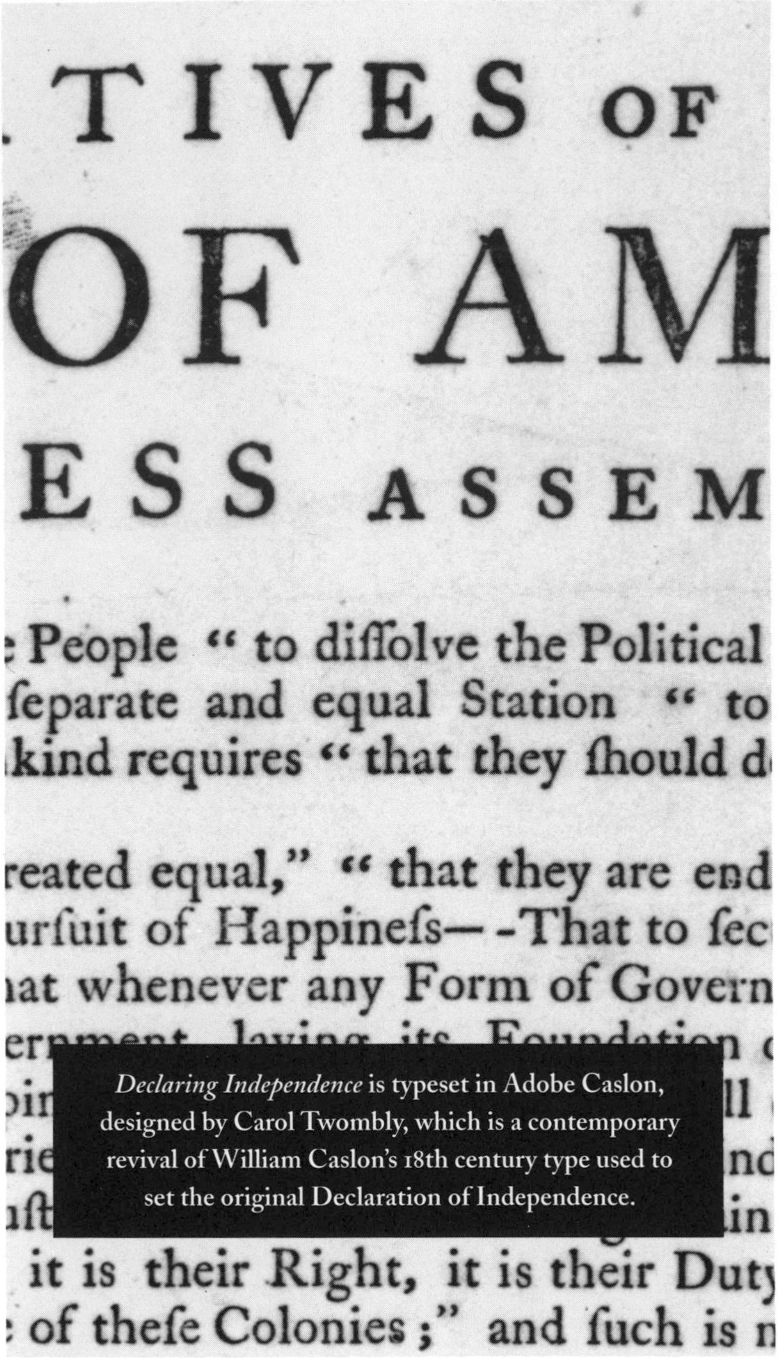

TIVES OF

OF AM

ESS ASSEM

People " to diſſolve the Political

ſeparate and equal Station " to

kind requires " that they ſhould d

reated equal," " that they are end

urſuit of Happineſs—-That to ſec

at whenever any Form of Govern

it is their Right, it is their Duty

of theſe Colonies;" and ſuch is n

Declaring Independence is typeset in Adobe Caslon, designed by Carol Twombly, which is a contemporary revival of William Caslon's 18th century type used to set the original Declaration of Independence.